Agenda for Africa's Economic Renewal

Agenda for Africa's Economic Renewal

■

Benno Ndulu, Nicolas van de Walle, and contributors:

Simon Appleton
Deborah Brautigam
Christopher L. Delgado
Ibrahim A. Elbadawi
E. Gyimah-Boadi
Sanjaya Lall
John Mackinnon
Frances Stewart

Transaction Publishers
New Brunswick (USA) and Oxford (UK)

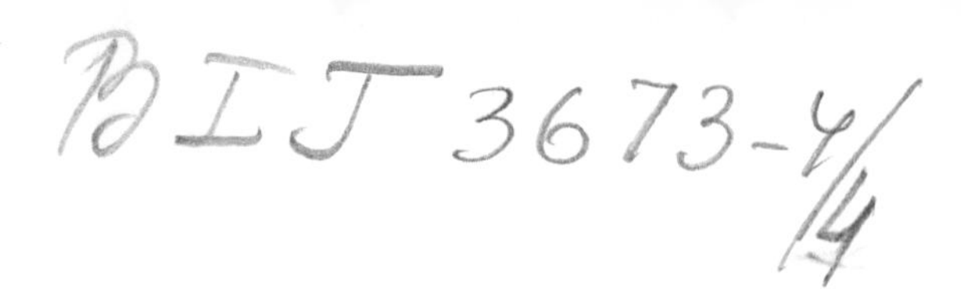

Library of Congress Cataloging-in-Publication Data

Ndulu, Benno J. and Nicolas van de Walle

Agenda for Africa's economic renewal/[edited by] Benno J. Ndulu and Nicolas van de Walle and contributors [et al.].

p. cm. (U.S.-Third World Policy Perspectives: No. 21)
Includes bibliographic references.
1. Africa, Sub-Saharan—Economic policy. I. Ndulu, B. J. II. van de Walle, Nicolas, 1957– . III. Series.

HC800.A623 1996 338.967—dc20 96-2923

ISBN: 1-56000-280-8 (cloth)
ISBN: 1-56000-900-4 (paper)
Printed in the United States of America

Director of Publications: Christine E. Contee
Publications Editor: Jacqueline Edlund-Braun
Edited by Michael Treadway and Elizabeth Reed Forsyth
Cover design: Ripe Studios
Book design: Tim Kenney Design Partners, Inc.

The views expressed in this volume are those of the authors and do not necessarily represent those of the Overseas Development Council as an organization or of its individual officers, program advisory groups, Board, Council, and staff members.

Contents

Foreword vii

Overview:
Africa's Economic Renewal: From Consensus to Strategy
Benno J. Ndulu and Nicolas van de Walle 3

Summary of Chapter Recommendations 33

Agenda for Africa's Economic Renewal

1. **Consolidating Macroeconomic Stabilization and Restoring Growth in Africa**
Ibrahim A. Elbadawi 49
Introduction 49
A Review of Macroeconomic Policy Reform in Africa 52
African Macroeconomic Reform and the Policy Frontier 61
From Stabilization to Growth 63
Conclusions 73

2. **State Capacity and Effective Governance**
Deborah Brautigam 81
What Is State Capacity? 83
African State Capacity in Historical and Comparative Perspective 85
Foreign Aid: What Has Been Done to Build Capacity and Why It Hasn't Worked 91
Foreign Aid and State Capacity 96
Strategies for Rebuilding State Capacity 100
Financing Improvements in State Capacity 104
Conclusions 104

3. **Enhancing Human Capacities in Africa**
Simon Appleton and John Mackinnon 109
Introduction 109
The Current Situation in Africa 110

Determinants of and Returns to Human Capacities at an Individual Level........ 114
Market Failure in Health and Education 121
Private and Public Financing of Education and Health........ 125
Provision of Education and Health Care.......... 137
Summary and Conclusions.......... 143

4. **Agricultural Transformation: The Key to Broad-Based Growth and Poverty Alleviation in Africa**
Christopher L. Delgado 151

Agricultural Transformation: What Is It and Why Is It Important?.......... 153
Promotion of Smallholder Agricultural Development on the Supply Side 160
Adding Back the Demand Side: Promoting Labor-Intensive Rural Development Through Agricultural Transformation 163
Strategies for Structural Change.......... 170

5. **Trade and Industrial Policy in Africa**
Sanjaya Lall and Frances Stewart.......... 179

Introduction 179
Industrial Policy in Africa in the 1960s and 1970s... 181
The Record of Structural Adjustment.......... 184
Adjustment and Industrial Performance in Africa... 189
The Record of Adjustment in Ghana.......... 194
Policy Implications 197
Conclusion.......... 206

6. **The Politics of Economic Renewal in Africa**
E. Gyimah-Boadi and Nicolas van de Walle 211

A Developmental State in Africa 212
Obstacles and Constraints 215
Prerequisites of the Developmental State.......... 220
Implications of the Argument 231

About the Overseas Development Council 241
About the Authors 243

Foreword

The last three decades have seen Sub-Saharan Africa lag behind all other continents in terms of economic growth and poverty alleviation. During the 1960s to early 1970s, African economies averaged a reasonable growth rate of 5.9 percent, but during the 1970s the growth rate declined to 4.1 percent and during the 1980s it declined even further to 2 percent. This deterioration in economic performance was registered against a rising population growth rate, which lead to a steeper decline in per capita income growth. Similar trends in human welfare—educational attainment, life expectancy, and infant mortality—indicate that development virtually stagnated during the latter half of the 1980s.

Africa's poor performance stands in stark contrast to the experience of the rest of the developing world, especially Southeast Asia, where there has been rapid economic growth and significant improvements in institutional capacity and in the lives of men, women, and children. Why after two decades of economic reform efforts has Africa's performance continued to deteriorate? In the rapidly changing international economic environment, what can African decision makers do to restore their countries to a development path in the years to come?

Agenda for Africa's Economic Renewal moves beyond critiques of particular reform programs to a much-needed, fresh look at a consolidated strategy for poverty-reducing growth in Sub-Saharan Africa. Starting with the considerable consensus among policymakers and scholars about what ails African economies, the authors identify and make recommendations in six key areas that need to be addressed for Africa to achieve economic renewal: consolidating achievements in macroeconomic stabilization; enhancing state capacity for development; promoting a dominant role for the private sector; transforming agriculture for broad-based growth and poverty alleviation; building human and state capacity; and diversifying the economy.

ODC was fortunate to have two extraordinarily qualified directors for this project. Benno Ndulu, one of Africa's foremost economists, is currently the Executive Director of the African Economic Research Consortium in Nairobi. Nicolas van de Walle is a Davidson Sommers Visiting Fellow on leave from Michigan State University and director of ODC's Project on Aid Effectiveness in Africa. The other contributors to this volume—from Africa, the United Kingdom, and the United States—have provided valuable analyses and proposals for national strategies that are at once pro-growth and anti-poverty.

Agenda for Africa's Economic Renewal is the latest in ODC's body of work on the development challenge presented by the continent. Most recently, as part of ODC's Policy Essay series, ODC published Nguyuru Lipumba's *Africa Beyond Adjustment*, a critique of structural adjustment programs, which also offers a different perspective on appropriate long-term development strategies for the region. Soon to be released by ODC, also in the Policy Essay series, is Nicolas van de Walle's *Improving Aid: The Challenge to Donors and African Governments*. This analysis, the synthesis of a collaborative project involving some fourteen research institutes and donor agencies in as many countries, reviews the effectiveness of aid and argues that the ability of recipient governments to integrate aid into their own development strategy is critical to the success of aid.

ODC gratefully acknowledges The Ford Foundation and The Rockefeller Foundation for their generous support of the Council's overall program, including the U.S.-Third World Policy Perspectives series of which this study is a part. ODC also wishes to acknowledge The Equitable Life Assurance Society of the United States for its support of the Davidson Sommers Fellowship on International Development Studies, which made possible Dr. van de Walle's research.

John W. Sewell
President
June 1996

Acknowledgments

The editors wish to thank the following people for having read and commented on different parts of the book: Bob Christiansen, Daniel Green, John Heilbrunn, Ravi Kanbur, Peter Lewis, Nguyuru Lipumba, Barbara Nunberg, Stephen O'Connell, Terry Ryan, Ann Velenchik, and Ernest Wilson.

Overview and Chapter Recommendations

Overview

Africa's Economic Renewal: From Consensus to Strategy

Benno Ndulu and Nicolas van de Walle

A consensus has emerged in the development policy community during the past decade about the causes of Africa's economic crisis and the prerequisites of renewed growth there. When Africa's economic crisis first emerged in the early 1980s, there was a great deal of disagreement about its origins and the best way to overcome it. Over time, thanks in part to policy experimentation and dialogue between the donors and African policymakers, those disagreements narrowed considerably, so that a broad consensus can be said to exist. The challenge now is to develop viable development strategies based on this consensus. It is important to identify the choices, priorities, and tradeoffs facing African governments that are committed to overcoming the current crisis, given the range of endowments and capacities found in the region and the current international environment.

This overview seeks to contribute to that discussion. Of course, each national development strategy will be somewhat different, conditioned as it should be by distinct country characteristics and the preferences of citizens. Our aim here is to suggest the broad parameters of the economic strategies that African decision makers need to develop. In particular, we identify six key areas that will have to be addressed for Africa to achieve economic renewal. First, economic stabilization efforts must be sustained and consolidated, because economic growth will not return without a stable and predictable macroeconomic environment. Second, the state has to enhance its capacity to undertake key economic functions. Third, governments must create an environment that encourages private sector investment so as to enhance its contribution to economic recovery and the process of growth. Fourth, countries need to achieve substantial improvements in the level of human capital present in the economy to enhance productive capacity. Fifth, both to alleviate poverty and to spearhead the growth process, governments need to promote substantial productivity growth in agriculture. Sixth, viable and outward-looking industrial sectors need to be developed. This overview sets out the broad justification for these six components and the relationships among them. The ensuing chapters then investigate in much greater detail the requirements and main obstacles facing African governments in each area.

This chapter is divided into four sections. We begin with a brief review of the lessons that can be derived from the current generation of reform programs. We outline several general principles that must guide development strategy in the future. Here and throughout this chapter, we emphasize the large diversity of country characteristics and policy stances that affect the prospects for economic renewal in the region. In the next section, we assess the key changes in the international environment that impinge on efforts being made to reverse economic and social decline in the region. We reject the view that the international environment increasingly represents a danger for Africa, arguing instead that current changes present both significant opportunities for and challenges to future strategic interventions for initiating and managing change. In a fourth section, we provide a brief outline of the six key elements of any national strategy for growth. We conclude with comments about the relationship between these components and the dilemmas they are likely to pose.

THE EMERGENCE OF A BROAD POLICY CONSENSUS

Developmentalists in the 1960s and 1970s argued that Africa's lack of modern economies, its poor infrastructural and human capacity, and dependence on outside economies were fundamental constraints. They emphasized investment, driven by the state's dominant role in hastening the modernization process. Little attention was paid to the productivity of committed resources or to the limited capacity of African economies to respond to shocks. As the economic crisis worsened in the early 1980s, the destabilizing impacts of a series of severe shocks and the poor quality of investment decisions led to a shift in focus. While African governments tended to blame adverse international shocks for their balance of payments difficulties, the donors put the blame squarely on government policies and excessive intervention in the economy. They emphasized the central role of a stable macroeconomic environment, a market-oriented incentive structure, and a much-reduced involvement of the state in economic activities as the fundamental tools for promoting growth through efficient resource use and supply response.

This shift in macroeconomic policy orientation was spurred by a notable theoretical shift in the policy community toward a development paradigm that was greatly influenced by what has been called the "new consensus on macroeconomics" and the "new political economy." The new consensus emphasized the threat of inflation more than the risk of unemployment (notably through its accent on monetary policy), focused on supply-side factors more than on effective demand for promoting growth, and highlighted the negative effects of fiscal deficits on private investment and price instability more than a proactive role for engendering and supporting growth.[1] The shift away from dirigisme complemented this approach by emphasizing the costs of government rather than the costs of market failures, which led them to advocate a "minimalist" role for the state in the development process.[2]

There is little doubt that this shift had an enormous impact on policymaking during the past decade and a half in what amounted to a global wave of economic liberalization. More specifically, the reform programs pursued in Sub-Saharan Africa throughout much of the 1980s were predicated on this paradigm, and access to multilateral and bilateral assistance became conditional on following policies inspired by it. Even access to commercial sources of finance was affected, as assessment of creditworthiness and investment opportunities incorporated the tenets of the paradigm in country risk assessment. Although the reform agenda also incorporated new issues as the decade wore on, western donors compelled often reluctant governments all over Africa to retrench the economic role of the state through privatization, liberalization, and deregulation.

The actual implementation of economic reform has been uneven and slow. Nonetheless, after more than a decade of experimentation, the following appraisal of reform is possible. First, the evidence suggests that growth has recovered very modestly relative to the effort committed to reform. Reform has not led to an appreciable and sustained increase in new productive investment that would presage a significant spurt of new economic growth.

Second, the modest success in restoring macroeconomic stability may not be sustained, given the excessive dependence on external resource flows to achieve it. External resource contributions to the financing of budgetary expenditures remains very high in many reforming countries. This situation remains in some countries despite significant gains in revenue collection or cuts in overall *real* expenditure. That the bulk of external debt servicing is primarily a fiscal burden has exacerbated the pressures associated with achieving fiscal viability.

Third, external viability of these economies continues to be elusive. Domestic resource gaps, measured as the difference between exports and imports of goods and services, continue to expand as a proportion of gross domestic product (GDP) and are in excess of viable external financing levels in the long term. Although reforming countries have achieved a modest recovery of export growth, averaging 3.2 percent during 1986–1993, this falls far short of the much higher growth rates of imports, averaging 6.4 percent over the same period.[3] Moreover, this recovery is fragile because the export basket remains undiversified, consisting mainly of primary products that face long-term declining price trends.[4] The rapid increase in the external debt overhang has further worsened the likelihood of achieving external viability. The burden of servicing this debt, particularly in the context of real exchange rate depreciation, constituted an external real outflow of resources and considerably added pressure to achieving external balance.

Fourth, the reform effort has brought about little improvement in human welfare. Although the group of countries pursuing economic reforms in earnest have achieved marginally higher rates of growth, higher growth has not notably improved welfare indicators such as life expectancy, infant mortality, and school enrollment.[5]

A new policy consensus is beginning to emerge that takes into account these lessons of experience. It suggests that Africa's economic stagnation can be explained by six key factors. First, low and inadequate human, technological, and institutional capacities have provided very poor basic conditions for growth. There is ample evidence to suggest that favorable initial conditions have been fundamental to successful long-term growth elsewhere in the developing world, perhaps most notably in East Asia.[6] Second, economic policy distortions in Sub-Saharan Africa have had undesirable and deleterious effects on growth and efficiency in resource use. Uncertainties arising from macroeconomic instability have proven inimical to private investment, while distorted incentive structures have spurred inefficient allocation of resources and hampered productivity growth. Third, the undiversified and highly dependent character of African economies has left them with a weak capacity to respond flexibly to external and natural shocks. Vulnerability to shocks has been exacerbated by the low creditworthiness of Sub-Saharan African countries, which have limited access to timely finance with which to ride out temporary and reversible shocks. Fourth, political instability and civil strife have disrupted the growth process in many countries in the region. The resulting deterioration of human and physical capital as well as risks to investors have curtailed the potential for growth and inflicted human misery. Unstable and war-torn states have harmful spillover effects on neighboring countries. Overflows of refugees, heightened ethnic tensions in some cases, and diplomatic conflicts have engaged large amounts of resources and effort in stable countries sharing borders with countries torn or threatened by civil strife. Thus, civil disorder is a broad problem for the region and warrants regional responses. Fifth, economic performance has been undermined by more general deficiencies in governance, including weaknesses in the capacity of the state to manage the development process, as well as pervasive corruption, rent seeking, and cronyism.[7] The recent wave of democratization provides the potential for significant progress on this front but must be further consolidated. Sixth, past growth strategies have paid inadequate attention to poverty alleviation. Although higher growth is a necessary condition for alleviating poverty, *broad-based growth* that spreads widely the benefits from economic expansion is needed to enhance the capacity of the majority to earn a decent income for satisfying basic needs.

To be sure, this emerging consensus is still fragile. On the one hand, the lessons to be learned from past policy experiments have still not been fully assimilated by some African policymakers. The disappointments of past reform attempts, as well as recent changes in the international environment, could well lead to a renewed critique of economic reform and calls for the protectionism and economic statism of the past. On the other hand, policymakers in Washington and other donor capitals may have lost their excessive faith in "the miracle of the market," but they lack the experience to implement the complex institutional and managerial reforms they now understand to be important.

Nonetheless, today there is more widespread agreement on what ails African economies than there was perhaps in the entire postcolonial period. Now this new consensus must be translated into viable national development strategies for Africa. Positing the importance of reducing poverty, say, or of increasing state capacity is not the same as devising and implementing effective strategies to achieve these objectives in a world of finite resources. The great paradox of the development process is that needs and the capacity to address them appear to be inversely related. Given the inherent difficulties of implementing economic policy reform and the limited financial and technical resources available to them, African countries will have to proceed strategically, make difficult choices, and establish priorities for action.

LESSONS OF EXPERIENCE

This policy consensus, built on the past decade of economic crisis and reform program implementation, allows us to generate several guiding principles that should be taken into account when devising any future development strategy.

National Variations

National development strategies should first take into account the important differences in resources, economic performance, and sociopolitical characteristics that distinguish the countries of Sub-Saharan Africa. For example, countries vary greatly in size and population, from Sudan with an area of 2.5 million square kilometers to the tiny Rwanda with 26,000 square kilometers or from Nigeria's estimated population of 101.9 million to Seychelles' population of 70,000. Natural resource endowments also vary significantly, from the quality of arable land to the concentration of mineral and oil wealth in half a dozen states.[8] Partly as a result, differences in the level of national income are greater than is commonly assumed. In per capita GDP, 8 of the world's 10 poorest countries are in Africa, as are 15 of the poorest 20. Nonetheless, per capita GDP in 1993 ranged from $6,347 for Seychelles to $77 for Ethiopia. The top one-fourth of the 47 countries in the region for which data are available had income per capita in excess of $800, comparing well with middle-income countries in other developing regions. Similarly, Sub-Saharan Africa's general economic decline disguises important differences across the region. National GDP growth during the 1980s ranged from 11.4 percent for Botswana to −1.9 percent for Liberia. Such contrasts in the resource base and in the size of the domestic market have profound implications for the kinds of strategies that will maximize economic growth and thus need to be taken into account when shaping national development policies.

The Importance of Governance

Countries that have deficient basic governance will not be able to undergo sustained economic growth. Belying a popular image of endemic civil strife and corrupt authoritarian regimes, the sociopolitical systems in the region also show great contrasts. At the most worrisome end are half a dozen states, such as Liberia and Somalia, that have collapsed amid civil strife. They are characterized by a widespread threat to life and property as well as a breakdown of public authority. These countries cannot pursue economic renewal until law, order, and public authority are restored. Where the strife is based on ethnic tensions, these countries have to pay more attention to the process of national integration.[9]

A second category includes countries with public authority but a high degree of political instability, where the risk of collapse is real.

Some of these states have experienced periods of relative stability and political tolerance in the past and could overcome their present difficulties, with creative leadership—for example, Nigeria, Sudan, and Zaire. For the time being, however, the state machinery is preoccupied with the survival of the regime in power, considerably detracting from sustained development initiatives. Often these countries are constrained from exploiting the opportunities for engaging in international economic activity as perceived risks keep away investors and official development assistance.

A third category, including roughly two-thirds of the countries in the region, can claim a stable civil environment and are today moving toward more open and contested political systems. These countries have benefited directly from the "third wave" of democratization and political liberalization. Half are engaged in earnest in political transitions,[10] which are likely to improve their governance, albeit initially in modest ways. The challenge here is to pursue economic and political reforms simultaneously, while also strengthening the functional effectiveness of the state, a conundrum analyzed in the last chapter of this volume.

A successful national economic strategy will obviously have to take these differences into account. In some countries, governance problems are so severe that reestablishing minimal national systems of legitimate authority and limited economic stabilization, notably through the reintroduction of effective central banking, needs to be achieved before long-term development strategies can be implemented.

Even in the third category of states, the mode of governance raises transaction costs and the level of uncertainty, thus discouraging productive investment. Legal structures are often incapable of enforcing contracts and property rights. Pervasive rent seeking within government motivates much of the state's regulatory apparatus and remains unofficially present, often even after deregulation and liberalization reforms. This behavior is deeply ingrained in the political system of some countries, where it is thought to be essential to political stability. Yet sustained economic growth requires that it be eliminated, or at least circumscribed, so that its negative impact on the economy is limited.

Sequencing and Timing

Any strategy for the future has to take into account the depth of the economic crisis in most countries of the region. The current problems have a long genesis: Sub-Saharan Africa's economic performance as a whole has declined over a long period. Country growth rates averaged reasonable rates of almost 6 percent a year during the 1960s to early 1970s but then declined to 4 percent during the 1970s and to 2 percent in the 1980s. Because of a rising population growth rate, per capita income growth rates have actually declined, from 1.9 percent during the 1970s to −0.4 percent during the 1980s and −1.7 percent in the first half of the 1990s.[11] True, a handful of countries such as Botswana, Cape Verde, and Lesotho achieved GDP growth rates in excess of 5 percent during the 1980s, and another five or so registered a respectable per capita growth rate of at least of 2.5 percent; at the same time, the 12 worst performers averaged an annual average decline of 3.3 percent in per capita GDP during the 1980s.

There is a growing acceptance of the negative effects of external shocks on the predictability and stability of Africa's small, open economies with limited access to international commercial finance.[12] The negative impact of deteriorating terms of trade has been particularly severe in Sub-Saharan Africa partly due to its higher dependence on the price-volatile primary products and partly due to relatively low accessibility to timely liquidity to help ride out these reversible shocks.[13] Moreover, the losses from deteriorating terms of trade more than offset external net transfers.

This vulnerability implies the need to design consistent packages of reforms to ensure that they remain credible and feasible. The appropriate sequencing of reforms is an important part of this. Trade and financial liberalization can increase the pressures on achieving fiscal viability. Loss of revenue from trade taxes before alternative sources emerge and reduced seigniorage income put pressure on the fiscal balance. Liberalization, in contrast, is sometimes pursued prior to instituting prudential behavior and adequate supervisory capacity, endangering confidence in the sector.

Future development strategies have to accept that progress will be slow and painful. Strategies must distinguish desirable objectives that can be attained in the short term from objectives that cannot be achieved quickly because structural weaknesses first need to be addressed, which will necessarily take time. Thus, macroeconomic stabilization can be undertaken relatively quickly because it does not imply strengthening basic economic institutions, while certain proactive sectoral policies will have to be deferred because they do require capacities currently not available to many governments in the region. Building up those capacities must be a priority but will not occur overnight.

Strengthening Domestic Institutions

Policymakers can no longer push into the background the need to develop the capacities of these countries to initiate and manage complex change—the essence of sustained development. Stronger institutions are needed at several different albeit overlapping levels. First, there is now a clear acknowledgment of the need for supportive institutions in a market economy. The ability of the private sector to fill the gap left by the retrenchment of the state has too often been presumed without establishing the necessary conditions for its development. Yet, markets in Sub-Saharan Africa are still shallow and typically lack a regulatory framework capable of ensuring their efficient operation. State structures often combine the authoritarian tendencies and pervasive corruption discussed above with little genuine competence for such basic tasks as the protection of property rights, the application of standards, or the administration of laws, without which markets will not function well. Yet the efficacy of macroeconomic policy and the strength of the supply response to a very large extent depend on the efficient operation of markets and a transparent institutional environment free of manipulation for rent-seeking purposes.

Second, the provision of basic public goods, whether in the area of basic public services or in infrastructure, has been undermined by the low capacity within the public sector. The underprovision of these public goods has clearly hurt economic growth in the past. Much the same could be said for the low capacity of most African states to design and manage economic policy: Even abstracting from the policies actually chosen, economic growth has been hurt by the inability of the state to collect statistics, monitor economic activity, and implement fiscal, monetary, and sectoral policies. It is hard to resist the conclusion that there can be no successful economic revival in Sub-Saharan Africa in the absence of a strong (as opposed to pervasive) and a competent government.

In this context, the region's reliance on outside capabilities for initiating and managing change has not helped the long-term prospects for growth. Despite the importance of overall flows, foreign aid has largely failed to build viable indigenous institutions or to strengthen local competence in development management.[14] The foreign-funded expertise that was convenient in the short term too often thwarted the need to improve indigenous deficiencies. The continued reliance on external capabilities for designing and managing development programs and projects is perhaps vividly illustrated by the presence of an estimated 50,000–100,000 foreign experts involved in development activities in Africa. The share of technical assistance in total aid flows has been estimated to range from 20 to 85 percent of bilateral aid.[15] Technical assistance has too often proven to be supply-driven, designed to perpetuate itself and to exercise donor control over projects rather than to maximize returns to committed resources. The training components of projects have yielded to the pressures of shorter-term objectives—procedural objectives and the demonstration of results—at the cost of long-term impact on local skills and capacities. Donor efforts cannot succeed unless they help build up long-term sustainable capabilities based on expertise supplied by personnel based in Africa who are knowledgeable about local circumstances.[16] This concern highlights the need for capacity-building strategies that put in place the capabilities fundamental for self-initiated and self-managed development programs.

Local Ownership

Local ownership of reform programs is critical to ensure their sustainability and effectiveness. Unless governments and a large proportion of the population understand and support the aims of the economic policies chosen, they are unlikely to remain committed to them for long, particularly when implementation entails substantial political costs. In this context, the large amounts of aid to Africa have not always helped, creating a sense of psychological dependence on outsiders and instilling passivity in the policymaking process. Typically, the process of drawing reform programs and monitoring their implementation has been driven by a dialogue between African governments and donors, with conditionality imposed by the latter serving as an external anchor. This approach entails minimal involvement of local nongovernmental interests, including key societal actors and intended beneficiaries of the reform process. The local population exercises exit options to frustrate reforms, where deemed not beneficiary, as exemplified by the preponderance of parallel markets in the past. Accountability, where effective, is to the donors.

Recent studies have shown that programs that emphasize local ownership have been more effective in producing results and sustaining initiative.[17] This implies a need for donors not to seek to preempt or replace national decision-making processes. Governments must be allowed to engage in more policy experimentation, based on enhanced policy analysis capabilities. Broader participation in policy formulation and decision making should be encouraged, whether by strengthening the oversight functions of the legislature or by opening up the policy process to nongovernmental organizations. Greater participation will lead to greater transparency and accountability for government decision makers, which can help ensure the legitimacy of the difficult policy decisions that need to be made.[18] Along with the ongoing efforts to promote economic liberalization, improved governance undermines the prevalent distributive and patronage politics that have thrived on access to and control of public resources and rental incomes. The essential point here is to root the interest of the reforms in the stakeholders, thus building a strong local constituency for sustaining the reforms and preventing willy-nilly reversals of them.

Poverty Alleviation and Growth

Policymakers need to pay greater attention to poverty reduction as an integral part of a growth strategy. All but five African countries are at present in the lowest category of human development as defined by the United Nations Development Programme.[19] Roughly half of Sub-Saharan Africa's population lives below the poverty line, and the depth of poverty is typically worse than anywhere else in the world and increasing. Average national human welfare indexes show a sluggish overall improvement through the mid-1970s and either stagnation or deterioration since then.[20] Some sharp national differences should be noted, however, because of their implications for the prospects for economic renewal. After rising from 43 years in 1965 to 50 in 1982, average life expectancy at birth was still only 52 years in 1992, but it ranged from 71 years for Seychelles, an industrial-world standard, to only 39 years for Guinea Bissau. Six countries in the region now have a life expectancy above 60 years. Similarly, infant mortality rapidly fell from 153 per 1,000 live births in 1965 to 120 in 1982 but has improved little since then. It varies from a still very high level of 162 infants out of 1,000 dying before they reach one year old in Mozambique to only 16 in Seychelles. After impressive increases during the 1970s, primary school enrollment actually declined from an average of 75 percent of school-age children in 1985 to 67 percent in 1992. Primary school enrollment ranges from a very high 119 percent of school-age children for Madagascar to only 24 percent for Mali.[21] The contrast for secondary school enrollment is from 50 percent of school-age children for Zimbabwe to a mere 4 percent for Mali. Although the median literacy rate for the region is almost 53 percent, 80 percent of Madagascar's adult population is literate, in great contrast to a mere 17 percent for Burkina Faso.

Poverty alleviation demands accelerated growth that is at the same time broad based and labor intensive. It thus implies an emphasis on the revitalization of agriculture in the strategies developed, because the agriculture sector supports the livelihood of 70 percent of the African population and provides perhaps the most promising opportunities for labor-using, income-generating activities. In addition, it is now recognized that growth in Sub-Saharan Africa crucially depends on the dynamic performance of agriculture. This view has been vindicated by the strong lead role played by agriculture in the recent revival of growth in countries that were more successful with reforms. Despite this, productivity in the sector, a key to growth and poverty reduction, has either stagnated or declined in most African countries and remains much lower than in other developing regions. The need to revive the initiative for transforming the sector cannot be overemphasized.

THE CHALLENGES OF A CHANGING INTERNATIONAL ENVIRONMENT

Sub-Saharan Africa faces a rapidly changing international economic environment in the 1990s. Major global changes are taking place in the trading and financial environment, due to increasing factor mobility, and these changes signal growing integration of the world economy.[22] In addition, following the end of the Cold War, official development assistance is beginning a perhaps irrevocable decline. Are these changes positive for Sub-Saharan Africa? Do they invalidate the lessons of the policy consensus we have been describing? In some circles, the growing integration of the global economy is a cause for concern. One prominent African observer has gone so far as to argue that globalization will exacerbate poverty in Africa.[23]

In fact, changes in the global economy raise the stakes for the conduct of domestic policies, because greater integration of world markets simultaneously expands opportunities and magnifies the costs of policy failures and structural weaknesses. Globalization will increase the markets, resources, and technologies available to Africa for its own development, but only if African governments increase their capacity to implement key policies and take advantage of the opportunities that present themselves. Otherwise, the small, open economies of Sub-Saharan Africa will be increasingly vulnerable to international forces over which they have little control. Thus, far from invalidating the emerging policy consensus, changes in the international environment make its implementation more urgent.

First, the trading environment is evolving toward freer trade, with reductions in tariffs and quantitative restrictions on the movement of goods and services. Average tariffs in industrial countries have fallen from 40 percent in 1950 to less than 5 percent today.[24] Developing countries intensified their own reductions during the 1980s and 1990s as they pursued unilateral liberalization in the context of economic reform programs. In addition, a large and growing share of world production and trade is accounted for by transnational corporations. The combination of these changes has resulted in unprecedented growth of world trade at approximately twice the rate of growth of world output.[25]

A stronger mechanism for binding these changes in world trade has been provided by the recent establishment of the World Trade Organization, with its unprecedented number of signatories (including most Sub-Saharan African countries) following the Uruguay Round. To be sure, some conditions set under the Uruguay Round may be considered a high price to pay in exchange for "guaranteed" market access. The downside risks in particular relate to the application of clauses for intellectual property rights and the removal of agricultural subsidies. The social cost of tightening protection of foreigners' intellectual property rights and removing agricultural subsidies may turn out to be high in terms of higher prices for basic necessities. There is also a risk that future negotiations will include clauses that undermine Africa's comparative advantage. For instance, there is increasing debate about the need for labor standards, which may serve to dampen the advantage that Sub-Saharan African countries have in products that are intensive in unskilled labor. In fact, proposals for introducing labor standards made by France and the United States prior to the Marakesh ministers' meeting in April 1994 were strongly resisted by the developing countries as an avenue for introducing protectionism. Similarly, calls have been made for linking trade measures to environmental concerns. Premature stringency in environmental standards may prove to be an excessively onerous burden to those countries still struggling to break away from the vicious cycle of poverty. When these standards are tied to trade issues, they could be used to camouflage protectionist motives. Indeed the benefits of trade liberalization may not extend to Sub-Saharan Africa if the industrial countries adopt a protective stance or pursue arrangements for deeper integration among themselves.[26]

Nonetheless, the rapid growth of world trade spurs the international economy and improves the economic prospects of Sub-Saharan African countries as it enlarges markets, promotes international investment, and increases access to better technology and learning. These opportunities are particularly significant for "late starters" who can benefit from technological innovation and investment. These opportunities may be out of reach, however, if new industries are unable to compete with solidly established industries. Sub-Saharan African countries will have to adopt outward-oriented strategies and policies to facilitate access to international markets, exchange, and investment. Concerted efforts need to be made to raise the volume of exports and to diversify the export base. Some of the primary commodity producers that were able to increase their volume of exports in response to a realignment of incentives toward the production of tradables were not able to raise real export earnings due to a sharp deterioration in the terms of trade.[27] Diversification away from dominance of primary commodity exports is therefore critical for sustaining higher earnings from exports. The success of diversification will require the development of export competence in nonprimary commodities sectors, particularly the capacity to produce higher quality goods to meet the more discerning consumer standards, improved market access, and infrastructure.

Second, a phenomenal growth in international capital markets has resulted from the removal of restrictions on financial flows. Cross-border equity flows, international bond trading, and international lending through banks (to a lesser extent) have increased significantly since the mid-1980s.[28] This increase has resulted both from push factors, such as the low real returns in "source" countries, and from pull factors related to improved creditworthiness in recipient economies. Speculation has also been facilitated by innovations in information technologies that have lowered transaction costs as well as by the requirements of servicing a larger volume of trade and the growing role of multinational corporations.

Although these changes ultimately widen opportunities for access to global finance, they impose considerable penalties on governments that ignore prudent conduct of domestic policies. The increased options and mobility of funds also increase the volatility of financial markets, particularly in "small economies." Short-term financial capital is particularly prone to this volatility. For most Sub-Saharan African countries, dealing with surges and ebbs of short-term capital flows is a new and daunting policy task. Dealing with hard landing during ebbs and maintaining stable real exchange rates and real interest rates during surges are difficult policy tasks. When a significant portion of these short-term flows is destined for highly liquid instruments, such as government securities and bills, monetary control becomes elusive as options for sterilization remain limited. This is exacerbated by the thinness of financial markets in these countries.[29] The pressure such flows have generated on the strengthening of the domestic currency has caused concerns regarding the erosion of international competitiveness that most of these countries are still struggling to reestablish. Moreover, these surges often lead to higher real interest rates with dire consequences for investment and the interest cost of domestic debt.

The stock of foreign direct investment has more than doubled in the past eight years.[30] Again, the trend is toward greater mobility and more competition among developing countries. This has raised the importance of international competitiveness, macroeconomic stability, and other policy and institutional requirements for attracting foreign capital. A close link to fiscal measures is also discernible as tax incentives have become a major instrument for raising after-tax returns. Although Sub-Saharan African economies have yet to benefit significantly from the recent boom in foreign direct investment, countries in the region are committing substantial effort and resources to attract such investment. Apart from inducing more private domestic investment, foreign direct investment influences growth through technological innovation and higher productivity.[31]

The literature shows, however, that the higher productivity obtains only if the host country has a minimum threshold stock of human capital (which is provided by secondary education). To attract a larger share of world foreign direct investment and to maximize its impact on their economies, African states need to put in place complementary measures, such as improved infrastructural services, more transparent property rights with a judiciary that can enforce them, and programs to ensure the training of skilled personnel to fit the requirements of foreign firms. A stable political and social environment is critical for the protection of property. These factors are more important than the investment incentives typically offered by countries seeking to attract foreign investors.

A third global change concerns the shift of official development assistance, following the end of the Cold War, and the growing perception that large amounts of aid to Sub-Saharan Africa have been ineffective over the past three decades in bringing about growth or alleviating poverty. Africa has grown used to large aid flows, which typically amount to a tenth or more of the domestic economy. As a result of the decrease in overall aid budgets and the emergence of large new demands placed on donors by the former Soviet Bloc, Sub-Saharan Africa faces a declining volume of aid resources in the foreseeable future.[32] The shifting approach to official development assistance emphasizes effectiveness rather than volume of aid and ex post conditionality to a more selective set of recipient states. Donor support will be extended increasingly only to governments that have demonstrated "good behavior," defined largely as adherence to the emerging consensus defined above.

The decline of official development assistance has several major policy implications for Sub-Saharan African countries. First, governments need to improve the effectiveness with which they use aid resources to engender growth and alleviate poverty. In addition to pursuing sound economic policies and promoting local ownership of and accountability for the use of aid resources, this should include efforts to strengthen local capacity to plan, initiate, and manage macroeconomic and sectoral policies, so that aid is better integrated into overall budgeting and development planning. It should also include efforts to reduce reliance on technical assistance over time, thus freeing up resources for program and project support. Second, governments need to create conditions conducive to diversifying sources of external finance, particularly from the private sector. There is a continuing need for external resources to complement domestic resource mobilization and to ensure that ongoing economic reforms are sustained and growth is revived. Third, however, governments must also step up domestic resource mobilization, including domestic saving, foreign exchange generation, and government revenue collection.

In short, Sub-Saharan African countries have to develop or enhance the policies and institutions that will allow them to survive with much less external assistance than they received in the past. Facing these challenges requires a concerted effort by recipients and donors in a strategic partnership that will eventually allow a successful transition to less dependence on aid. This transition will take time to materialize, and continued assistance will be desirable in the immediate future. Nevertheless, countries need to move away from the traditional aid relationships and operational procedures if the transition is to succeed.

The last, but by far not the least important, global change is on the technological front. One currently sees a technological revolution led by very rapid developments in informatics.[33] This revolution has the potential to raise productivity by improving the organization of work and by linking the globe through information superhighways. Access to the benefits of this technology depends critically on the quality of human skills available in the domestic economy. It also requires incurring large costs to reorganize production systems, and it may impose high levels of structural unemployment. It is apparent that developing countries, such as those in Southeast Asia, that have positioned themselves well for using this new technology have been successful in closing not only income gaps but to a very large extent also the technological gap. To avoid technological marginalization and, more important, to gain access to this efficiency-enhancing technology, Sub-Saharan African countries will have to invest more in human competence. Because the cost of hardware for this form of technology is not as prohibitive as that of purely mechanical technology and continues to decline, it may offer some opportunities for African economies that upgrade their pool of skills to leapfrog technologically.

TOWARD NATIONAL STRATEGIES FOR ECONOMIC RENEWAL

In sum, the lessons learned from almost two decades of experimenting with economic reform and the changing nature of the international environment signal the need to put together new strategies for poverty-reducing growth in Sub-Saharan Africa. The vision is to employ a more effective government to promote broad-based growth by strengthening the human capital base and thereby increasing labor productivity, to encourage private initiative so as to enhance its contribution to the process of growth, and to provide a stable institutional environment (economic and political) that favors the long-term commitment of resources for economic expansion. External cooperation should be sought to complement these initiatives. In light of past experience, and based on the lessons discussed above, we single out six major areas as central to the national strategies for economic renewal in the future.

Consolidating Achievements in Macroeconomic Stabilization

First, the recent achievements in macroeconomic stabilization pursued by a large number of African economies need to be consolidated. Sustainable macroeconomic stability is a prerequisite of growth because it helps countries to avoid the stop-and-go cycles prompted by the need for painful adjustments to periodic, severe resource gaps. With adjustment finance becoming more scarce, large adjustments will disrupt the growth process and have high welfare costs. Where such finance is available, it should be aimed at reducing uncertainties in resource availability. Furthermore, a stable and sustainable macroeconomic environment boosts the confidence of private investors, for whom improved creditworthiness is key. Potential foreign investors pay great attention to whether or not efficient mechanisms for allocating resources are in place as well as to growth and export performance. Their confidence in the economic prospects is key, because their investments allow countries to diversify away from the high dependence on diminishing official development assistance.

The design of the adjustment process itself needs to minimize the costs associated with policy reform by providing appropriate sequencing and timely access to flexible medium-term financing. Building an internal consensus about sharing the burdens imposed by the adjustment process is probably more important than obtaining financing for ensuring that the adjustment process is sustainable. In this regard fiscal adjustment is probably the most sensitive and has tended to be the most elusive of the stabilization measures adopted. As Elbadawi argues in Chapter 1, Sub-Saharan African countries need to raise their effort to collect revenue. The potential for substantial increases in revenue can be judged from recent successful experiences in Ghana, Kenya, Malawi, and Uganda. To a large extent, success in this effort hinges on three main areas of action. First, governments need to reduce leakages from tax obligations and to raise the tax system's productivity by reducing exemptions and opportunities for evasion. Improved and simplified tax structure, stronger tax administration, improved incentives to collectors, and firm action against misconduct are essential for plugging the leakages. Second, the tax base must be enlarged, most notably by extending it to previously untaxed earners in the agricultural and informal sectors. Third, voluntary compliance should be increased through tax education and efforts to engender fairness in treatment. Demonstration of value for money on the side of government expenditure, simplified tax structures, and avoidance of prohibitive tax rates are conducive to voluntary compliance.

Even if governments manage to mobilize more domestic resources, they must also reduce the large overhang of external debt. This cannot be overemphasized. The burden of debt servicing prevents governments from making much-needed developmental investments. Reductions in the debt burden are critical not only for sustaining both external and fiscal balance but also for engendering confidence to encourage private sector investment. What makes matters worse is the close link between external and fiscal constraints on growth in these countries, because the bulk of external debt has to be serviced through the mobilization of fiscal resources.[34] When the recent buildup of internal debt through domestic borrowing from the public is taken into account, establishing fiscal viability faces immense odds.

Chapter 1 by Elbadawi elaborates on the nature and sources of uncertainties related to the existence of a large debt overhang. In general, a key element in securing policy credibility is the adequacy of finance and assurance of its continuation.[35] Investors are concerned about future tax burdens and potential reversals of policies that are not fully compensated by expected returns to investment.[36] The result of these uncertainties is a tendency to "wait and see." Some debt relief and the promise of stable official aid flows are both critical to reducing these fears. Stability, policy credibility, and a clear commitment to maintaining both reduce uncertainty and raise creditworthiness. In this context, regional cooperation can be used to protect gains made in macroeconomic stability through collective action, as Elbadawi argues, and should be encouraged.

Enhancing State Capacity for Development

A successful development strategy in Africa must include a constructive role for the state in fostering and managing the development process. The role of the state in efforts to initiate, implement, monitor, manage, and evaluate policy change is now increasingly recognized, as is the need to strengthen the present capacity of the state, even as the scope of its activities is circumscribed. But the policy implications of current state weakness have not been fully assimilated.

Rapid economic growth of the kind witnessed in East Asia probably requires the state to take a more proactive role than simply providing basic public goods like stable property rights, basic infrastructure, and law and order. In the immediate run, all African governments should make sure that they are capable of providing these basic public goods. The longer-term challenge for African governments is to overcome the weak capacities of current public institutions so that governments can play a more proactive role. For instance, given various disadvantages and constraints facing private investors, states probably need to implement targeted policies to favor key sectors, subsidize the acquisition of needed technologies and skills in the working-age population, or to protect infant industries judiciously and encourage small and medium enterprises. Until the state's current weaknesses are alleviated, however, to be effective, such a proactive role will have to be undertaken rarely and with caution, notably regarding its budgetary sustainability and administrative implications.

As emphasized by Brautigam in Chapter 2, enhancing state capacity to perform these ambitious tasks has several components. First, it implies meaningful civil service reform.[37] In many countries, substantial improvements in the working conditions are needed to enhance the effectiveness of public institutions. It is not unusual for the level of real wages to have declined by 90 percent over the past 25 years, leading to low morale, moonlighting, and high turnover. Improving material incentives is particularly overdue at higher grades and skill positions. Civil service reform also involves a host of other measures, including paying more attention to manpower planning and training issues, establishing promotion and pay systems based on merit, reclassifying positions, and enacting measures to instill an esprit de corps among staff. Given the resources available to most African states, upgrading the performance of the civil service is a long-term proposition, which cannot be expected to pay immediate dividends. Reform should initially focus on enhancing the policymaking capacities of a small number of core state institutions that are most central to macroeconomic stability and growth.

Second, economic reforms that dismantle state controls or divest the state of public enterprises can help promote state effectiveness, by concentrating the state's limited resources on a limited number of functions. It is important for governments and their citizens to set priorities for the activities of the state and to ensure that adequate resources are devoted to higher priority activities, before lower priority ones are addressed.

Third, in the past, economic policymaking suffered from the pervasive interference of private interests, through clientelism, rent seeking, and patronage.[38] At the same time, performance suffered from the lack of institutions that could promote the transparency of decision making and enforce the accountability of decision makers. Improved decision making implies both protecting state decision makers from political pressures and ensuring the accountability and transparency of their actions.[39] Political leadership initially plays a critical role by covering the senior civil servants who will be in charge of implementing politically difficult policies.

Although it cannot replace leadership, the current process of democratization in Africa is an important part of this agenda in that it increases public participation and competition, both of which can pressure the state to open up and improve its performance. Indeed, many observers have suggested that improved economic performance in Africa is not possible without democratization or at least significant changes in governance.[40] At the same time, as Gyimah-Boadi and van de Walle suggest in Chapter 6, unless the state is strengthened, it is not clear that it will have the capacity to respond to the new demands put on it. A difficult balance must be struck between enhancing participation in decision making and overburdening decision makers with constituency pressures that do not serve long-term national interests.[41] Part of the solution is to strengthen state administrative structures so that they are capable of processing, channeling, and, when necessary, rejecting demands. The importance of the institutional capacity of the state to define and pursue realistic long-term development policies cannot be overemphasized. In addition, what Paul Collier has called agencies of restraint must be established. These are institutions that can protect certain critical policy processes from day-to-day political pressures.[42] Even as increased contestation and inclusiveness open up the political process, the implementation of policy must be insulated and protected.

Promoting a Dominant Role of the Private Sector

Accelerating rapid growth will necessarily require the prominent involvement of investors, entrepreneurs, and enterprises from the private sector. Mobilizing domestic and foreign private capital and know-how is a critical prerequisite of recovery: The experience of the past three decades clearly demonstrates the limits of government-led development strategies. In some countries, recent years have been marked by the flight of large amounts of capital; ensuring its return will help spur growth and increase the confidence of potential foreign investors. Foreign direct investment will help compensate for local capital shortages and can provide valuable learning opportunities for the local economy by introducing new production and marketing technologies and by opening new export markets. Experience suggests that job creation is most dynamic within small and informal private sector enterprises.

This does not mean that the state does not have a critical role to play; it does mean that governments need to encourage, stimulate, regulate, and complement the private sector, rather than compete with it or attempt to displace, discourage, and exploit it, as too often happened in the past. Governments should do both more and less than they have been doing. They should intervene less in competitive markets, notably by continuing the process of liberalization and privatization many have already begun. They should eliminate various disincentives for foreign direct investment, and they should lighten the burden of administrative controls and regulations on private sector activity.

The promotion of private investment entails changing the relationship between the public and private sector, which too often has been characterized by suspicion and rent seeking. Creating a climate favorable to investment requires establishing a partnership between the government and the private sector on the basis of greater transparency in public administration and strong intermediate organizations, such as chambers of commerce, business councils, and professionals associations, that can engage the state in a regular dialogue.

At the same time, governments need to do more than in the past to provide an enabling environment that encourages productive investment. This includes, first and foremost, ensuring low inflation and macroeconomic stability through sound and sustainable policies, as the World Bank has long argued. In addition, governments should provide basic public goods such as secure property rights, an effective legal system, and more generally effective governance,[43] as well as an adequate public infrastructure. Surveys of business attitudes consistently emphasize the quality of communications and transportation infrastructure in determining investment decisions.[44] Governments need to establish effective and transparent regulatory systems in order to protect consumers or lessen monopoly power in certain sectors. Private markets will not function well and investment will not increase until governments perform these basic economic responsibilities adequately, even if they have managed to eliminate inflation.

Transforming Agriculture for Broad-Based Growth and Poverty Alleviation

The renewal of growth will need to start in the countryside, and agricultural transformation thus needs to be reinstated onto the development agenda. Thirty-five percent of Sub-Saharan Africa's GDP and 70 percent of Africa's population depend on agriculture, and poverty alleviation will depend on agriculture's performance for the foreseeable future. Although recent measures have focused on incentive structures to elicit increased supply from existing capacity, neither donors nor governments have paid adequate attention to improving agricultural productivity and aggregate production capacity, yet these are fundamental to the sector's development and to the health of the overall economy. Agricultural yields have more or less stagnated in Africa in contrast to their rapid rise elsewhere. A thriving agriculture is an important prerequisite of rapid industrialization because it can provide markets for industrial output and contribute toward foreign exchange earnings on which the successful operation of the industrial sector is particularly dependent. It is also a key component of a sustainable effort to alleviate poverty.

Previous attempts at agricultural transformation in Africa were not successful due to problems with the design and implementation of strategies. In a large number of cases, state involvement substituted for grassroots initiatives. Committed resources were inadequate, while policies heavily taxed agriculture to obtain resources for other economic sectors. That the thrust of modernization was placed on industrialization rather than on agriculture is evidenced by the very low investment going into the sector. A fresh look at the transformation of agriculture needs to incorporate strategies for strengthening human capabilities, redefine the roles of the public and private sector in the transformation process, focus on investments in rural infrastructure, and enhance the rural institutions needed to promote longer-term investments in the sector, in particular land tenure and credit institutions. To address poverty concerns more directly, transformation ought explicitly to target poverty reduction and equity, as Delgado suggests in Chapter 4.

Delgado also offers an agenda for the transformation of agriculture. The thrust of the strategy focuses on the pursuit of investment in new sources of productivity growth. These sources of growth revolve around the reduction of transaction costs in the sector, particularly in relation to transport costs, the adoption of technological innovations to enhance supply responsiveness, and the creation of schemes aimed at reducing risks so as to enable specialization according to ecological comparative advantage. Institutional innovations to engender more decentralization and privatization of supportive services to agriculture are key factors for lowering the transaction costs facing smallholders. To the extent that the public sector's role in the modernization of agriculture will continue to be dominant for the foreseeable future, policies ought to focus on addressing market failures and promoting (not necessarily providing) those services with potentially large benefits to the sector that cannot be captured privately.

Building Capacity

Long-term economic success will depend on building the human capital base to promote modernization of the economy. This requires, first, considering basic education and health not solely as consumption items for improved welfare (needs) but also as investment in productive competence. Much of the debate on provision of these services has focused on the relative merits of efficiency versus equity concerns and has been driven largely by the extent of budgetary exposure, given the dominance of public provision of these services at present. The key instruments to resolving this tension include enhancing efficiency via better technology and cost-effective delivery as well as private sector and community participation in service provision. As Appleton and Mackinnon show in Chapter 3, this is particularly true for postprimary education, where the high private returns generated justify a larger role for private provision.

Second, a policy to build human capital should also aim to develop a broad array of technical, managerial, and scientific skills needed to sustain rapid growth. Technological progress should be seen more broadly to encompass skill formation. A supportive incentive structure should reward the acquisition and building up of such competence. The issues here range from the most cost-effective ways of achieving basic human competence involving the private and the public sector; the use of technological choice and competition policy as the means to promote skill formation; the roles of foreign investment and transnational corporations in effective technological transfer, including skill formation, through learning by doing; and the role of research and development.

Third, technocratic capabilities and supportive institutional structures need to be enhanced to enable local formulation and implementation of sound macroeconomic and sectoral policies. This emphasizes the need to support capacity building for the analysis and design of policy and the monitoring of implementation of development programs. Civil service reforms currently being pursued in a number of African countries are one part of this initiative. Previously the focus was on downsizing the civil service with the objective being mainly to reduce government expenditure. Increasingly, and correctly so, more attention is being paid to enhancing the effectiveness of governments to enable them to deliver services efficiently and to provide the required development management leadership. Strong governmental structures, competent and confident civil servants, controls on the expenditure system, and the ability to direct policy are necessary for an effective government.

Capacity-building initiatives are not confined to governmental entities alone. The private sector, particularly the informal sector, needs to acquire skills to manage enterprises efficiently. Enhanced institutional capacity for providing information on markets and investment opportunities can go a long way to improve the overall efficiency of the economies. In the same view, so as to allow local communities to contribute meaningfully to development, there is need to strengthen the capacities of communities to plan and execute local development projects. Support has been received through nongovernmental agencies and local governments in this regard, but there is need to coordinate their activities in unison with national development strategies.

Diversifying the Economy

The final area concerns appropriate industrialization and trade strategies. The earlier concerns about the diversification of African economies through industrialization remain valid. The issues here pertain to the approaches adopted for achieving a healthy and dynamic industrial sector with strong linkages to the resource base and the internal demand structure. Import substitution industrialization buttressed by protective trade policy has constrained productivity growth, an essential feature for industrial development in today's competitive world. Export-led industrialization has played an important role in Southeast Asia's phenomenal growth. Although a trade policy stance that fosters openness and competition has played an important role in the success stories, lowering the costs of innovation and technological learning and carefully designing strategic interventions have also played a major role. The same experience also shows that a healthy industrialization process need not come at the expense of productivity growth in agriculture. What, then, are the appropriate ingredients for an industrialization strategy in African economies that builds on past investments in the sector and draws lessons from successful industrialization experience of other developing countries?

As Lall and Stewart point out in Chapter 5, efforts should be directed at building an efficient export-oriented industrial sector. To do so, African governments need to go beyond the provision of a stable macroeconomic environment and import liberalization—although these are critically important—to address the problems of weak technological capabilities and to develop export competence. Lack of technological capabilities is likely to continue to constrain sustained supply response.

Although cheap labor is likely to be a major source of comparative advantage for most industrializing African economies and should be aggressively pursued, as Lall and Stewart observe, the ability to compete internationally in the new global economy requires a level of productivity and managerial and technical skills that is presently lacking in these countries. In light of the significant contribution of small-scale enterprises to industrial output and employment, there is need to create conditions for further development of this subsector so as to exploit its potential. In addition to eliminating biases against the sector, it is necessary to promote technology and credit institutions to service its requirements.

In pursuing these measures, care must be taken regarding the speed and sequencing of relevant reform measures in order to minimize the likely cost of deindustrialization in the short term. The roles of governments and private actors in the process of industrialization need to be reappraised so as to allow strategic complementarities between the two. Government has a role to play in undertaking limited judicious strategic interventions to address market failures and provide public goods such as infrastructure and basic training necessary to build industrial capabilities. In addition, however, given managerial deficiencies and limited state capacities, governments will need to rely on the private sector to spearhead the process.

CONCLUDING REMARKS

The different elements of the development strategies that are needed are discussed at much greater length in the chapters that follow. Here, we note the interrelated nature of the different components of this strategy. Thus, industrialization and increased exports almost certainly hinge on macroeconomic stability, private sector development, and greater civil service effectiveness; achieving the transformation of agriculture requires both private markets and the development of greater technical capacity in public institutions than is available today. Because all of the elements are connected, many African economies have been stuck in a vicious circle, in which lack of progress on one front has undermined the sometimes considerable efforts on another. To a great extent, these linkages are not unique to economic policymaking in Africa, but institutional and financial resource scarcities and general economic vulnerability provide Africa with less margin for error than other, richer states.

How, then, can African economies put themselves on a virtuous cycle, where, on the contrary, effort in one area pays general dividends?

First, as is now widely agreed, any strategy must begin with coherent macroeconomic policies that generate the climate of stability and certainty without which there can be no investment and growth. Only in a climate of stability can governments begin to plan for the long term. Thus, there is no escaping the need for sometimes politically difficult fiscal and monetary adjustment. Luckily, the evidence suggests that implementation of stabilization does not require additional institutional capacities and can be expected to yield economic benefits within a couple years.

Second, it makes considerable sense to focus on the measures that are within grasp right away, given available resources. On the one hand, stabilization can be achieved within several years. Similarly, no extra resources are needed to assemble and empower small teams of qualified senior civil servants to implement the economic policies that have been decided upon by the government and its citizenry. On the other hand, as Brautigam rightly insists, creating stronger state institutions is a long-term process that cannot be expected to pay dividends for some time. A markedly more effective civil service should be an immediate objective in many countries in the region, but progress on achieving this will take many years. Similarly, a highly interventionist industrial policy along the lines pursued by East Asia may well be desirable at some point in the future, but it is unrealistic today. What is immediately possible, however, and should be emphasized right away is ensuring an institutional and policy environment that does not actively discourage investment. Governments should pursue the latter, while at the same time beginning to develop its capacities to undertake more proactive policies. In all cases, even as they work to expand their own capacities, governments should be aware of their present limitations.

Finally, a lesson throughout this book is that successful development strategies in Africa will require establishing clear priorities to make the best use of existing scarce financial and managerial resources. In the short run, at least, the choices may well be stark and may involve the deferral of some desirable policy objectives. More expenditure on primary and secondary education, for instance, may imply less public support for tertiary education, which may instead have to rely on creative use of private sector provision. It is only armed with this newfound realism that Africa will be able to forge the development strategies that will allow it to overcome the present crisis and renew with growth.

Notes

[1] UNCTAD, *Trade and Development Report 1994* (New York: United Nations, 1994).

[2] See, for instance, Gerald M. Meier, ed., *Politics and Policymaking in Developing Countries: Perspectives on the New Political Economy* (San Francisco: Institute of Contemporary Studies Press, 1991). See also Tony Killick, *A Reaction Too Far: Economic Theory and the Role of the State in Developing Countries* (London: Overseas Development Institute, 1988).

[3] Michael T. Hadjimichael et al., "Effects of Macroeconomic Stability on Growth, Savings, and Investment in Sub-Saharan Africa: An Empirical Investigation," IMF Working Paper WP/94/98 (Washington DC: International Monetary Fund, 1994), Table 9.

[4] C. M. Reinhart and P. Wickman, "Commodity Prices: Cyclical Weakness or Secular Decline?" IMF Working Paper WP/94/7 (Washington, DC: International Monetary Fund, 1994).

[5] World Bank, *Adjustment in Africa Reforms Results and the Road Ahead* (New York: Oxford University Press, 1994); Hadjimichael et al., op. cit.

[6] R. Barro and J. Lee, "Losers and Winners in Economic Growth," paper presented at the annual conference on development economics, World Bank, Washington, DC, World Bank, May 1–2, 1993; William Easterly, "Policy Technology Adoption and Growth," in *Economic Growth and the Structure of Long-Term Development*, ed. Luigi Pasinetti and Robert Solow (New York: St. Martin's Press, 1994) pp. 75–89; Ibrahim Elbadawi and Benno Ndulu, "Growth and Development in Sub-Saharan Africa: Evidence on Key Factors," World Congress of the International Economic Association, Tunis, December 17–22, 1995.

[7] Gyimah-Boadi and van de Walle discuss these deficiencies at length in Chapter 6 in this volume.

[8] Six countries (Botswana, Guinea, Sierra Leone, Zaire, Zambia, and Zimbabwe) are categorized as mineral rich, while another five (Angola, Cameroon, Congo, Gabon, and Nigeria) are categorized as oil rich.

[9] See I. William Zartman, ed., *Collapsed States: The Disintegration and Restoration of Legitimate Authority* (Boulder, CO: Lynne Rienner Publishers, 1995).

[10] Between 1990 and 1994, authoritarian incumbents in 11 countries were ousted from power through free and fair multiparty elections, and many of these, it can be argued, are working democracies today, albeit fragile and imperfect ones. In another five, the incumbent won multiparty elections but has maintained various political and social rights. For more on this, see Michael Bratton and Nicolas van de Walle, *Democratic Experiments in Africa: Regime Transitions in Comparative Perspective* (New York: Cambridge University Press, forthcoming 1996).

[11] Ibrahim Elbadawi and Benno Ndulu, "Long-Term Development and Sustainable Growth in Sub-Saharan Africa," in *New Directions in Development Economics,* ed. M. Lundahl and B. Ndulu (London: Routledge, forthcoming 1996).

[12] Reginald Green, "ESAF Renewal: Project Decision or Structural Entry Point?" *Compendia of Studies,* Vol. 3, UNCTAD GID/G24/3 (New York: United Nations, 1993).

[13] Gerald Helleiner, "External Resource Flows, Debt Relief, and Economic Development," in *From Adjustment to Development in Sub-Saharan Africa,* ed. G. Cornia and G. Helleiner (London: Macmillan, 1993); Elbadawi and Ndulu, op.cit.; Green, op. cit.

[14] See K. Forss et al., *Evaluation of the Effectiveness of Technical Assistance Personnel Financed by the Nordic Countries* (Copenhagen: DANIDA, 1990); Elliott Berg, *Rethinking Technical Cooperation: Reform for Capacity Building in Africa* (New York: United Nations Development Programme and Development Alternatives Inc., 1993); Uma Lele and R. Jain, "The World Bank's Experience in the MADIA Countries: Agricultural Development and Foreign Assistance," in *Aid to African Agriculture: Lessons from Two Decades of Donors' Experience,* ed. Uma Lele (Baltimore, MD: Johns Hopkins University Press, 1992).

[15] See Lele and Jain, op. cit., who argue that it is considerably less for multilateral donors.

[16] Ibid.

[17] World Bank, "Financial Flows to Developing Countries: Current Developments," *Financial Flows and the Developing Countries: A World Bank Quarterly* (Washington, DC: World Bank, March 1992).

[18] Gerald Helleiner, "From Adjustment to Development in Sub-Saharan Africa, Conflict, Controversy, Convergence, and Consensus," in *From Adjustment to Development in Sub-Saharan Africa,* ed. G. Cornia and G. Helleiner (London: Macmillan, 1993).

[19] Cited in United Nations Development Programme, *United Nations Human Development Report 1994* (New York: Oxford University Press, 1994). The exceptions are Botswana, Gabon, Mauritius, Seychelles, South Africa, and Swaziland.

[20] The statistics used in this paragraph come from World Bank, *World Tables 1994* (Baltimore, MD: Johns Hopkins University Press, 1994); and from World Bank, *World Development Report* (New York: Oxford University Press, various years).

[21] Gross enrollment ratios may exceed 100 percent when some pupils are younger or older than the country's standard primary school age, due to early or late entry, repeated grades, etc.

[22] Vito Tanzi, *Taxation in an Integrating World,* Integrating National Economies Series (Washington, DC: Brookings Institution, 1995).

[23] Adebayo Adedeji, "An Alternative for Africa," in *Economic Reform and Democracy,* ed. Larry Diamond and Mark Plattner (Baltimore, MD: Johns Hopkins University Press, 1995).

[24] Tanzi, op. cit.

[25] Ibid.

[26] See Anne O. Krueger, *Trade Policies and Developing Nations,* Integrating National Economies Series (Washington, DC: Brookings Institution, 1995), and comments by Benno Ndulu and Dani Rodrik in the same.

[27] See, for example, Hadjimichael et al., op. cit.; World Bank, *Adjustment in Africa,* op. cit.

[28] E. Fernando-Arias and P. Montiel, "The Surge in Capital Inflows to Developing Countries: Prospects and Policy Response" (World Bank, Washington, DC, 1995, mimeo); and Tanzi, op.cit.

[29] P. K. Asea and C. M. Reinhart, "Real Interest Rate Differentials and the Real Exchange Rate: Evidence from Four African Countries," paper presented at the African Economic Research Consortium Workshop, Nairobi, May 27–June 2, 1995.

[30] Tanzi, op. cit.

[31] K. Jansen, "Macroeconomic Effects of Direct Foreign Investment—The Case of Thailand," *World Development,* Vol. 23, No. 2 (1995), pp. 193–210; and E. Borensztein, J. Gregorio, and J. Lee, "How Does Foreign Direct Investment Affect Economic Growth?" NBER Working Paper No. 5057 (Cambridge, MA: National Bureau of Economic Research, 1994).

[32] Helleiner, "External Resources Flows," op. cit.

[33] C. Brundenius, "How Painful Is the Transition? Reflections on Patterns of Economic Growth, Long Waves, and the ICT Revolution," paper presented at the international colloquium New Directions in Development Economics Growth Equity and Sustainable Development, SAREC, Stockholm, 1995.

[34] Jose Fannelli, Roberto Frankel, and Lance Taylor, "The *World Development Report* 1991: A Critical Assessment," in *International Monetary and Financial Issues for the 1990s,* ed. UNCTAD, Vol. 1 (New York: United Nations, 1992).

[35] Helleiner, "External Resources Flows," op. cit.

[36] See also Benno Ndulu, "Foreign Resource Flows and Financing of Development in Sub-Saharan Africa," in *The International Monetary and Financial System: Developing-Country Perspectives*, ed. G. K. Helleiner (New York: St. Martin's Press, 1996); Benno Ndulu, "International Governance and Implications for Development Policy in Sub-Saharan Africa," in *Global Governance and Development Fifty Years After Bretton Woods: Essay in Honour of G. K. Helleiner,* ed. A. Berry, R. Culpeper, and F. Stewart (Ottawa: North-South Institute, forthcoming 1996).

[37] In addition to Chapter 2 by Brautigam, see David Lindaeur and Barbara Nunberg, eds., *Rehabilitating Government: Pay and Employment Reforms in Africa* (Washington, DC: World Bank. 1994); and World Bank, *Adjustment in Africa,* op. cit.

[38] See Goran Hyden, *No Shortcuts to Progress: African Development Management in Perspective* (Berkeley: University of California Press, 1983); Richard Sandbrook, *The Politics of Africa's Economic Stagnation* (Cambridge, UK: Cambridge University Press, 1985).

[39] Deborah Brautigam, "Governance, Economy, and Foreign Aid," *Studies in Comparative International Development,* Vol. 27, No. 3 (Fall 1992), pp. 3–25.

[40] See "Democracy and Growth: Why Voting Is Good for You," *The Economist* (August 24, 1994); World Bank, *Sub-Saharan Africa: From Crisis to Sustainable Growth: A Long-Term Perspective Study* (Washington, DC: World Bank, 1989).

[41] On this point, see Thomas Callaghy, "Civil Society, Democracy, and Economic Change in Africa: A Dissenting Opinion about Resurgent Societies," in *Civil Society and the State in Africa,* ed. John W. Harbeson, Donald Rothchild, and Naomi Chazan (Boulder, CO: Lynne Rienner Press, 1994), pp. 231–54; Richard Jeffries, "The State, Structural Adjustment, and Good Government in Africa," *Journal of Commonwealth and Comparative Politics,* Vol. 31, No. 1 (March 1993), pp. 20–35.

[42] Paul Collier, "Africa's External Economic Relations, 1960–1990," in *Africa, 30 Years On: The Record and Outlook After Thirty Years of Independence,* ed. Douglas Rimmer (London: James Currey, Ltd., 1991).

[43] The role of these kinds of governance issues in the development process is the subject of Mick Moore, ed., "Good Government?" *Institute of Development Studies Bulletin,* Vol. 24, No. 1 (special issue, January 1993); World Bank, *Governance and Development* (Washington, DC: World Bank, 1992); and World Bank, "Financial Flows to Developing Countries," op. cit.

[44] Breakdowns in public infrastructure impose significant burdens on businesses. In Nigeria, a 1990 survey of 179 firms found that 92 percent had their own electricity generators, 37 percent owned radio equipment, and 44 percent owned their own boreholes. Cited in Tony Hawkins, "Industrialization in Africa," in *Africa, Thirty Years On,* ed. Douglas Rimmer (London: James Currey, 1991), p. 148.

Policy Perspectives

Summary of Chapter Recommendations

Consolidating Macroeconomic Stabilization and Restoring Growth in Sub-Saharan Africa

Ibrahim A. Elbadawi

Save for some remarkable progress in a few countries, the overall outcome of economic reforms in Sub-Saharan Africa has so far been modest, if not disappointing, even in those African countries that escaped major political instability or protracted civil wars. The continent has the dubious distinction of being the only developing region of the world that experienced zero average per capita growth over the last 30 years, including negative growth rates over the last two decades. In contrast, other developing regions fared much better, and in some cases spectacularly so as in the case of the East Asian "miracle" countries. It is not surprising, therefore, that out of the 20 poorest countries of the world, 16 are from Sub-Saharan Africa. Given the current tragedy of economic development in Africa, avoiding major policy reversal—let alone deepening the reform process—is still a major concern. Restoring growth in the short run following macroeconomic stabilization, creating conditions (e.g., structural diversification and flexibility against external and natural shocks) for its sustainability in the medium to long runs, and ensuring that growth is sufficiently equitable and broad based to achieve meaningful poverty reductions are minimal conditions for generating a self-enforcing reform process.

Based on Africa's own reform experience and the lessons from other development experiences—most notably that of East Asia—a broad convergence (and not necessarily consensus) is emerging that emphasizes relevant elements from the traditional statist development strategy as well as the more recent market-oriented reform programs (market discipline, private sector, and a redefined but critical role for the state). The broader elements of this paradigm are the following:

- *structural adjustment*, encompassing macroeconomic stabilization measures such as fiscal and monetary restraint and exchange-rate reform to correct macroeconomic imbalances and to change the structure of incentives, as well as supply-side measures, such as trade liberalization, financial-sector reform, and public-sector reform, to eliminate microeconomic distortions;
- restoring and sustaining growth in the medium to long term, requiring policies and institutions that facilitate *rapid accumulation of physical and human capital* (as in the East Asian experience); and
- *sustained growth in per capita income* to achieve sustainable reduction in poverty.

This strategy, however, provides only the *necessary* (and by no means *sufficient*) conditions for sustained growth and reductions in poverty. It also does not provide sufficient guidance for making the switch from adjustment to growth. To bridge the gap between necessity and sufficiency, several major issues need to be addressed. For example, one such issue is how countries are to develop the capacity to manage their own affairs in an uncertain internal, regional, and world environment. Clearly a broader development vision (which should include a strategy for external economic relations) is needed to guide the reform process, taking into account the role of national capacity in determining the success of reforms as well as the efficacy of state intervention and therefore its role in economic development.

While the overall macroeconomic adjustment in Africa has been substantial, it is still well below that of the East Asian economies, which is judged to be consistent with sustainable growth. Therefore, consolidating the initial macro-based fiscal stabilization with deeper structural reform in fiscal policy institutions and other supportive structural reforms should clearly be a top priority for Africa. Subscribing to the above analysis, a combination of four policy measures and external initiatives needs to be in place to effect the switch from stabilization to growth in the short run following stabilization.

First, a massive debt reduction for Africa is required to resolve the market coordination problem facing the reforming countries of the region and to allow the resumption of growth in the short run, and hence the sustainability of reform, as well as to level the playing field for achieving and sustaining longer-term growth. A key feature of a new strategy of external support for Africa could be based on full or partial replacement of the balance-of-payments support with drastic debt reduction and/or debt freeze for a very substantial period.

Second, African states can and should help effect the transformation to a more diversified economy by investing in education and human capital, so that domestic production of capital goods will eventually become internationally competitive. To make this possible, however, African economies need a significant reduction of their debt overhangs to release resources for investment and growth.

Third, to the extent that the current African democratization process generates more transparent, participatory, and open governance, it could strengthen commitment to reforms and foster credibility in the longer run. In the short run, however, it could make some aspects of the reforms more difficult to implement.

And, finally, there is a window of opportunity for African countries to use regional integration as a supranational mechanism to foster national policy credibility and as a means for pooling risks between otherwise vulnerable small economies; to resolve conflicts and minimize political risk; to exploit complementarities; and to develop regionally based links on a reciprocal and mutually beneficial basis.

State Capacity and Effective Governance

Deborah Brautigam

Since the early 1980s, observers have highlighted the critical role played by a strong and capable state in the remarkable development performance of East Asian economies, and yet the thrust of reforms in Africa has been not to build, but to shrink the state. At the close of the twentieth century, state capacity in Africa remains inadequate for economic renewal. Although high levels of debt and reduced taxation revenues significantly affect state capacity, the weakness of African states is only partly a matter of finance. Too many governments fail to link budgeting with planning, collect information on their own debts, or audit their internal accounts. Corruption, low skill levels, low morale, and a lack of accountability are all growing problems.

Increasing state capacity is a long-term process. Compared to other developing areas, African states are very new—the vast majority of them being formed during colonial rule and taken over by the first generation of African leaders scarcely a generation ago. Most of today's countries inherited the mantle of statehood without first building a nation. By comparison, colonialism ended in most of Latin America in the mid-nineteenth century, and many of the high performing Asian countries had long histories of bureaucratic development before the arrival of the Europeans.

Four dimensions of state capacity are critical for economic renewal. Regulatory, or legal, capacity enables the state to set and enforce the rules of economic and social interaction, leading to greater predictability. Technical capacity gives the state specialized abilities to assist producers and manage macroeconomic policy, leading to greater stability. Extractive or taxation capacity allows the state to raise revenues to pay for its programs. And administrative capacity encompasses the management skills that provide effective government service.

Although governments and aid agencies have paid a great deal of attention to training and higher education, technical assistance, and civil service pay and employment reforms, these efforts have had little impact on the growing problem. When leaders make arbitrary policy decisions rather than relying on careful analysis, ruling mainly through patrimonial ties rather than rational-legal norms, there will be little demand at the top for more effective governance. Donor strategies for building state capacity must start with local initiatives and serve primarily to reinforce demand for better governance when it clearly exists, supporting local ownership of state capacity building programs.

This chapter outlines a strategy for government leaders committed to building state capacity. A committed government might begin by rebuilding professionalism and a sense of mission in the civil service, by establishing clear rules and transparent, merit-based procedures for hiring and promotion, by institutionalizing review procedures that evaluate and reward good performance, and by using the money saved through attrition and the elimination of fictitious "ghost" employees to raise government salaries to approximately market levels. This should directly reinforce administrative capacity. Second, governments are more likely to succeed in their reforms if they adopt a realistic strategy of concentrating reforms in a few critical bureaus first, shifting politically important patronage opportunities to slightly less vital agencies. An excellent starting place for reform would be the internal revenue service and the customs bureau as a means of strengthening the critical element of extraction capacity. These reforms can help finance other aspects of capacity, while more directly building demand among citizens for effective governance. Third, agencies critical for economic stability and the rule of law will perform better if they can be insulated from patronage pressures and short-term political demands. This is especially important for the central bank and the judiciary. Fourth, capacity outside the public sector can reinforce capacity within. This is particularly true of the professions of law, accounting, medicine, and engineering, all of which have deeply held professional values as well as technical expertise. Nongovernmental development organizations also often share strong values and expertise. Strong professional associations, professional schools, and other nongovernmental entities can provide sources of information and technical expertise; through membership activities, professional training, and joint implementation efforts, they can help create demand for a more capable and effective state, while reinforcing core professional values in both state and society.

Enhancing Human Capacities in Africa

Simon Appleton and John Mackinnon

Countries in Sub-Saharan Africa have relatively low levels of attainment in health and education. Some observers argue that health and education are normal goods, for which demand is positively related to income. Thus low levels of achievement are simply a result of Africa's poverty. However, various forms of market failure reduce the levels of health and education below what would be possible and desirable given the resources available to the economies concerned. Moreover, health care and education are not pure consumption goods whose availability depends on income. Rather they are investments in human resources that can help to generate future income as well as save lives. There is a role for state action, but extensive failures within the public sector raise questions of political economy and management as well as of economic policy.

In general, after independence Africa experienced remarkable improvements in educational access and life expectancy. Progress slowed during the 1980s, however, and future gains are uncertain given the economic outlook and the AIDS epidemic. By comparison, the present state of health and education is far worse in Africa than in the rest of the developing world. In Africa gross primary school enrollment ratios average around 69; in the developing world as a whole they average more than 100. Life expectancy for Africa is around 51 years compared with 63 for the developing world.

Although much research finds economic returns to investments in education and health, the evidence is limited because it is typically nonexperimental and is almost always concerned with private, as opposed to social, returns. Consequently, the existing state of knowledge does not quantify the overall gains from public investments in human resources. Some commonly made claims in this area—such as the supposed high returns to primary education in wage employment—are probably not true for Africa in the 1990s. Moreover, insofar as these claims concern only private returns to wage employment (a minority activity in Africa), they are largely irrelevant. More empirical work is needed in this area (for example, to identify the effects of education on productivity in agricultural and nonagricultural self-employment). In health care, systematic application of cost-effectiveness tools, as those presented in the *World Development Report 1993*, would help to guide allocation decisions. However limited the existing evidence may be, it does suggest that both education and health services save lives and can bring sizable economic returns.

There are strong a priori grounds for believing that without public action investments in human resources will be inequitable and inefficient. Subsidies are justified on a number of grounds: distributional objectives (both within and among households), extensive informational failure, secondary market failure, and externalities. The distributional argument is straightforward: making progress to universal provision of basic services will tend to benefit individuals from more disadvantaged households and, in the case of education, the more disadvantaged within households (often girls). Because information is limited, it cannot be assured that individuals will privately purchase optimal levels of health care and education. Secondary market failure refers to the absence or imperfect functioning of the credit and insurance markets often needed to fund private education and health. Positive externalities are the benefits that accrue to others from investments in one individual. Public health measures are a classic example, but more recently the "new economic growth" models have stressed the network externalities arising from education.

Three distinctive features of health care and education are relevant to this discussion. First, education decisions—and many decisions about health care—are made by parents on their children's behalf. Second, education and health care consist largely of the transmission of information, and hence it is not surprising that consumers are often ill-informed. And third, the consumption of health and education services entails substantial time and transport costs, which means that demand is finite even when services are provided free.

Once the need for public action is established, the question becomes how much health and education should be subsidized. Without reliable quantification of the social benefits, this question cannot be settled once and for all. However, significant improvements in education and health are achievable with commitments of resources that are not prohibitive for most African countries. The required interventions need to be selective, such as investments in textbooks rather than reductions in class size or investments in public health campaigns targeted at villages rather than in national hospitals. For most African countries, it is sensible to aim for universal free provision of basic health and education, but what counts as basic services will have to be carefully delimited. There is widespread agreement that primary education and many primary health services should be included. For many countries, hard choices must be made concerning secondary education and more expensive curative health services. Often, these further services will have to be rationed (by academic ability or medical need), will require cost-sharing, or, for some individuals, will be left to private and nongovernmental providers.

The recommendation that public finance in both health and education needs to move from tertiary to primary facilities has been made widely, because African governments are financing expensive social services for a small elite, while failing to provide cheaper services for the bulk of their populations. Political-economy reasons have prevented the adoption of this recommendation until now, but this situation may be changing. Nevertheless, tertiary education also exhibits important secondary-market failure; in this case a graduate income tax seems the most feasible way of making beneficiaries pay.

The private sector currently plays a major role in health care and education in most of Africa. In the case of education, there are few grounds for heavy regulation. In Africa, many private schools cater to children whom the state cannot afford to educate further. The best private schools set standards or introduce diversity, which may ultimately benefit the public sector. In the case of health, consumer ignorance raises grounds for regulation. This is perhaps clearest in two cases: tobacco products, which unregulated threaten a future epidemic of smoking-related disease, and medical drugs, which, through reliance on overpriced brand-name products, currently cost Africa eight times what they should.

Public provision of health care and education could be improved in a variety of ways. The current mix of inputs may be suboptimal. For example, teaching materials are likely to be better investments in learning than smaller classes. More generally, there should be payoffs in the form of incentives, decentralization, and competition traditionally associated with the private sector. Various reforms could achieve those payoffs. Given the size of the public sector in most countries, it is possible to carry out pilot tests of some of these reforms at relatively little cost or risk. Such efforts to improve the quality of social service provision would naturally strengthen the case for expanded public funding.

Agricultural Transformation: The Key to Broad-Based Growth and Poverty Alleviation in Africa

Christopher L. Delgado

A strategy for the agricultural transformation of Africa should involve a series of closely related initiatives, beginning on the supply side, incorporating potential for growth on the demand side, and fully mobilizing local resources.

First and foremost, rural people living in areas where agricultural transformation is in its early stages need research and extension to cut the unit costs of producing items for which a local market exists. It does not greatly help to promote nontradables at this point, including services and micro-scale local manufactures, because they lack an expanding local market. Instead, it seems more fruitful to cut the costs of production for those items for which rural people already have a broad market and that can absorb production increases without large price declines. This means promoting agricultural and livestock exports, in most cases.

At early stages of agricultural transformation, it is unrealistic to think that the private sector could replace public agencies in providing research and extension services. This will be possible later, in higher stages, particularly where benefits are capturable. Cases in point are cash crop projects, such as tea out-growers or hybrid maize sales, both of which are more likely to occur in later stages. In early stages, the risks are too great and the returns are too hard to capture. In a given country, both private and public systems can co-exist, if they do not try to do each other's job.

Finally, the debate between observers who think that Africa has lots of unused agricultural technology on the shelf and those who think that such technology is not appropriate for local conditions will soon become moot. Reforms of policies that held back the adoption of shelf technology have been under way for some time. Technologies that shift the supply curve for nontradables will probably stagnate, despite market reforms and despite being technically sound. In contrast, demand for technologies that alleviate supply constraints for tradables will grow.

Freeing up the movement of goods and services in Africa is the second highest priority. Some of this can be accomplished by direct policy action; some will require major infrastructural investments. Liberalization of road transport has been slower to occur in Africa than liberalization of other areas, yet most rural goods move by truck when they move over long distances. Removing 80 percent tariffs on spare parts or charges imposed by local police forces, as in the central corridor of West Africa, would reduce agricultural transport costs. Beyond such initiatives, there is little alternative to improving the central grid physical infrastructure, as expensive as it is.

In the absence of major technological change in staple food production, an important means of developing smallholder agriculture is to promote production of higher value products on the farm. Most high-value products such as nontraditional agricultural exports, dairy products, and aquaculture products are subject to especially high transaction costs. These products have high costs because of high perishability; large quality differences related to handling and end product; lumpiness of initial investments (economies of scale) in production, processing, and marketing; inflexibility and lags in production plans; and seasonal variability in output.

Supportive policies to lower the transaction costs facing smallholders wishing to become involved in these activities will require significant institutional innovation. In Africa's changing political and fiscal environment, many of these innovations will involve decentralization and privatization of functions once thought to be more appropriate to parastatal activity. They will involve both grassroots producer organizations and trader associations. Such institutions will need to function within market principles and to deal with the public goods nature of some of the issues.

One of the harshest challenges facing Africa during the 1980s was the need to diversify the base of agricultural exports. Food and beverages typically account for well over half of merchandise exports in nonoil-exporting countries of Sub-Saharan Africa, excluding South Africa.

Despite the concentration of exports at the national level, African agriculture is extremely diverse across zones, within villages, and even on individual farms. At the farm level in Africa, crop and livestock diversification is largely management of risk, and, as elsewhere, technological progress and commercialization will probably require more specialization of households in addition to diversification across households. Similarly, in the future farmers in dry areas perhaps should concentrate on raising livestock for trade as opposed to producing foodgrains under difficult conditions. Better transport links between zones producing different commodity groups would help, but it is not enough.

To reap the growth benefits of the division of labor and to permit both commercialization and technological progress to proceed, public policy in countries at an early stage of agricultural transformation will need to reduce the risks associated with farm, village, or regional specialization. It would be irresponsible to advocate such specialization in current conditions, which include unpredictable food supplies, only partially liberalized linked markets, and arbitrary policy shifts. Nevertheless, previous regimes successfully introduced cash crops by guaranteeing the availability of food. It is hard to see how agricultural transformation will occur in countries subject to the unpredictable climate shifts facing most of Africa unless some form of public agency shares with farmers the risks of food security.

The key to fostering rural employment in Africa is to promote widespread and sustained increases in income for large numbers of rural people from sources that are not dependent on local demand. Higher smallholder production of tradable crops and livestock as a result of lower unit costs of production and distribution is the best bet for having this widespread impact. Once the engine of growth is in place, then policy must facilitate the supply response of the products, especially food items, that rural people wish to buy when their incomes rise. This will help to ensure that higher rural demand is translated into higher production, rather than higher prices for wages and goods.

The instruments with which to commercialize agriculture include spatially diffused rural infrastructure, functioning rural institutions, and a dynamic agriculture based on technological progress. Because the required interventions are often commodity-, location-, and time-specific, national and local decision makers will have to have the will and the ability to assess specific constraints on and potential for rural production and marketing.

Only participatory local institutions will be capable of mobilizing the local knowledge and the immense resources required to promote agricultural transformation. Only African political processes can arrive at the right form of local government for a dynamic countryside. Donors can still prioritize the flow of resources to countries that have demonstrated real commitment to bringing farm people into the political class. Donors and national governments must strengthen the national capacity to conceptualize national problems.

Trade and Industrial Policy in Africa

Sanjaya Lall and Frances Stewart

Industrialization is an essential aspect of long-run development. In nearly all economies, the manufacturing industry has been a critical agent of the structural transformation from a primitive, low-income state to one that is dynamic, sustained, and diversified. Consequently, the objective of industrial policies in Africa must be to build up an efficient industrial structure that will permit the long-term expansion of manufacturing exports.

Industrial policies in much of Africa during the 1960s and 1970s emphasized heavy import protection, subsidized credit and tax incentives, and considerable regulation. The pattern of industrialization was, for the most part, inefficient, with very low linkages to the rest of the economy and very low levels of exports. As a result, the returns were not commensurate with the resources invested. The structural adjustment programs that were put in place in many countries at the beginning of the 1980s with the help of the World Bank sought to eliminate all the distortions that prevented the realization of market-driven competitive solutions. However, these reform programs were based on economic assumptions that are not appropriate for African economies. The rapid and sweeping liberalization recommended by structural adjustment programs was incapable of promoting industrialization or increasing exports.

The results of structural adjustment programs in 45 African countries can be grouped into three categories: those with "improved" policies, those with policy "deterioration," and those that did not undergo adjustment during the period 1980–93. Nothing can be concluded, however, about the general effects of adjustment on gross domestic product or industrial growth, export performance, or competitiveness. This is not to deny that good macroeconomic policies are desirable in Africa, but rather to suggest that causal inferences must be drawn with much more care about the impact of rapid liberalization on low-income economies such as those in Africa. The case of Ghana, which has undergone substantial reform to its trade and industrial regime, illustrates clearly the limits of orthodox adjustment strategies. Pervasive market failures raise the costs of adjustment to import competition and hold back the creation of new manufacturing activities and exports in response to the new incentives.

Instead, two components are essential to the satisfactory development of industry. First, industrialization policies must be efficient, so that resources are not wasted and the sector may eventually become a significant source of exports. Second, indigenous capabilities must be built up so that Africans perform more and more major managerial and technical functions. The policies of the 1960s and 1970s emphasized protection of African industry but placed little emphasis on efficiency. The adjustment policies of the 1980s focused almost exclusively on efficiency and paid no attention to capacity-building. For the future, then, it is necessary to steer a delicate course between these two extremes.

Thus, bearing in mind the dual objectives of developing efficient industrialization and building up capabilities, policies for reform and stabilization must emphasize five areas. First, different policies must be put in place to encourage African ownership of industry, through joint ventures between the public sector and private sector firms and between foreign and local firms.

Second, structured markets are needed to avoid a common bias against the small-scale sector. Various measures can be promoted to ensure that adequate resources are allocated to small firms. In particular, technology and credit institutions must be designed to serve small firms. Third, a more gradual and nuanced strategy of liberalization is needed. This would include a slower, more realistic pace that would give enterprises the time to adjust and improved capabilities that would ensure the government's ability to mount pervasive interventions in support of industrialization. Fourth, regional integration should be promoted through efforts in finance, trade, and infrastructure. Policies should encourage greater liberalization of restrictions on trade within the African continent. Fifth, supply-side measures should be pursued, including development of skills, support and extension of technology, improvement of infrastructure, and provision of adequate financial support for industrial restructuring and upgrading.

The Politics of Economic Renewal in Africa

E. Gyimah-Boadi and Nicolas van de Walle

The major obstacles to Africa's economic renewal are institutional. Pro-growth economic policies will not emerge there without the development of more effective political institutions. Such institutions are likely to emerge under specific circumstances.

States that create and sustain a policy climate that promotes productive investments, exports, growth, and human welfare are called developmental states. They are characterized by three key factors. First, they are endowed with a professional and skilled central administration that provides the state with the capacity to implement sound policies effectively. Second, they have a central government that enjoys broad legitimacy. Finally, they are deeply committed to economic growth. Most African states lack all three of these characteristics.

Various obstacles inhibit the emergence of developmental states in Africa. First, the weak capacity of existing state structures militates against the emergence of effective states. In most countries of the region, the states inherited at independence possessed very little capacity. Economic crisis probably undermined what capacity had been built up in the years after independence. Building more effective state administrations will require time. Second, the roots of the African state are found in neopatrimonialism, which also militates against the emergence of more effective states. State elites often lack the political incentives to improve state capacity.

These obstacles to economic and institutional reform are structural and highly unlikely to change in the short run. Moreover, past, largely unsuccessful, attempts at reform have created a great deal of skepticism about the long-term sustainability of policy change, which makes successful reform more difficult today. The willingness of donors to try to micro-manage the reform process, sometimes in the face of little governmental commitment to reform, worsens this situation.

Several factors have been identified as prerequisites to the emergence of states capable of bringing about rapid economic growth in Africa. First, democratization and the empowerment of civil society have been identified as necessary to bring about rapid development. Yet the current wave of democratization will result in slow change, because many of the key institutions of democratic politics are too weak for multiparty elections to change economic governance dramatically. Second, a change in the social coalitions that dominate African politics has been identified as a necessary precondition for the adoption and sustaining of pro-growth policies. A new, pro-growth coalition is emerging in some countries, but it is nascent at best and will become dominant only if and when economic reform becomes viewed as legitimate and thus sustainable and only if it is organized and led by an effective political force.

Third, a broader and more sophisticated debate about economic policy is needed by African elites. Africans are usually poorly informed about the nature of the economic choices their economies face. A broad-based policy debate is needed for the African public and elites to engage in "policy learning," a process through which perceptions of available options and choices are altered.

Fourth, effective political leadership is needed to overcome obstacles to economic and institutional reform. Few African leaders seem to have developed a positive political strategy for sustaining fundamental economic reforms that would promote growth. Yet, for leaders who are committed to reform, a host of strategies are available to lessen resistance to painful economic reform and to restore credibility to the reform process. Even the most committed leadership will not make much of a difference, however, if that commitment is not backed up with organizational and mobilizational capacity. That is the purpose of political parties, which can mobilize popular support for governmental policies.

This argument has several implications. African states are not completely hemmed in and are capable of putting into place and sustaining pro-growth economic policies. Macroeconomic stabilization should be an urgent priority of all African states. Stability is needed if African economies are to attract productive investment, and instability is having a disastrous long-term impact on institutional capacities, which must be addressed urgently.

It is at the same time important for governments to integrate institutional reform into the reform process from the outset, rather than to defer it to a later phase, as has typically been done in recent reform programs. Civil service reform, or the strengthening of the judiciary, needs to be undertaken right away. At the same time, the state apparatus will need to devote its limited resources and capacities to a circumscribed set of essential functions for the foreseeable future. Finally, the past pattern of donor-government relations, characterized by a combination of ineffectual conditionality and micro-management of the reform process, has been counterproductive and needs to be changed.

Building the developmental state in Africa will take much more time than has typically been allowed for in public policy debates about economic reform in Africa. Creating capable institutions both inside and outside the state will require years of effort.

Agenda for Africa's Economic Renewal

Chapter One

Consolidating Macroeconomic Stabilization and Restoring Growth in Africa

Ibrahim A. Elbadawi

INTRODUCTION

With a few remarkable exceptions, the countries of Africa[1] have so far seen at best a modest and in many cases a disappointing payoff from economic reform. Even those countries that have escaped major political instability or protracted civil war have little to show for their reform efforts.[2] The African continent has the dubious distinction of being the only developing region of the world that has experienced zero average growth in GDP per capita over the last 30 years, and the only one to suffer negative growth on average (at an annual rate of –0.35 percent) over the last two decades. During the more recent period from 1987 to 1992, only a few countries—Botswana, Chad, Ghana, Guinea-Bissau, Mauritius, Mozambique, Nigeria, Tanzania, and Uganda—achieved growth rates of real GDP per capita exceeding 1 percent per year. This performance contrasts sharply with that of the countries of East Asia and the Pacific, which achieved spectacular growth in real GDP per capita of over 5 percent per year on average during 1965–1990, and even with that of Latin America, which grew at an average rate of almost 2 percent per year.

It is not surprising, then, that of the world's 20 poorest countries, 16 are in Africa, and that the relative standing of most African countries in more tangible human terms, such as infant mortality, life expectancy, and calorie intake, is alarming.[3] During the 1980s, for example, infant mortality in Africa averaged 125 per thousand births, compared with only 58 in Latin America and the Caribbean, 38 in East Asia and the Pacific, and 11 among the industrial market economies of the Organization for Economic Cooperation and Development (OECD). Life expectancy at birth averaged 48 years for the African countries, compared with 64, 65, and 74 years for the other three regions, respectively, and daily caloric intake averaged 2,122 calories in Africa, compared with 2,721, 2,617, and 3,417 calories for the other regions.

Given the tragedy of economic development in Africa and the political infeasibility of sustaining reforms, policymakers in the region find themselves hard pressed just to avoid major policy reversal, let alone deepen the reform process. Reforms have not yet become self-sustaining, nor will they until the following minimum conditions are met: a restoration of growth in the short run following macroeconomic stabilization; structural diversification, to give the economy the flexibility to withstand both external economic and natural shocks; and measures to ensure that growth is sufficiently equitable and broad-based to achieve meaningful reductions in poverty. This paper attempts a partial assessment of the recent experience with macroeconomic reform in Africa, with the objective of proposing some future direction of policy toward sustained and equitable development.[4]

The quest for macroeconomic reform in Africa and the adoption of a new development paradigm have dominated academic and policy circles in the continent itself and in the international development community since the beginning of the 1980s. This new approach has come in the wake of the failed development strategies of previous decades, which emphasized development finance and a dominant role for the state in the development process (while tending to ignore the shortcomings of an overextended state, such as rent seeking and inefficiency) and belittled the roles of the private sector and market discipline in development. But the evolution of the new paradigm has followed a costly learning curve as well. As Benno Ndulu has observed, in its earlier phases the new development strategy "focused on macroeconomic stabilization at any cost and the restructuring of incentives and other supply-side factors to encourage output growth. Concerns for other development fundamentals, including national capacities to initiate and sustain change, were pushed to the background."[5]

From Africa's own reform experience and that of other developing regions—most notably East Asia—a broad convergence of policies (if not necessarily a consensus) is emerging, which emphasizes elements of both the old and the new development strategies, stressing market discipline and involvement of the private sector, but also acknowledging a critical, although redefined, role for the state. The broad elements of this emerging paradigm are the following:

■ *structural adjustment,* encompassing macroeconomic stabilization measures such as fiscal and monetary restraint and exchange-rate reform, to correct macroeconomic imbalances and to change the economy-wide structure of incentives, as well as supply-side measures such as trade liberalization, financial-sector reform, and public sector reform, to eliminate microeconomic distortions;

■ policies and institutions that will facilitate the *rapid accumulation of physical and human capital* (using the East Asian experience as a model), to restore and sustain growth in the medium to long term within an enabling macroeconomic environment; and

■ *sustained growth in income per capita,* to achieve a sustainable reduction in poverty.

This strategy, however, establishes only the necessary (and by no means sufficient) conditions for sustained growth and sustained reduction in poverty.[6] Nor does it provide sufficient guidance for making the transition from adjustment to growth.[7] The gap between necessity and sufficiency is considerable. For example, one major issue that still needs to be addressed is how countries are to develop the capacity to manage their own affairs in an uncertain internal, regional, and world environment. Clearly a broader development vision (which should include a strategy for external economic relations) is needed, taking into account the role of national capacity in determining the success of reforms as well as the efficacy of state intervention and therefore its role in economic development.

To set the stage for a discussion of these issues, the next section of this paper reviews the recent experience with macroeconomic reform in Africa. The review emphasizes the centrality of fiscal adjustment, because it is the most fragile component of reform yet can determine the chances for sustainability and progress for the entire reform program. The section that follows compares the current macroeconomic policy stance in Africa with the policy frontier, that is, best contemporary policy practice as proxied by that of the most successful Southeast Asian countries. The paper then addresses the issue of how to move from stabilization to growth; here the emphasis is on the key role of external support in consolidating fiscal positions as well as the critical problem of market coordination: of inducing a timely response by private investors to the opportunities created by reform. Three further requirements for restoring growth are also discussed: the need to enhance economic flexibility as a defense against shocks; the need to foster regional cooperation and regional complementarities; and the need to reduce political risks.

A REVIEW OF MACROECONOMIC POLICY REFORM IN AFRICA

The macroeconomic and sectoral policy stance in most African countries deteriorated rapidly after the mid-1970s, for a variety of reasons including mismanagement of the commodity export booms that Africa had enjoyed during that decade. The problems reached crisis proportions in the early 1980s: For the region on average, government consumption as a percentage of GDP rose steadily from the late 1960s on, eventually exceeding the average for the other developing regions by a staggering 50 percent in 1977. Average GDP per capita declined by 15 percent between 1977 and 1985. The severity of these problems compelled many countries in the region to embark on comprehensive adjustment programs, assisted by the World Bank, the International Monetary Fund (IMF), or both. Almost all of these countries started their adjustment from a position of low and declining real incomes; worsening fiscal imbalances and mounting current account deficits, external debt and debt service burdens; very low national saving and nvestment rates (and what investment remained was relatively inefficient); and declining agricultural output, external competitiveness, and export performance. This dismal policy stance, coupled with the inflexibility and structural disarticulation (i.e., weak linkages between sectors within the economy) that characterize these economies, provided the makings of a crisis when the continent experienced the severe external shocks of the late 1970s and early 1980s.

A recent comprehensive World Bank study reviewed the record of economic reform in Africa over the second half of the 1980s and concluded that macroeconomic adjustment efforts so far have been substantial, but have not yet reached the policy frontier adequate for restoring growth and reducing poverty.[8] However, in analyzing the timing of the crisis in Africa and the policy response to it, an important distinction needs to be made between the fixed-exchange-rate economies of the two CFA monetary unions[9] and the "flexible"-exchange-rate economies elsewhere in the region. The World Bank's broad characterization largely applies to the situation in the non-CFA countries. The countries of the CFA zone, on the other hand, benefited from the discipline of monetary union and the depreciation of the French franc (to which their common currency, the CFA franc, was pegged) against the U.S. dollar and were able to weather (or at least delay) the effects of the external shocks of the late 1970s and early 1980s. After 1986, however, the CFA zone economies started to experience serious adjustment problems due to the strengthening of the French franc, a precipitous decline in their terms of trade, accumulated fiscal imbalances, and an inability to achieve real depreciation of their currencies without devaluation, given that initial inflation rates were already very low.

Thus, even as many non-CFA African countries were consolidating their reforms and adjusting to external shocks during the second half of the 1980s, the CFA countries experienced substantial real overvaluation of their common currency, loss of competitiveness, and protracted recession.[10] Preliminary evidence following the devaluation of the CFA franc by 50 percent in 1994 suggests that the countries of the CFA zone have finally begun to address this problem: Some progress has been made toward depreciating the CFA franc in real terms, strengthening fiscal positions, and restoring export competitiveness and growth.[11] However, the anticipated future strengthening of the French franc is bound to generate problems for these countries in the not too distant future.

Against the background just described, it is not surprising that macroeconomic reform (at least in the non-CFA countries of Africa), although substantial, has not yet reached the policy frontier. This section provides a brief overview of the evidence, focusing on three main areas of macroeconomic policy: fiscal, exchange-rate, and monetary policy. This analysis seeks to motivate the analysis of the two sections that follow, by underscoring the centrality of fiscal reform—which by no coincidence is also the most fragile component of reform—for the sustainability of the overall macroeconomic reform process in Africa, and hence the scope for restoring and sustaining growth in the long term.

Fiscal Policy

As Table 1 shows, the record of fiscal policy in Africa is fragile at best. The median fiscal balance for the region as a whole worsened steadily over the 1981–1992 period, with the median ratio of the overall fiscal deficit (excluding grants) to GDP increasing from 7.6 percent in 1981–86 to 8.5 percent in 1987–1992, and reaching 8.7 percent in the last two years of the latter period. The median ratio for the overall deficit including grants has remained stationary, at 6.2 and 6.1 percent of GDP for 1981–86 and 1987–1992, respectively, and during the last two years of the latter period it declined by half a percentage point of GDP, to 5.6 percent. These numbers reflect the steady rise in net official grants, from 1.4 percent of GDP in 1981–86 to 2.4 percent in 1987–1992 and to 3.1 percent in 1991–92.

This story of worsening overall fiscal deficits needs to be balanced, however, by the remarkable progress made in cutting primary fiscal deficits (a measure that excludes expenditures for debt service). The average primary fiscal deficit among the African countries rose from 2.6

TABLE 1. MACROECONOMIC POLICY STANCE IN AFRICA, 1981–92 (percentage of GDP except where noted)

	All Countries			CFA Countries			Non-CFA Countries		
Indicator	1981–86	1987–92	1991–92	1981–86	1987–92	1991–92	1981–86	1987–92	1991–92
Fiscal policy									
Overall fiscal deficit									
Excluding grants	7.6	8.5	8.7	7.5	9.4	7.5	10.1	8.5	9.1
Including grants	6.2	6.1	5.6	6.0	6.4	5.8	7.3	4.7	5.4
Total revenue	18.4	17.3	17.0	18.4	16.9	16.7	18.4	17.7	19.2
Expenditure									
Total	27.9	26.0	26.0	28.5	26.1	23.8	27.3	25.9	27.7
Current	17.9	18.0	18.2	16.2	17.3	15.8	20.2	19.7	19.3
Capital	8.7	n.a.	6.1[a]	10.6	n.a.	5.8[a]	6.8	n.a.	6.4[a]
Monetary policy									
Seigniorage[b]	1.1	0.7	1.1	1.0	–0.3	–0.1	1.6	2.0	2.3
Inflation rate (percent per year)	10.5	7.5	9.4	6.6	0.2	0.2	18.4	22.5	23.4
Real interest rate on deposits[c] (percent per year)	–0.7	1.0	5.5	2.0	6.0	7.9	–5.2	–4.7	–4.4
Exchange rate policy									
Change in the real effective exchange rate index (percent)[d]	n.a.	n.a.	n.a.	–7.6[e]	11.4[f]	n.a.	60.0[e]	47.6[f]	n.a.
Parallel market premium[g] (percent)	n.a.	n.a.	n.a.	n.a.	n.a.	n.a.	59.7	36.5	22.2[h]

Note: All data are medians for the country group indicated. n.a. = not available.

[a]Data are for 1990–91.
[b]Calculated as $(M1_t - M1_{t-1})/GDP_t - g_t * (M1_t/GDP_t)$, where $M1_t$ is the stock of money at the end of period t, GDP_t is gross domestic product at time t, and g_t is the rate of real GDP growth.
[c]Calculated as the difference between the nominal interest rate and the inflation rate in the following year, divided by one plus the inflation rate in the following year.
[d]An increase in the index indicates a real depreciation.
[e]Data are for 1981–92.
[f]Data are for 1980–92.
[g]Difference between the parallel market exchange rate and the official exchange rate at the end of the period.
[h]Data are for 1993.

Sources: World Bank, *Adjustment in Africa: Reforms, Results, and the Road Ahead* (New York: Oxford University Press, 1994); and Lawrence Bouton, Christine Jones, and Miguel Kiguel, "Macroeconomic Reform and Growth in Africa: Adjustment Revisited" Policy Research Working Paper No. 1394 (Washington, DC: World Bank, December 1994).

percent of GDP in 1986 to a peak of 4.4 percent in 1988, before steadily declining to about 2 percent in 1993. This contrasts, however, with a steep rise in debt service payments, from an average of 3.9 percent of GDP in 1986 to 5.7 percent for 1987–92; in 1993 the average debt service burden reached 5.9 percent of GDP—almost three times the primary deficit ratio. Furthermore, the decline in revenue by 1.4 percentage points of GDP for the average country between 1981–86 and 1991–92, coupled with the steady rise in the debt service ratio, was not matched by the substantial cuts in capital expenditure, which declined from a median of 8.7 percent of GDP in 1981–86 to 6.1 percent in 1990–91.[12]

This review of the overall fiscal policy stance in Africa not only exposes the fragility of African economic reform and its strong dependence on foreign aid, but also highlights the very high debt service ratios now prevailing and the adverse conditions they create for future growth: The need to service debts not only diverts resources from investment in human and physical capital but creates economic uncertainty as well. It is also clear that many countries have no option but to resort to distortionary taxes or distortionary fiscal practices (e.g., the so-called inflation tax in the non-CFA countries and arrears in the CFA countries) to finance their remaining deficits, which are still very high.

This overall characterization of fiscal adjustment in Africa, although valid both for the major groupings (CFA versus non-CFA) and for most individual countries, at the same time hides some very important differences among countries—and some important policy lessons. Table 1 highlights several differences between the two major groups.

First, the overall fiscal deficit (excluding grants) of the non-CFA group in 1981–86 was much higher, at 10.1 percent of GDP, than that of the CFA countries, at 7.5 percent. However, these positions were reversed in the 1987–1992 period, when the deficit declined to 8.5 percent of GDP for the first group but rose to 9.4 percent for the second. The modest (1.6 percent of GDP) but important improvement in the fiscal balance of the non-CFA region reflects the payoffs of the initial efforts at macroeconomic stabilization (mainly currency devaluation and reduction of inflation) and not the effects of institutional fiscal reform or other types of structural reform (such as divestiture of public enterprises) that could allow for significant improvement in the fiscal balance. The deterioration of the fiscal balance for this group over the 1991–92 period (the fiscal deficit rose to 9.1 percent of GDP) corroborates this point, since it appears that the initial effect of stabilization has subsided, as very little progress was made on more structural fiscal reforms. On the other hand, the deterioration of the fiscal balance in the CFA group between the two periods is consistent with the deep recession that depressed tax revenue in the CFA zone, and with the worsening terms of trade, which could not be countered by devaluation.[13]

Second, in some of the higher (relative to other Sub-Saharan African countries) income African countries with large fiscal deficits (Congo, Côte d'Ivoire, and Zimbabwe), significant further reductions in the deficit may have to come from cutting current expenditure, not from raising revenue. For example, government revenue in Zimbabwe already stands at more than 35 percent of GDP (more than double the median for the region, and comparable to ratios in the OECD), and current expenditure at 36.4 percent (also more than double the African median). The two CFA countries in this group, Côte d'Ivoire and Congo, have high revenue-GDP ratios by African standards (in excess of 22 percent), yet these ratios are more than 10 percentage points of GDP below their own 1981–86 averages. Therefore, there appears to be some scope in the longer run for these two countries (and for Gabon as well) to maintain their historically high revenue shares and to reduce their large deficits. However, as in Zimbabwe, a more realistic option is to cut current expenditure, which averaged more than 30 percent of GDP in 1991–92. Côte d'Ivoire and Congo may have to experience even more drastic cuts in current expenditure than Zimbabwe in order to provide for more capital expenditure, which on average declined from a very high 15 percent of GDP in 1981–86 to less than 4 percent in 1990–91, while in Zimbabwe it rose from 6.0 percent to 8.5 percent.

Third, for countries such as Kenya, where fiscal performance in terms of overall deficit and revenue ratios has been close to the regional median, a combination of moderate cuts in current expenditure and, more important, further enhancements of revenue would be most appropriate. On the other hand, for countries such as the Central African Republic, Niger, Uganda, and even Ghana, with high deficit ratios but very low revenue ratios, the only option for fiscal policy reform is to boost revenues sufficiently to allow for higher total expenditure, especially capital expenditure, while also reducing the deficit.

Fourth, those countries that have achieved substantial reductions in fiscal deficits did so mainly through even more drastic reductions in capital expenditure. For example, Tanzania and Senegal brought down their overall fiscal deficits to 2.8 percent and –0.3 percent of GDP (i.e., a surplus), respectively, in 1991–92, from levels of 5.8 percent and 2.4 percent over the whole 1987–1992 period. However, to accomplish this, Tanzania had to slash its capital expenditure budget from 6.8 percent of GDP in 1981–86 to 3.9 percent in 1991–92, and Senegal had to reduce a much lower initial budget share for capital outlays (only 3.8 percent in 1981–86) to just 2.7 percent in 1990–91.

In summary, the rather low total revenue ratios and especially low capital expenditure ratios in both the CFA and the non-CFA group suggest that scope for further improving the fiscal policy stance (both in terms of aggregate balance and in terms of the quality of expenditure) can only come from currency devaluation (in the case of the CFA group), to allow capital expenditure to recover in the short run, and, more important, from substantial structural reform and meaningful debt relief, to allow more sustainable and more significant revenue enhancement and steady increases in capital expenditure.

Monetary Policy

Monetary policy in Africa is still by and large determined by the need to finance the fiscal deficit. In addition to official (and usually concessional) external lending, three other forms of financing are available: seigniorage and the inflation tax, domestic borrowing with or without financial repression (e.g., through negative real interest rates on deposits), and private foreign capital flows (both direct investment to finance capital expenditure, and interest-bearing inflows). Excessive use of any of these three types of deficit financing carries dangers, for each corresponds (approximately) to a particular macroeconomic imbalance. Money creation to finance the deficit often leads to high inflation. Domestic borrowing crowds out private-sector consumption and investment and, if accompanied by negative real interest rates, can also lead to financial disintermediation and inefficient resource allocation. External financing leads to current account deficits and further indebtedness, and to exchange-rate disequilibrium (overappreciation of the currency) when capital inflows are speculative and unsustainable.

In the countries of the CFA zone, monetary discipline (the rate of domestic credit expansion may not exceed a specified fraction of previous-year fiscal revenue) effectively rules out the use of seigniorage and the inflation tax, while currency convertibility and very low inflation limit the scope for financial repression through negative real interest rates. Seigniorage revenue,[14] already very low at 1 percent of GDP in 1981–86, declined to a barely negative level of –0.1 percent in 1991–92. Meanwhile the median real interest rate on deposits in the CFA countries was positive and rising: from 2.0 percent in 1981–86 to 6.0 percent in 1987–1992, including a rise to 7.9 percent in 1991–92. This leaves only the options of external finance and domestic borrowing to finance a median deficit (net of external grants) in the CFA zone of about 6 percent of GDP in 1991–92. Many of the high-deficit countries of the zone (such as Côte d'Ivoire and Congo) had great difficulty raising enough revenues through these channels during the severe economic recession and the near collapse of the financial sector during the second half of the 1980s. These countries therefore resorted to such desperate measures as simply running arrears against the private sector, which were quite substantial in the case of Côte d'Ivoire, for example.

The non-CFA countries have a broader array of options for financing their deficits, but these options are also more distortive of their economies. For example, in 1991–92 almost all these countries generated seigniorage revenues in excess of 1.5 percent of GDP, the level beyond which an economy is considered likely to fall into a high-inflation trap. Six of these countries (Guinea-Bissau, Kenya, Madagascar, Nigeria, Sierra Leone, and Zambia) currently have a median seigniorage ratio well above 3 percent, which indicates major macroeconomic imbalance.[15] It is not surprising, therefore, that this group has a median inflation rate of more than 50 percent and includes some countries with much higher inflation (e.g., 142 percent in Zambia, 82 percent in Sierra Leone, and 72 percent in Guinea-Bissau). The evidence likewise suggests that the non-CFA countries have resorted to financial repression to finance their deficits: Real deposit rates in these countries stood at less than –4 percent in 1991–92.

More recently the combination of financial liberalization, tighter monetary policies (mainly driven by IMF conditionality), and even more demanding deficit financing requirements have led many non-CFA countries (e.g., Ghana, Kenya, Tanzania, Uganda, and Zambia) to resort to the sale of treasury bills (in some cases at auction and at exorbitantly high real interest rates) as a means of financing public expenditure. This has resulted in substantial private capital inflows and dramatic real currency appreciation. Available evidence suggests that, perhaps except in Ghana and Tanzania (given the latter's small fiscal deficit), these capital inflows were mainly of a speculative nature (as the recent crash of the Zambian kwacha indicates). This suggests that this new phenomenon of large private capital inflows not only adds to the fragility of African fiscal reform but also, to the extent that the inflows push up the value of the currency, risks reversing earlier gains on the competitiveness front achieved by sustained real depreciations.

Exchange-Rate Policy

A number of countries were obliged to undertake substantial exchange-rate policy reforms in the wake of currency crises during the 1980s. These had been precipitated by the dramatic expansion of aggregate demand, facilitated by commodity price booms, in the 1970s and the subsequent failure to adjust following the terms-of-trade reversals after 1980. Rather than attempt to contain aggregate demand, policymakers in most African countries have responded by increasing exchange and trade controls to avoid a balance-of-payments crisis. These policies, buttressed with increased reliance on foreign aid, have enabled some countries to maintain their apparently unsustainable levels of aggregate demand for a while. However, the inconsistency between their fixed and rigid exchange-rate and trade regimes, on the one hand, and their underlying aggregate demand policies and the external environment (declining external finance and worsening terms of trade), on the other, created the conditions for the emergence of parallel markets in foreign exchange (in the non-CFA countries[16]), capital flight, and substantially appreciating (and possibly overvalued[17]) currencies.

In the non-CFA countries the extent of real overvaluation and the tendency of parallel and illegal dealings in foreign exchange to develop into major markets, usually at very high premiums, have been a major concern of policymakers. Mounting empirical and theoretical evidence suggests that both overvaluation and a very high premium in parallel markets not only complicate macroeconomic management but are also harmful to long-term growth, especially export-oriented growth. Both are considered very distortionary forms of taxation, biased against the country's tradable sectors, and the premium is a visible signal that macroeconomic policy lacks credibility. Therefore policymakers have given high priority, as part of their macroeconomic reforms, to unifying the exchange-rate regime by integrating the parallel markets into the regular economy, eliminating or substantially reducing the parallel premiums, and, most important, achieving substantial real depreciation of the currency.

In many adjusting African countries, reform of the foreign exchange market has been gradual but persistent. Specific measures have included large one-time devaluations (followed by implementation of a crawling peg regime, in which the currency is devalued gradually but steadily over time), reforms in the allocation of foreign exchange (beginning with special windows for purchase of foreign currency for imports, followed by foreign exchange auctions and then interbank markets), and trade liberalization.[18] These policies have been largely successful in achieving the two objectives of real depreciation and reduction of parallel market premiums in many African countries. For example, in the non-CFA group, currencies depreciated in real terms by a median rate of 48 percent from 1980 to 1992, and by 60 percent over the same period, and a few countries achieved more dramatic depreciations: The domestic price of foreign currency rose by 1,174 percent in Uganda, 390 percent in Ghana, 360 percent in Nigeria, and 176 percent in Tanzania. The parallel market premium (calculated as the percentage difference between the parallel market exchange rate and the official rate) declined from a median of about 60 percent in 1981–86 (with premiums in individual countries as high as 1,899 percent in Mozambique and 1,098 percent in Ghana) to just 22 percent in 1993, and premiums fell to negligible levels in countries such as Ghana (1.4 percent) and Tanzania (1.7 percent). Mozambique even recorded a discount of the market to the official rate of 4.6 percent. There have been reversals, however: In Nigeria the premium increased from 37 percent in 1987–1992 to 129 percent in 1993.

In the CFA zone, monetary discipline and the depreciation of the French franc allowed member countries to escape serious real overvaluation during the first half of the 1980s, despite severely negative terms-of-trade shocks and a worsening fiscal stance. However, things have changed dramatically since 1986, when a precipitous deterioration in the terms of trade and the strengthening of the French franc, coupled with the precarious fiscal situation, led to massive overvaluation. From 1980 to 1991–92 the CFA zone achieved a median rate of real depreciation of about 11 percent, too small to be consistent with the dramatic terms-of-trade deterioration of the 1980s. Moreover, the 1987–92 period actually witnessed a median real appreciation of about 7 percent relative to 1981–86, and there were huge appreciations of 32, 25, and 13 percent in Cameroon, Côte d'Ivoire, and Senegal, respectively. Given the pattern of change in the fundamentals, it is generally agreed that the zone has experienced substantial real overvaluation since the mid-1980s.[19]

In summary, exchange-rate policy reform has been by far the most successful (and perhaps the easiest) component of macroeconomic adjustment in the non-CFA countries of Africa but has been until recently the most elusive aspect of reform in the CFA zone. In the non-CFA group the modest fiscal adjustment, but more importantly monetary retrenchment and adequate devaluations, have allowed substantial reductions of the parallel market premium. There has also been a considerable real depreciation of the CFA franc toward its equilibrium, caused by sustainable changes in the fundamentals, most notably a worsening in the terms of trade and liberalized trade regimes. More recently, however, there has been a slowdown of real depreciation in many countries and a reversal in others—changes substantially dictated by fiscal policy considerations.[20] In the end, therefore, the sustainability of the earlier gains in exchange-rate competitiveness in the non-CFA countries and the more recent ones in the CFA zone will depend greatly on further institutional and policy reforms on the fiscal front.

AFRICAN MACROECONOMIC REFORM AND THE POLICY FRONTIER

A comparison of the current macroeconomic policy stance in Africa with the policy frontier, as represented by the policies of three Southeast Asian countries (Indonesia, Malaysia, and Thailand),[21] clearly suggests that Africa needs to undertake further adjustment. Table 2 compares several macroeconomic indicators in these three countries in 1980–1990 with those in selected African countries in 1991–92. Whereas the three Southeast Asian countries recorded fiscal deficits equivalent to 1.8, 2.3, and 10.7 percent of their respective GDPs in 1980–1990, the median deficit-GDP ratio for Africa in 1991–92 was 5.6 percent—more than twice the average for Indonesia and Thailand during the 1980s—and a few countries (Burundi, the Central African Republic, Côte d'Ivoire, and Congo) had deficits that exceeded even Malaysia's average for the 1980s. On the other hand, a few African countries (such as the Gambia, Mauritania, Senegal, and Tanzania) achieved during 1991–92 a fiscal policy stance at least as healthy as that of Indonesia or Thailand during the 1980s.

However, a simple comparison of budget ratios can be misleading. For example, Malaysia saved a third of its GDP during the 1980s, achieving one of the highest saving rates in the world. Therefore it is not surprising that Malaysia could finance a large fiscal deficit internally while holding inflation to 3.2 percent and keeping its debt ratios manageable throughout the 1980s. Clearly a "sustainable deficit" analysis, taking into consideration GDP growth rates, saving rates, and debt ratios, would show that the fiscal policy stance in Africa is substantially short of the Asian standard.[22]

A top priority for many African countries is to consolidate their initial, macroeconomics-focused fiscal stabilization with deeper structural reform of fiscal policy institutions such as the revenue boards and other supportive structural reforms (e.g., further liberalization of domestic goods and financial markets as well as of external trade, restructuring and privatization of state enterprises, and deregulation of private-sector production and investment). In terms of political economy this is the more difficult phase of the economic reform agenda, but it is also potentially the more rewarding. For example, a recent study of fiscal deficits in Chile, Ghana, and Zimbabwe concluded that "active fiscal policies are both the main culprits in fiscal crises and effective instruments in bringing about fiscal stabilization and adjustment."[23] The authors found that fiscal policy variables are by far the dominant factor in these countries' fiscal adjustment or deterioration. External and domestic macroeconomic shocks play a minor, and often even negative,

TABLE 2. THE AFRICAN POLICY STANCE RELATIVE TO THE POLICY FRONTIER
(percent)

Country	Overall budget deficit (including grants) as a share of GDP[a]	Real annual interest rate on loans[b]	Average annual rate of inflation[a]	Parallel market exchange rate premium[c]
Southeast Asia				
Indonesia	1.8	13.2	8.6	8.0
Malaysia	10.7	6.2	3.2	9.0
Thailand	2.3	11.7	4.4	2.0
Africa				
Cameroon	7.2	9.5	0.1	n.a.
Côte d'Ivoire	13.6	4.1	2.6	n.a.
Ghana	6.0	8.0	14.0	1.4
Kenya	4.6	n.a.	24.7	32.0
Mali	5.8	3.1	4.1	n.a.
Nigeria	6.8	–22.7	28.8	128.5
Senegal	–1.1	7.8	–0.9	n.a.
Tanzania	–0.6	n.a.	22.2	1.7
Zambia	4.3	–48.3	142.5	33.3
Zimbabwe	7.7	n.a.	32.7	22.2
Medians				
All Africa	5.6	5.5	9.4	22.2
CFA countries	5.8	7.9	0.2	n.a.
Non-CFA countries	5.4	–4.4	23.4	22.2

Note: n.a. = not available.

[a]The data cover the periods 1980–90 (Southeast Asia) and 1991–92 (Africa).
[b]The data cover the periods 1986–90 (Southeast Asia) and 1991–92 (Africa).
[c]The data cover the periods 1986–91 (Southeast Asia) and 1993 (Africa).

Source: David L. Lindauer and Michael Roemer (eds.), *Asia and Africa: Legacies and Opportunities in Development* (San Francisco: Institute for Contemporary Studies Press, 1994), Table 1 and Tables 4.1 to 4.3.

role in the cyclical variation and the structural changes in public-sector budgets.

Moreover, despite its potentially contractionary short-run effect (which depends on whether and which of an economy's markets suffer from rigidities and on their openness to international transactions), fiscal adjustment is likely to be expansionary in the long run. This expansionary effect works through two channels: the recourse contribution to higher domestic investment and the reduction of financial and monetary market distortions and macroeconomic instability. However, empirical evidence suggests that whereas fiscal adjustment contributes significantly to growth by reducing macroeconomic instability, its effect through the provision of more resources for domestic investment is at best weak.[24]

The consolidation of fiscal adjustment and other macroeconomic reforms, in the hope of creating conditions for sustained growth in the future, requires that public capital expenditures including human capital expenditures rise, that public enterprises be divested, and that public employment be reduced. Such changes should substantially modify, and in many areas eliminate or sharply reduce, the role of the state in the economy. However, these aspects of reform—rewarding though they may be—also present some serious problems of political economy, for example when they require civil service retrenchment.[25] First, market liberalization implies a shift in the structure of incentives, so that educated people and urban dwellers are induced to shift their human capital investment toward private endeavors, including trade. However, the existing stock of human capital may not be well suited to compete in privately productive activities at world prices. Hence, incumbent public sector employees will very naturally try to postpone liberalization, in the hope of never having to realize what for them is a human capital loss. Second, those who expect to see their tenure in the public sector shortened may have strong incentives to seize immediately as large a share as possible of the rents they now enjoy, before those rents disappear. This may increase corrupt activity in the short run. To the degree that the fragility of fiscal adjustment comes down to problems of this sort, there would appear to be a strong argument for front-loaded external aid—for example, in the form of debt cancellation—to buy off the generation that would otherwise block reforms.

FROM STABILIZATION TO GROWTH

Although structural fiscal reforms should have considerable payoffs in all countries, especially those (such as Uganda) where revenues are very low as a percentage of GDP, the reform effort will be substantially limited by heavy debt service burdens. Generating an adequate investment and growth response to macroeconomic reform in Africa may therefore require major and visible external support for the reform program in the form of fundamental debt relief. Also important to this effort are measures to enhance the flexibility of the African economies to withstand external shocks, to reduce political risk, and to foster the credibility of policy reforms through collective commitment.

Coordination Failure and the Role of External Finance

The path dependence of economic growth (on policy variables as well as other fundamentals) is now a well-accepted analytical construct, fostered both by the new theoretical growth models and by recent practical development experience in the high-performing East Asian economies. For African policymakers and scholars and their partners in the wider development community, the findings of this literature represent both challenges and opportunities, now that economic policy could have lasting effects on growth. However, the new models describe economies characterized by relative price flexibility, which ensures full capacity utilization along the path of potential output growth. Certainly this is a useful paradigm for guiding growth strategy in the medium to the long run, but the more immediate issue facing Africa is the challenge of restoring growth in the short run following a stabilization program. One of the main difficulties in restoring growth in the short run is that firms' willingness to invest in export expansion or in domestic import substitution following adjustment may be heavily influenced by concerns that the new policies might be reversed. The problem is one of coordinating private responses with public initiatives. If there is no substantial front loading of incentives in the reform program—which may be difficult politically since it involves further redistribution of income—firms may prefer to take a "wait-and-see" approach, which could delay the restoration of growth by several years.[26]

It has been observed in the aftermath of stabilizations, first in Latin America and now in Africa, that capital (whether it be new or flight capital) does not quickly return, or if it does return is usually placed in liquid rather than in tangible productive assets. Anecdotal evidence suggests that the recent repatriation of flight capital and the flow of new private capital into Africa—in the case of Kenya, for example, but also in Tanzania, Uganda, and Zambia—is largely speculative. This happens because potential investors exercise the option of waiting "until the front-loading of investment returns is sufficient to compensate them for the risk of relinquishing the liquidity option of a wait-and-see position."[27] Formal modeling of the option value of waiting solves two equilibriums: "in one case when domestic rate of returns is not sufficient to warrant the risk of repatriation, no capital comes in. In the other case, because enough capital returns, the risk is low, and therefore the required excess returns falls off to nothing."[28]

Thus, stabilization by itself may not be enough to trigger a virtuous cycle from stabilization to growth to still greater stability. There is a need, therefore, for an external mechanism to resolve this failure of coordination and break the tendency of market participants to wait on the sidelines. In the case of Africa this external mechanism should take the form of substantial debt relief. Admittedly, the continent has been receiving considerable support from both bilateral and multilateral donors in the form of grants and concessional lending. On the other hand, in terms of the ratio of the debt stock to GDP, Africa is the most indebted of all developing regions: The debt to GNP ratio in 1992 reached a staggering 117 percent, which is more than three times the ratio for South Asia.[29] As is argued below, the external finance currently being extended to Africa cannot by itself undo the continent's looming debt overhang—not only is the magnitude of that finance too low but, much more critically, its modality (basically balance-of-payments support) does little to reduce the debt. As a recent study indicated, "in [many low income countries] the debt crisis has halted development. . . . Although financial difficulties are not the only barriers to development in these countries, no policy for growth in the short term could be contemplated without resolving the debt problem at the same time."[30]

One of the key rationales for balance-of-payments support for reforming economies is to leverage policy change through conditionality. However, this mechanism of external support, which dominated African economic reform for more than a decade, has been subject to two major criticisms. First, as a threat-making mechanism it has been challenged by Collier and by Collier and Gunning as largely ineffective and inherently "alien," administered and monitored by outside institutions.[31] Instead these authors have proposed a collective threat-making mechanism in the form of a participatory reciprocal regional arrangement with an industrial-world partner, namely, the European Union. The industrial partner provides a guarantor (or anchor) for the arrangement, which will confer credibility to economic policy reforms. The reciprocal threat-making mechanism works to enforce compliance with jointly agreed policies by member countries. Perhaps a more devastating criticism is that balance-of-payments support tends to take on a life of its own and begins to act as a substitute for exports. This could deprive the economy of the other benefits of having a dynamic export sector. For example, exports may fail to play their natural role as a "conveyor belt" for the import and adoption of new technologies, and as a vehicle for "the learning by doing and learning by looking processes that contributed so successfully to human capital and entrepreneurial skills—as the East Asian miracle has clearly demonstrated."[32]

If one accepts debt relief for Africa as a precondition for sustaining the continent's reforms and enhancing its prospects for sustained growth, through what modality should this relief be effected? Is there a need for some sort of conditionality? Some analysts maintain that debt relief should be heavily conditional and *ex post* (that is, disbursed only after the debtor has demonstrated good progress).[33] Others, however, argue that for debt relief to be credible and effective it has to be both unconditional and *ex ante*.[34]

Three arguments support the latter view. First, governments that are genuinely committed to reforms may not be able to implement them if external creditors cannot credibly precommit themselves to rewarding rather than penalizing short-term effort. Cutting debt today is credible; promising to consider the issue tomorrow is significantly less so, and any debt that remains on the books represents a potentially high future tax on success. Second, the essential contribution of debt relief is not to change the direction of net flows, but rather to remove a major distraction from overburdened African governments that now have to deal with gross flows far out of proportion to the net flows that really matter. The prospective net flows alone give donors plenty of leverage over African economic policy and political development. The additional leverage afforded by gross flows is simply dysfunctional, frustrating the development and "ownership" of home-grown institutions that are so crucial for African governments. Third, the literature on irreversible investment suggests that increased uncertainty leads to postponement of investment. This provides an argument for *ex ante* debt relief that is related to—but distinct from—the argument advanced above based on failure of market coordination. There is clearly a tension between reducing uncertainty (through *ex ante* debt relief) and providing the right incentives (through *ex post* relief), but arguably the former concern should be overriding in the case of Africa and tip the scale in the favor of *ex ante* debt relief.

To summarize, massive debt reduction is required to resolve the market coordination problem that reforming African countries face and to allow the resumption of growth in the short run, and hence the sustainability of reform, as well as to level the playing field (that is, to eliminate the disadvantage that high- indebted reforming countries face) for achieving and sustaining growth over the longer term. The key features of a new strategy of external support for Africa could be based on two broad principles:

- full or partial replacement of balance-of-payments support with *ex ante* and essentially unconditional, drastic debt reduction and/or a debt freeze for a very substantial period, and
- maintenance of traditional conditionality for project lending, which could experience further expansion as reforms consolidate.

Massachusetts Institute of Technology economist Rudiger Dornbusch argues that "a minimal step in that direction is for industrial countries to support the complete suspension of external debt service—to commercial banks and to official creditors—for a substantial period."[35] Dornbusch also notes that "work by the League of Nations in the 1920s provided such programs, and the same are required today."

Economic Diversification and External Shocks

The economies of Africa are structurally weak and disarticulated and hence arguably more vulnerable than other developing economies to external shocks. In addition to the direct cost of such shocks, economies that are perceived to be too inflexible to accommodate adverse external and natural shocks may be unable to attract the additional investment that is the reward for sustained adjustment, because an economy vulnerable to such shocks poses risks similar to those caused by political uncertainty. Diversification of the export base to help stabilize earnings, as well as transformation of the economy to reinforce the links between domestic production and domestic resources and demand, should therefore be at the top of the poststabilization policy agenda for Africa.

EXTERNAL SHOCKS AND AFRICAN ECONOMIES.[36] It is widely acknowledged that any successful strategy for economic management and development in Africa has to be developed and "owned" by the African nations themselves. But many authors have argued all along that, in the case of Africa, the external environment nevertheless matters considerably. For example, African economists Ibrahim Elbadawi and Benno Ndulu offer two arguments emphasizing the extreme vulnerability of growth in Africa, as well as of African domestic economic policy, to both the magnitude and the variability of external shocks.[37] The authors first examine the transmission of external shocks and highlight the structural features that enhance Africa's vulnerability to them. They then look at the types and relative magnitudes of external shocks faced by African countries and how they differ from those affecting other developing countries.

On the first issue, the African economies are structurally dependent, in their quest for imports to sustain production and investment, on uncertain revenue from exports, on the one hand, and on exogenous external resources to finance them, on the other. This dependence is critically important to understanding the extreme vulnerability of these economies to external shocks. A large proportion of Africa's exports are of primary commodities, subject to extreme price volatility in world markets and to supply rigidities. In 1986, for example, 40 percent of African merchandise exports were agricultural, versus 29 percent for the average low-income country worldwide.[38] Meanwhile a large proportion of external resource inflows into Africa is in the form of official development assistance. Exports in turn are largely supply-constrained and significantly dependent on imports for expansion. This intensifies the significance of the foreign exchange constraint on growth.[39] Domestic saving cannot be converted into investment unless foreign exchange is available with which to import capital goods; and once created, productive capacity cannot be effectively utilized without imports of intermediate goods. In this way both capacity and output expansion depend on the availability of foreign exchange. That, in turn, is determined by factors for the most part unrelated to the dynamics of the African economies themselves—it is exogenous. It is this exogeneity of foreign exchange constraints that determines the relative exogeneity of Africa's growth performance and its sensitivity to exogenous shocks.

Second, Elbadawi and Ndulu analyze three types of external shocks: those due to changes in the terms of trade, changes in interest rates, and net transfer effects, which are net capital inflows net of debt payments and other transfers abroad. They find that, for the period from 1970 to 1990, terms-of-trade shocks clearly dominate, accounting for an income loss of 3.8 percent of GDP twice the 1.9-percentage-point loss for other developing countries in the sample.[40] The periods 1973–76, 1979–1980, and 1987–89 witnessed the most severe terms-of-trade shocks. Import price increases were relatively more significant drivers of negative terms-of-trade shocks during 1973–75 and 1979 1980, both because the price changes themselves were larger and because shares of imports in GDP were higher.[41] Between 1970 and 1990, Africa suffered a net income loss of 2.1 percent from all these external shocks combined, compared with 1.6 percent for the other developing countries in the sample.[42]

Recent empirical studies on the international terms of trade for primary commodity exports relative to manufactured goods show that the recent trend against primary commodities is indeed part of a long-run secular decline, as preeminent structuralist scholars Prebisch and Singer hypothesized.[43] Using a sophisticated econometric model, Georgetown University economists Cuddington and Feyzioglu find the terms of trade of commodity-exporting countries to be characterized by a statistically significant negative time trend.[44] The same view is echoed almost word for word by IMF economists Reinhart and Wickham, who also draw an important policy implication from their findings: ". . . irrespective of the technique used, the downward trend has obviously steeped in recent years, implying that the design of stabilization efforts should incorporate this feature of commodity price behavior."[45]

TOWARD AN EXPORT DIVERSIFICATION STRATEGY FOR AFRICA. If, as these findings suggest, the deterioration in the terms of trade facing Africa's major exports is secular in nature (and even the temporary shocks tend to persist over several years), export diversification becomes a development objective of paramount importance for the African countries. The key question is, then, how best to achieve diversification.

A key implication of the Prebisch-Singer hypothesis is that the state should play a proactive role in determining a country's pattern of specialization. Decreasing terms of trade for primary goods lead to increasing relative prices of capital goods and therefore provide an incentive for starting up a capital goods sector. It may also be tempting to recommend to developing countries that they should reduce their imports of foreign capital goods.[46] However, as UNCTAD economist Ziesemer has pointed out, relative productivities matter, and for each price path one can imagine a path of relative labor productivities such that capital goods production does not become profitable, because productivity in that sector is growing more slowly than in other sectors.[47] Ziesemer argues, however, that government can appropriately influence the pattern of specialization when there are significant externalities (spillover effects) from investment and when investments have the character of a public good.

Human capital provides a case in point. When a scarcity of technical progress-enhancing human capital makes the production of capital goods too expensive to be internationally competitive, public investment in education can reduce the cost of producing capital goods and hence influence the pattern of specialization. This view appears to be corroborated by the successful experience of the East Asian countries. Industrialization in these countries at first mainly exploited their comparative advantage in unskilled labor. However, as the industrial experience of these countries grew, as real wages rose, and as the educational attainment and skill composition of their labor forces increased, new industries with comparative advantage in skilled labor emerged.[48] Skill formation and an increase in technological capabilities were thus part of the experience in successful industrialization and not merely a precondition for it. This points to an important feedback from the process of industrialization to building these capabilities and ultimately enabling shifts in comparative advantage.

In summary, African states can and should help effect the transformation to a more diversified economy by investing in education and human capital, thus permitting domestic production of capital goods to become internationally competitive. Mauritius, which succeeded in weaning itself from dependence on sugar exports by focusing on wage restraint and export subsidies in the manufacturing sector, provides an example of a possibly useful strategy for the transition to industrialization, before the payoffs from earlier investments in human capital are fully internalized.

Unfortunately, the policy and international environment facing many reforming African countries has changed profoundly from what it was when Mauritius started its transitional strategy. First, public budgets are shrinking, and the task of reconciling improved human capital formation with declining public expenditure requires considerable attention to ordering the state's priorities. Second, the challenge of promoting manufacturing exports will be stronger in a world that is less tolerant of activist industrial policies, including aggressive export subsidization, than in earlier decades. The important role of industrial policies in the phenomenal industrial transformation and growth of the East Asian economies suggests that reforming African countries will have a hard time replicating the East Asian miracle.[49] However, a significant reduction in the debt overhang could go a long way toward leveling the playing field. Given the dominance of public debt in African countries' debt servicing requirements, such a reduction would help boost public investment in particular, and through it stimulate private investment and increase the absorptive capacity of these economies for growth. Human capacity would benefit in particular from public investment in education and health.

Minimizing Political Risk

No part of the world is worse beset by political instability than Africa south of the Sahara. At its worst this instability manifests itself in protracted civil wars, which arguably also constitute the most spectacular economic shocks affecting the continent, leading some to suggest that "investing in peacekeeping policy might plausibly offer the best social rate of return among African investment opportunities."[50] Obviously, if political instability, and especially civil war, could be avoided, not only would the direct negative externality be eliminated, but the prospects for international and regional support for national reform programs would be enhanced. Evidence suggests that *both* national and regional political instability can have deleterious effects on national economic growth.[51] The recent tendency in the international development community has been to write off those countries suffering from prolonged civil war or from a total collapse of social and political order, such as Angola, Liberia, Rwanda, Somalia, Sudan, and Zaire. Obviously it is hard to find reason for optimism about these countries' prospects. However, these countries not only constitute about one-fifth of the population of Africa but can impose substantial negative neighborhood effects (both political and economic) on other, more promising countries. Hence, understanding the underlying political economy of the African countries so as to avoid civil strife is a pertinent issue within an overall African development strategy.[52] Here African regional institutions can make themselves useful, in this case by providing a mechanism for conflict resolution. For example, the Inter-Governmental Authority for Drought and Desertification (IGADD) has been making considerable efforts to mediate a peaceful resolution of the civil war in Sudan. More recently, the Southern African Development Community (SADC) has started to assume an increasingly important role in resolving the Angolan problem.

Meanwhile the rest of Africa has been swept by a wave of democratization. Despite some major reversals (e.g., in Nigeria and Sudan), and despite the fact that, in many cases, the political opposition still is not fully legitimized or is only reluctantly accepted, there is no doubt that the African political landscape has changed profoundly, not least with the emergence of a democratic South Africa. The advent of democratic rule presents both opportunities and dangers for economic reform and development. One of the dangers is that this new openness will provide an opening for the better organized African bureaucrats and other elites to regain the political power they lost during the adjustment era. Should this happen, the result of democratization could be a reversion to the earlier bias of development policies toward urban areas.[53] Worse yet, multiparty democracy could in some cases legitimize divisive tribal politics, to the detriment of nation building and development. On the other hand, the openness and transparency of the democratic process "may result in a contestable political market," making bureaucratic power more accountable to the people.[54] In any case, the problems of tribalism and other forms of divisive social behavior are part of the substructure of African society and are not likely to go away (and may even worsen) in the absence of transparency and openness.

More transparent, participatory, and open forms of governance are generally considered among the major prerequisites for successful economic reform and successful development in general. Hence it is not surprising that overall assessments of the likely impact of African democratization on the future of economic reform have ranged from cautiously optimistic[55] to upbeat.[56]

Regional Cooperation and Integration to Foster Policy Credibility

Economic cooperation can have a positive impact on the credibility of national policy, as it provides a mechanism for collective commitment to economic reform in the context of a reciprocal threat, such as denying market access to violators of agreements.[57] Deeper regional economic integration can also permit the regional economy to expand to the critical threshold scale at which much-needed strategic complementarities are triggered. An integrated regional economy may be able, where individual countries are not, to attract the levels of investment required for the development of modern manufacturing cores and the transfer of technology within the region.[58] Empirical studies also support the notion that economic integration has growth-enhancing effects. The most significant finding of this literature is that, once spillover effects (such as those due to public investment or political instability) are accounted for, the process of economic growth in Africa can be fully explained by variations in growth fundamentals.[59] Regional cooperation is one of the main factors credited for the stellar performance of the Southeast Asian countries. According to Ibrahim Elbadawi, these factors are, "first and foremost, a strong country-specific and regional economic performance in terms of economic growth, which in turn was substantially enhanced by collective policy credibility and investment spillovers brought about by regional cooperation; second, measured but effective regional cooperation; and, third, policy coordination in the area of external economic relations."[60]

The key question raised by this analysis is whether the existing regional institutions in Africa are up to the task of achieving market integration. In a comprehensive study, Canadian researcher Jeffrey Fine and deputy director of London-based Centre for Economic Policy Research Stephen Yeo argue against renewed integrative efforts in Africa along traditional lines, in which, despite their repeated failure in the past, existing regional schemes are called upon to attempt to promote regional trade directly.[61] These schemes, they argue, are inappropriately structured, designed to pursue the now-outmoded development strategy based on import substitution. Fine and Yeo instead propose a new paradigm for African regional integration, inspired by the experience of postwar Europe and more recently that of East Asia. They propose that regional integration initiatives be designed to achieve the twin objectives of fostering national policy credibility and the rapid accumulation of physical and human capital—the latter triggered by enhanced foreign direct investment initially and by saving and investment surges within the region in subsequent stages. Fine and Yeo exhaustively review the evidence linking regional integration to these two objectives, which are now accepted as the fundamental driving forces behind East Asia's economic miracle.

The key element of this strategy adopts the proposal of Oxford economist Paul Collier and Dutch economist Jan Gunning for "participatory supranational agencies of restraint" in which national economic policy would be tied in a reciprocal threat-making arrangement to an industrial-country anchor (the European Union).[62] Fine and Yeo then pose the question: Why might the European Union be interested in playing such a role? Unlike in the case of Eastern Europe, enhancement of trade, fears of mass migration, and imminent security concerns cannot be major factors. Instead Fine and Yeo suggest that the precedent of UEMOA;[63] the vast interest of the European nations in South Africa; the realization that the African, Caribbean, and Pacific (ACP) agreement—which is administered by the European Commission—has met with limited success; and growing concerns within the European Union about political stability as a prerequisite for economic growth may prompt a more active policy toward Africa.[64]

In conclusion, there may be a window of opportunity for African countries to use regional integration as a supranational mechanism to foster the credibility of their individual national policies, and as a means for pooling risks between otherwise vulnerable small economies; to resolve conflicts and minimize political risks; to exploit complementarities; and to develop regionally based links on a reciprocal and mutually beneficial basis. Reciprocity is key here, because it is the only guarantee against the possibility that strategic cooperation with a dominant economic and political core might stifle an indigenous initiative on the part of African nations to "own" and undertake their own development vision.[65] This, however, remains a challenge, since most of the existing arrangements so far have been genuinely responsive to industrial-country interests and have in large measure tended to divide rather than integrate Africa (e.g., along the Anglophone-Francophone fault line). Although ties mediated through the multilateral institutions may not be perfect, they have nevertheless operated at arm's length from the narrowest national interests of the donor countries. In this context any new African regional scheme should also take into account "the incentives facing the government bureaucracy and the private sector; address the issues of concentration and agglomeration, and the distribution of gains and losses; attempt to deal creatively with the problems of 'hub and spoke'; and create strong institutions that can effectively implement integration measures."[66]

CONCLUSIONS

This paper has attempted to assess the recent macroeconomic reforms in Sub-Saharan Africa, focusing on fiscal, monetary, and exchange rate policy, with the objective of proposing some ideas that might help sustain and deepen reform, restore growth in the short run, and create the conditions for its sustainability in the longer term. The review of the experience of macroeconomic reform in Africa emphasizes the centrality of fiscal adjustment, because although it is the most fragile component of the reform, it has the capacity to determine the chances for the sustainability and progress of the entire reform program. The story of the overall fiscal policy stance in the African countries clearly exposes not only the fragility and the extreme dependence of their economic reforms on foreign aid, but also their very high debt service ratios and the adverse conditions they create for future growth. Moreover, the recent slowdown in real currency depreciation in many countries and its reversal in others have been substantially dictated by fiscal policy considerations. In the end, therefore, the sustainability of previous gains in exchange-rate competitiveness in the non-CFA countries and the more recent gains in the CFA zone will very much depend on further institutional and policy reforms on the fiscal front.

Although overall macroeconomic adjustment in Africa (especially in the non-CFA countries) has been substantial, it is still well short of that achieved at the Asian policy frontier and judged to be consistent with sustainable growth. Therefore, consolidating the initial, macroeconomically based fiscal stabilization with deeper structural reform in fiscal policy institutions and other supportive structural reforms is clearly a top priority.

This paper identifies four policy measures to effect the switch from stabilization to growth in the short run following stabilization. First, generating an adequate investment and growth response to macroeconomic reform in Africa may require some major and visible form of external support in terms of fundamental debt relief. Also important are measures to enhance the flexibility of African economies against external shocks, to reduce political risks, and to foster the credibility of policy reforms through collective commitment.

Massive debt reduction for the African countries is required to resolve the market coordination problem facing the reforming countries of the region and to allow the resumption of growth in the short run, and hence the sustainability of reform, as well as to level the playing field for achieving and sustaining longer term growth. A key feature of a new strategy of external support for Africa could be full or partial replacement of balance-of-payments support with drastic debt reduction and/or a debt freeze for an extended period.

African states can and should help effect the transformation to a more diversified economy by investing in education and human capital, so that domestic production of capital goods will eventually become internationally competitive. To make this possible, however, African economies need a significant reduction of their debt overhangs to release resources for investment and growth.

To the extent that the current African democratization process generates more transparent, participatory, and open governance, it could strengthen the commitment to reforms and foster credibility in the longer run. In the short run, however, it could make some aspects of the reforms more difficult to implement.

There is a window of opportunity for African countries to use regional integration as a supranational mechanism to foster national policy credibility and as a means of pooling risks between otherwise vulnerable small economies; to resolve conflicts and minimize political risks; to exploit complementarities; and to develop regionally based links on a reciprocal and mutually beneficial basis.

Notes

The views expressed in this paper do not necessarily represent the official view of the African Economic Research Consortium. The paper benefited from very helpful and extensive comments by Stephen O'Connell on an earlier draft. Contributions from other participants at a meeting of the contributors to this volume at the Overseas Development Council in Washington are also acknowledged. However, all remaining errors and omissions are the sole responsibility of the author. The author acknowledges the research assistance of Sheila Nyanjui.

[1] Throughout this paper, "Africa" refers only to those African countries south of the Sahara (i.e., Sub-Saharan Africa). The countries included in this and other regional groupings mentioned are those used in official World Bank documents.

[2] For a review see: Ibrahim Elbadawi and Benno Ndulu, "Economic Growth and Long-Term Development in Sub-Saharan Africa," paper presented at SAREC's International Colloquium on "New Directions in Development Economics: Growth, Equity, and Sustainable Development," Stockholm, October 1994; M.T.D. Hadjimicheal et al., "Effects of Macroeconomics Stability on Growth, Saving and Investment in Sub-Saharan Africa: An Empirical Investigation," IMF Working Paper No. WP/94/98 (Washington DC: International Monetary Fund, 1994); and William Easterly and Ross Levine, "The Tragedy of African Growth" (Washington DC: World Bank, 1994).

[3] Easterly and Levine, op. cit.

[4] A comprehensive agenda for reform and a vision for Africa's development is provided by the classic World Bank study, *Sub-Saharan Africa: From Crisis to Sustainable Growth* (Washington DC: World Bank, 1989); see also Jean-Paul Azam, "Development Policy for Africa: A Research Agenda," paper presented at the OECD Development Centre Experts meeting on "What Future for Africa?" Paris, September 1994. More recent work that includes an elaborate critical review of African structural adjustment from a long-term, development-oriented perspective include Nguyuru H. I. Lipumba, *Africa Beyond Adjustment,* Policy Essay No. 15 (Washington, DC: Overseas Development Council, 1994); and Erik Thorbecke and Solomane Kone, "Performance in Sub-Saharan Africa Under Adjustment and Components of Long Term development Strategy," paper presented at the OECD Development Centre Experts Meeting on "What Future for Africa?" Paris, September 1994.

[5] See Benno Ndulu, "Economic Reforms and Development in Sub-Saharan Africa: What Have We Learned and What Are the Challenges Ahead?" paper presented at the Global Coalition for Africa Meeting, Washington DC, April 1995.

[6] See Michael Bruno, "Will Growth Last: Will It Spread?" keynote address, 1994 Annual Bank Conference on Development Economics, Washington DC, 1994.

[7] See Rudiger Dornbusch, "Policies to Move From Stabilization to Growth," in *Proceedings of the World Bank Annual Conference on Development Economics,* ed. S. Fischer, D. de Tray, and S. Shah (Washington DC: World Bank, 1990).

[8] See World Bank, *Adjustment in Africa: Reforms, Results, and the Road Ahead* (New York: Oxford University Press, 1994); and Lawrence Bouton, Christine Jones, and Miguel Kiguel, "Macroeconomic Reform and Growth in Africa: Adjustment Revisited," Policy Research Working Paper No. 1394 (Washington DC: World Bank, December 1994). These studies exclude the small economies of Cape Verde, Comoros, Djibouti, Equatorial Guinea, São Tomé and Principe, and Seychelles, as well as Angola, Ethiopia, Liberia, Somalia, Sudan, and Zaire, because of protracted civil wars or major political instability that affected their economies during the period of the study.

[9] The CFA zone, which covers the area of former French domination in West Africa, is made up of two separate monetary unions: the West African Monetary Union (Union Monétaire Ouest-Africain, or UMOA) and the countries that have formed the Bank of Central African States (Banque des Etats de l'Afrique Centrale, or BEAC). UMOA includes the countries of Benin, Burkina Faso, Côte d'Ivoire, Mali, Niger, Senegal, and Togo; BEAC consists of Cameroon, Central African Republic, Chad, Congo, Equatorial Guinea, and Gabon.

[10] See, for example, Ibrahim Elbadawi and Nader Majd, "Fixed Parity of the Exchange Rate and Economic Performance in the CFA Zone: A Comparative Study," Policy Research Working Paper No. 830 (Washington, DC: World Bank, January 1992); and Shanta Devarajan and Lawrence Hinkle, "The CFA Franc Parity Change: An Opportunity to Restore Growth and Reduce Poverty" (World Bank, Washington DC, April 1994, mimeo).

[11] Devarajan and Hinkle, op. cit., p. 17, provide a persuasive argument in favor of the parity change in the CFA zone as an essential step for restoring growth and reducing poverty. However, they also recognize that devaluation was only a first step and must be "followed by a program of economic reforms to generate export-led growth; create more flexible, competitive private sector oriented economies; strengthen regional financial and trade policies; and accelerate poverty reduction and human resource development."

[12] Hadjimicheal et al. (op. cit.) reports even deeper cuts: from an average of 3.28 percent in 1986 to 2.3 percent in 1991–92.

[13] See Klaus Schmidt-Hebbel, "Fiscal Adjustment and Growth: In and Out of Africa," paper presented at the Bi-annual Research Workshop, The African Economic Research Consortium, Nairobi, Kenya, May 1994.

[14] Seigniorage revenue is taken from the World Bank, *Adjustment in Africa,* op. cit. and is calculated as: $(M1_t - M1_{t-1})/GDP_t - g_t{}^* (M1_t/GDP_t)$, where $M1_t$ is the stock of money at the end of period t, GDP_t is gross domestic product at time t, and g_t is the rate of real GDP growth during period t.

[15] See Stanley Fischer and William Easterly, "The Economics of Government Budget Constraint," *The World Bank Research Observer,* Vol. 5, No. 2 (July 1990), pp. 127–42.

[16] Currency convertibility has insulated the CFA zone from the emergence of parallel markets. Recently, however, as restrictions on convertibility were imposed in an attempt to contain capital flight, small parallel markets have emerged in several CFA countries. These markets continue to function even after the recent devaluation.

[17] A currency is said to be overvalued when its real exchange rate, generically defined as the relative price of tradables to nontradables, is lower than the corresponding equilibrium rate. The equilibrium exchange rate is determined by the sustainable evolution of certain fundamentals, such as taxes, international terms of trade, the trade regime, capital and aid flows, and technology.

For more details on model-based estimates of real exchange-rate misalignment in Africa, see Dan Ghura and Thomas Grennes, "The Real Exchange Rate and Macroeconomic Performance in Sub-Saharan Africa," *Journal of Development Economics,* Vol. 42 (1993), pp. 155–74; Ibrahim A. Elbadawi, "Estimating Long-Run Equilibrium Real Exchange Rates," in *Estimating Equilibrium Exchange Rates,* ed. John Williamson (Washington, DC: Institute for International Economics, 1994), pp. 93–131; and Allechi M'Bet and Niamkey

Madeleine, "External Shocks, Macroeconomic Adjustment and Behavior of CFA Economies Under a Flexible CFA Pegging Scenario: The Case of Côte d'Ivoire and Burkina Faso," report presented to the African Economic Research Consortium Workshop, Nairobi, Kenya, December 1994.

For example, Ghura and Grennes found, consistent with the analysis in this paper, that most of the non-CFA countries were substantially overvalued during the 1972–1997 period, but those of the CFA countries only moderately so (e.g., the extent of overvaluation was estimated at 152 percent for Ghana, 146 percent for Uganda, and 40 percent for Nigeria, but only 12 percent for Côte d'Ivoire and 18 percent for Cameroon). On the other hand, M'bet and Madeleine found the currencies of Côte d'Ivoire and Burkina Faso to be overvalued by about 40 percent during the second half of the 1980s.

[18] See Miguel Kiguel and Stephen O'Connell, "Parallel Exchange Rates in Developing Countries: Lessons from Eight Case Studies," Policy Research Working Paper No. 1265 (Washington, DC: World Bank, 1994).

[19] See, for example, Devarajan and Hinkle, op. cit.; and M'Bet and Madeleine, op. cit.

[20] For example, the Ugandan shilling appreciated in real terms (relative to domestic inflation) from 178 in December 1991 to 140 in December 1993. This appreciation was caused by a relatively high fiscal deficit (including grants) of around 4 percent of GDP and its financing through sales of so-called counterpart funds (foreign exchange in the form of grants or program loans). See James Duesenberry et al., "Improving Exchange Rate Management in Sub-Saharan Africa" (Harvard Institute for International Development, Cambridge, MA, September 1994, mimeo).

[21] For a more comprehensive comparison of the economic development experience in Asia and Africa, see David L. Lindauer and Michael Roemer (eds.), *Asia and Africa: Legacies and Opportunities in Development* (San Francisco: Institute for Contemporary Studies Press, 1994).

[22] For a review of the literature on assessing the sustainability of fiscal policy, see Schmidt-Hebbel, op. cit.

[23] William Easterly and Klaus Schmidt-Hebbel, "The Macroeconomics of Public Sector Deficit: A Synthesis," in *Public Sector Deficit and Macroeconomic Performance,* ed. William Easterly, Carlos Rodriguez, and Klaus Schmidt-Hebbel (Oxford: Oxford University Press, 1994).

[24] See Schmidt-Hebbel, op. cit.

[25] The author is indebted for Stephen O'Connell for pointing this out in his discussion of an earlier draft of this paper.

[26] See Dornbusch, "Policies to Move from Stabilization," op. cit. There are two additional factors impeding the restoration of growth in the short run: first, if deficit reduction leads to reduced real wages and hence reduced internal demand, there is no guarantee that the freed-up resources will automatically go into the export or the import substitution sector; second, even though a competitive real exchange rate will eventually support vigorous export growth, in the short run a real depreciation does exert a contractionary effect on demand.

[27] Ibid.

[28] Ibid. Examples from this literature include Rudiger Dornbusch, "The New Classical Economics and Stabilization Policy," *American Economic Review,* Vol. 90, No. 2 (May 1990), pp. 143–47; Mario Blejer and Alain Isze, "Adjustment Uncertainty, Confidence, and Growth: Latin America After the Growth Crisis," IMF Working Paper No. 89/106, (Washington, DC: International Monetary Fund, 1989); and Sweder van Wijnbergen, "Trade Reform, Aggregate Investment, and Capital Flight: On Credibility and the Value of Information," *Economic Letters,* Vol. 19 (1985).

[29] For more detail, and for an analysis of various arguments in favor of debt relief for Africa, see Siddig A. Salih, "Impact of Africa's Growing Debt on Its Growth," Research for Action Paper (Helsinki: World Institute for Development Economics Research, or WIDER, 1994).

[30] J.-C. Bethelemy and A. Vourc'h, *Debt Relief and Growth,* Development Centre Studies (Paris: OECD, 1994)(note that this quotation was taken from Thorbecke and Kone, op. cit.).

[31] See Paul Collier, "Africa's External Economic Relations: 1960–90," *Economic Affairs,* 1991; and Paul Collier and Jan Gunning, "Linkage Between Trade Policy and Regional

Integration," paper presented at African Economic Research Consortium Conference on "Regional Integration and Trade Liberalization in SSA," Nairobi, December 1993.

[32] See Thorbecke and Kone, op. cit., p. 62.

[33] For example, Dornbusch, "Policies to Move from Stabilization," op. cit.

[34] The author is indebted to Stephen O'Connell for pointing out this critique of conditional debt relief and the arguments for the alternative view in favor of unconditional debt relief.

[35] See Dornbusch, "Policies to Move from Stabilization," op. cit., p. 45.

[36] This section draws from Elbadawi and Ndulu, op. cit., and from Ibrahim Elbadawi, "The Structure of Incentives, the External Environment, and Agricultural Supply Response in Sub-Saharan Africa," paper presented at the Second International Conference on African Economic Issues, Arusha, Tanzania, October 1994.

[37] Elbadawi and Ndulu, op. cit.

[38] World Bank, *World Development Report 1988* (New York: Oxford University Press, 1988).

[39] Mohsin Khan and M. Knight, "Import Compression and Export Performance in Developing Countries," *The Review of Economics and Statistics,* Vol. 70, No. 2 (1988), pp. 315–21.

[40] The measurement of the terms-of-trade shock appropriately uses export and import shares of GDP as weights on prices, so that the relative importance of shocks from the export and the import side is determined. In the analysis of shocks stemming from foreign real interest rate changes and their impact on debt servicing, the real rate of interest is measured in "effective" terms by dividing interest payments by total debt, adjusted by the U.S. GNP deflator. The magnitude of the shock is thus measured as a ratio of changes in real interest payments to GDP (see Elbadawi and Ndulu, op. cit., section III.2).

[41] Africa suffered further terms-of-trade losses in 1991 (*The Economist,* January 11, 1992). For a detailed account of individual country experiences see Gerald Helleiner, "Trade Policy, Exchange Rates, and Relative Prices in Sub-Saharan Africa: Interpreting the 1980s," paper prepared for a conference in Gothenburg, Sweden, September 6–8, 1992.

[42] Accounting only for official development assistance (ODA), Helleiner, op. cit., calculates that out of 15 Sub-Saharan African countries that lost from terms of trade deterioration over the 1980s decade, only 6 have received increased ODA that more than compensated their losses.

[43] See John Cuddington and T. Feyzioglu, "Long-Run Trends in Primary Commodity Prices: Resolving Our Differences Using the ARFIMA Model" (Economic Department, Georgetown University, Washington, DC, 1993, unpublished mimeo); and Carmen Reinhart and P. Wickham, "Commodity Prices: Cyclical Weakness or Secular Decline," IMF Staff Papers, Vol. 41, No. 2 (June 1994), pp. 175–213. Reinhart and Wickham analyze the manufacturing unit value (MUV)-deflated price indexes for food, beverages, metals, and all commodities for the 1900–1990 period. Their comprehensive analysis investigates stationary properties, distributional characteristics, volatility, decomposition into permanent and transitory components, and the persistence of cyclical shocks. Cuddington and Feyzioglu applied a robust time-series model (the autoregressive fractionally integrated moving average, or ARFIMA) to similar commodity price data measured by the MUV-deflated commodity price index.

[44] Cuddington and Feyzioglu, op. cit.; and Reinhart and Wickham, op. cit.

[45] Reinhart and Wickham state: "Whether the trend component is modelled by a simple broken deterministic linear trend or by a stochastic process using alternative methodologies, the recent decline in commodity prices appears to be primarily secular." Reinhart and Wickham, op. cit., p. 198.

[46] See Lance Taylor, "South-North Trade and Southern Growth: Bleak Prospects from the Structuralist Point of View," *Journal of International Economics,* Vol. 2, 1981.

[47] T. Ziesemer, "Economic Development and Endogenous Terms-of-Trade Determination: Review and Reinterpretation of the Prebisch-Singer Thesis," Discussion Paper No. 87 (Geneva: United Nations Conference on Trade and Development, July 1994).

[48] See Anne Krueger, "Export-Led Industrial Growth Reconsidered," in *Trade and Growth in the Advanced Developing Countries in the Pacific Basin,* ed. Wontack Hons and Lawrence Krause (Seoul: Korean Development Institute, 1981), pp. 3–27.

[49] See Dani Rodrik, "King Kong Meets Godzilla: The World Bank and the East Asian Miracle," and Robert Wade, "Selective Industrial Policies in East Asia: Is the East Asian Miracle Right?" in *Miracle or Design? Lessons from the East Asian Experience,* Policy Essay No. 11 (Washington DC: Overseas Development Council, 1994).

[50] See Azam, "Development Policy for Africa," op. cit.

[51] See, for example, Robert Barro and J. Lee, "Losers and Winners in Economic Growth," paper presented at the Annual Conference on Development Economics, World Bank, 1993; and A. Ades and H. Chua, "Regional Instability and Economic Growth: Thy Neighbor's Curse," Center Discussion Paper No. 704 (New Haven, CT: Economic Growth Center, Yale University, 1993).

[52] The literature in this area is small but growing. See, for example, Jean-Paul Azam, "Democracy and Development: A Theoretical Framework," *Public Choice,* forthcoming 1995; Jean-Paul Azam, "How to Pay for the Peace? A Theoretical Framework with References to African Countries," *Public Choice,* forthcoming 1995; Robert Bates and Paul Collier, "Wars of Secession" (Harvard University, Cambridge, MA, 1995, unpublished mimeo); J. Buchanan and R. Faith, "Secession and the Limits of Taxation: Toward a Theory of Internal Exit," *American Economic Review,* Vol. 77, No. 5 (1987), pp. 1023–31; and R. Findlay, "Towards a Model of Territorial Expansion and the Limits of Empire" (Department of Economics, Columbia University, New York, 1994, unpublished mimeo).

[53] See Robert Bates, *Beyond the Miracle of the Market: the Political Economy of Agrarian Development in Kenya* (Cambridge: Cambridge University Press, 1989).

[54] Azam, "Development Policy for Africa," op. cit.

[55] Nicolas van de Walle, "Political Liberalization and Economic Policy Reform in Africa," *World Development,* Vol. 22, No. 4 (1994), pp. 483–500, concludes that ". . . the emergence of more participatory politics will not necessarily make successful reform less likely. Although the instability of political change will exact an economic cost in the short run, in the long run political liberalization provides opportunities as well as risks for economic reforms. It will probably make some macroeconomic reforms more difficult, but it provides a window of opportunity for significant progress on governance issues. The net impact will vary across states; in most countries, the prospects for economic reforms will not be dramatically altered, because political reform does not alter some of the structural characteristics of economic policy making in Africa."

[56] See, for example, a recent World Bank document, *A Continent in Transition: Sub-Saharan Africa in the Mid-1990s* (Washington, DC: World Bank, 1995).

[57] See Collier, op. cit.

[58] See, for example, Paul Krugman, *Geography and Trade* (Cambridge, MA: Massachusetts Institute of Technology Press, 1991).

[59] See H. Chua, "Regional Spillovers and Economic Growth," Center Discussion Paper No. 700 (New Haven, CT: Economic Growth Center, Yale University, 1993); and H. Chua, "Regional Public Capital and Economic Growth," (Economic Growth Center, Yale University, New Haven, CT, 1993, unpublished mimeo). See also Easterly and Levine, op. cit., who eliminated the African dummy variable by using an index of neighbors' average growth as an indicator of regional spillover effects.

[60] See I. Elbadawi, "The Impact of Regional Trade/Monetary Schemes on Intra-Sub-Saharan African Trade," in A. Oyejide, I. Elbadawi, and P. Collier (eds.), *Regional Integration and Trade Liberalization in SSA: Vol. 1* (New York: MacMillan, forthcoming 1996). See also Collier and Gunning, op. cit. They identified country-specific multilateral trade liberalization; policy harmonization and regional cooperation on a limited set of areas (e.g., infrastructure, power, and communication); and a strong and coordinated strategy for external relations as the best options for Africa to foster both growth and regional integration (without actively promoting it), as well to avoid marginalization in the global economy.

[61] Jeffrey Fine and Stephen Yeo, "Regional Integration in SSA: Dead End or a Fresh Start?" paper prepared for the African Economic Research Consortium Project on "Regional Integration and Trade Liberalization in SSA," Nairobi, Kenya, 1994.

[62] See Collier, op. cit.; and Collier and Gunning, op. cit.

[63] Communauté Economique de l'Afrique de l'Oust (CEAO) has recently been integrated with the West African Monetary Union (UMOA) in a new bloc, the Economic and Monetary Union of the West African States (UEMOA).

[64] See D. Cobham and P. Robson, "Monetary Integration in Africa: A Deliberately European Perspective," *World Development,* Vol. 22, No. 3 (1994), pp. 285–99, who adopt similar arguments for assigning the European Union the role of an external anchor in the context of monetary integration in Africa.

[65] Fine and Yeo, op. cit.

[66] Ibid.

Chapter Two

State Capacity and Effective Governance

Deborah Brautigam

In 1967, at the University of California, Los Angeles, a group of African and Africanist academics met at a monthly colloquium to discuss the institution-building challenges facing the new African nations. Over the course of the year, as Arnold Rivkin later related, "It became clear that the endemic political instability, the widespread economic stagnation, and the epidemic of military coups d'état of the decade of the 60s are direct manifestations of the African institutional gap. . . . There seems no detour around the gap; it must be bridged if development is to take place, . . . [and] it may well prove to be the most intractable and difficult problem of all."[1]

Rivkin and his colleagues were right. Just as the rest of the world has begun to acknowledge the critical role played by a strong and capable state in the remarkable economic performance of the East Asian countries, it has become all too clear that Africa's development crisis is compounded by an often profound weakness in the capacity of the state to promote development. Although high levels of debt and reduced revenues from taxation deeply affect this capacity, the weaknesses of African states are only partly a matter of finance. Brain drain, wage erosion, indiscipline, low morale, and lack of accountability are all growing problems. Increasingly, other institutions are substituting for the state. In East Africa, nongovernmental organizations (NGOs), local communities, and the private sector provide half of the funding and facilities for water, education, and health.[2] With more than 100,000 expatriate advisers and professionals costing more than $4 billion annually, African governments depend more on external assistance today than they did at independence.[3]

This chapter addresses the critical role that state capacity plays in Africa's economic renewal. Since the early 1980s, the thrust of reforms has been to shrink the state. Now, in order to lay the foundation for renewal, African states need to focus the same level of attention on the institutional reforms necessary to build an effective government that can raise revenues to meet expenditures, ensure economic stability, heighten predictability, and provide effective public service. This is a long-term process. The chapter begins by outlining four dimensions of state capacity (regulatory, technical, extractive, and administrative). This is followed by a review of African state capacity in historical and comparative perspective, which points out that poor leadership and economic crisis have eroded the wages, status, working conditions, and values of committed civil services across Africa. The third section reviews the experience of foreign aid in building African state capacity, particularly training and higher education, technical assistance, and civil service pay and employment reforms. In concluding that foreign aid may have served as much to weaken as to strengthen states, the chapter argues that any strategy for building state capacity must start with local ownership. Shifting to locally owned programs will require either that foreign aid for state capacity be channeled through a foundation or fund mechanism that is truly demand-driven or that aid become more performance-based, with support given on an ex post basis once local leaders have initiated reforms or programs.

The last section outlines a strategy for government leaders who are committed to building state capacity. A committed government might begin by rebuilding professionalism and a sense of mission in the civil service. This entails establishing clear rules and transparent, merit-based procedures for hiring and promotion, institutionalizing review procedures that evaluate and reward good performance, and using the money saved through attrition and the elimination of "ghost" employees to raise government salaries and benefits to approximately market levels. Governments are more likely to succeed in their reforms if they adopt a realistic strategy of concentrating reforms in a few critical bureaus first, shifting politically important patronage opportunities to slightly less vital agencies. An excellent starting place would be to reform the internal revenue service and the customs bureau, which would directly strengthen the state's extraction capacity. Insulating the judiciary and the central bank from patronage pressures and short-term political demands enhances the independence of these critical agencies. Finally, capacity outside the public sector can reinforce capacity within. Strong professional associations, professional schools, and other nongovernmental entities can provide sources of information and technical expertise. Through membership activities, professional training programs, and joint implementation efforts, they can reinforce the values and professional norms within the state.

WHAT IS STATE CAPACITY?

State capacity is a measure of the ability of a government to implement its policies and accomplish its goals.[4] At a minimum, state capacity rests on administrative control of a given territory, a minimum contested in more than a few African states today. Also central to capacity are an effective bureaucratic machinery, skilled and committed leaders and officials, and ample financial resources. State capacity has four dimensions: regulatory, administrative, technical, and extractive.

Regulatory capacity involves the ability of the state to establish and enforce the rules that guide, or regulate, societal behavior. In the broadest sense, this means establishing the rule of law, but especially in Africa, where traditional and religious legal systems coexist alongside systems of constitutional, civil, and commercial laws often little amended from the colonial period, it means enforcing the rules preferred by the state, especially when they conflict with those preferred by society. For example, many African governments still struggle unsuccessfully to eliminate widespread black markets, abolish trials by ordeal through traditional justice systems, and ensure that all children, including girls, attend the required years of schooling.

Administrative capacity involves the routine ability to manage the personnel and resources of the state and to ensure accountability and efficiency in service delivery. It is based on objective hiring and promotion practices, adequate accounting staff to audit public expenditures, working systems of information, stable and rule-based authority, and internal coherence between goals and the resources, personnel, and tools available to carry them out.

Technical capacity includes the expertise and knowledge required to make and implement technical decisions—whether in science and engineering or in macroeconomics—as well as the policy tools and instruments necessary to implement those decisions effectively. These might include establishing and monitoring standards for pharmaceutical imports, managing a crawling peg exchange rate, or evaluating the engineering plans for a proposed hydroelectric dam.

Finally, the most important element of capacity may be *extractive capacity*: the ability of the state to raise the revenues it needs to pay for the expenses of implementing its policies and goals. As sociologist

Theda Skocpol notes, "A state's means of raising and deploying financial resources tell us more than could any other single factor about its existing (and immediately potential) capacities to create or strengthen state organizations, to employ personnel, to co-opt political support, to subsidize economic enterprises, and to fund social programs."[5]

How do we know capacity when we see it? The following indicators offer some direct and indirect ways in which levels of capacity can be determined and compared.[6] An indicator of regulatory capacity is the ability of the state to enforce its rules, including contracts, protection of property rights, defense, and public order. The extent to which alternative power holders (regional warlords, guerrillas) compete with the state for authority is one indicator of this capacity. In addition, the ability of society to evade the state's rules can be seen in the toleration of a substantial black market for foreign exchange or imported goods. For administrative capacity, indicators might include the turnover or stability of top officials over time, the ratio of expatriate personnel involved in government operations, and some measure of the level of service delivered by government (for example, the percentage of population with access to safe water or electricity). For technical capacity, indicators might include the scope and timely production of statistical and information services, the level of local enrollment in science and engineering, the number of trained accountants in the public sector, or the presence of effective policy instruments such as a central bank, economic planning bureau, or development finance agency. Indicators of extractive capacity include the ratio of revenues to gross national product (GNP), the relative weight of different categories of revenue (taxes on trade require less capacity to collect than income or value added taxes), and the ratio of fiscal self-reliance (aid receipts compared with total domestic revenue).

These indicators are offered with some caveats. In general, states with higher capacity will have better development indicators than states with lower capacity, yet outcomes (per capita domestic food production), as opposed to specific policy outputs (number of extension agents per 1,000 farmers), are subject to numerous intervening influences, from weather to commodity price trends. A more difficult problem is implied by the fact that some of these indicators (access to safe water, for example) may reflect the capacity of NGOs, foreign aid agencies, and the private sector more than the capacity of the state. Finally, an important indicator of capacity—the ability of a government to deliver services—might be affected by income level. Although this can be addressed by comparing outputs in countries with similar levels of per capita income, this comparison tends to reinforce the idea that capacity is also related to government commitment. For example, Sierra Leone ranks just below Vietnam in per capita GNP but has only 21 percent literacy, while Vietnam has almost 90 percent literacy.

AFRICAN STATE CAPACITY IN HISTORICAL AND COMPARATIVE PERSPECTIVE

In other parts of the world, the development of relatively high state capacity took many centuries. In Europe, the boundaries of the first modern states were carved out only after centuries of struggle. As historian Charles Tilly has pointed out, state-building in this context was almost ancillary to war-making.[7] To support and finance their wars, rulers developed centralized control over what were originally private armies, developed institutions to adjudicate disputes, improved systems of taxation, and established rules and courts to control the behavior of the people within their boundaries. These rulers drew on early forms of technical assistance to strengthen their state capacity: In the eighteenth century, Prussia brought in French fiscal experts to strengthen the taxation system, while Russia imported engineers to staff its government training institute.[8]

Like many African states today, early modern states in Europe were characterized by patrimonial politics and predatory leadership. Developing professional bureaucracies took many generations. Not until the nineteenth century did expectations grow in Europe that the civil service would be staffed by disinterested and honest public servants. Only in 1816 did Great Britain's civil servants begin receiving formal salaries, marking the decline of the widespread practice of distributing offices as spoils and prebends.[9] The Northcote-Trevelyan reforms of the British civil service in 1854 heralded the self-conscious construction of a professional meritocracy shaped by the rule of law.[10] Although African states, not only as late industrializers but also as late state-builders have the advantage of being able to learn from the experience of others, building a modern and effective state apparatus takes time.

Compared with other developing areas, African states are very new, the vast majority being formed during colonial rule and taken over by the first generation of African leaders scarcely a generation ago. By comparison, colonialism ended in most of Latin America in the mid-nineteenth century, and many of the high-performing Asian countries had long histories of bureaucratic development before the arrival of Europeans. The European colonial powers partitioned most of Sub-Saharan Africa into colonies only at the Berlin Conference of 1884–85, and each power constructed colonies out of the former empires and tribal areas it occupied. With small governments intended primarily to maintain law and order and assist resource extraction, the colonial powers did little to build more sophisticated regulatory, extractive, technical, or administrative capacity. For example, by 1945, in the Portuguese colonies only 1 percent of people were literate, and in 1960, only 36 percent of Sub-Saharan school-age children were enrolled in primary school.[11] This is in sharp contrast to the experience under Japanese colonization where, for example, in Taiwan, 79 percent of primary school-age children were enrolled in classes by the late 1930s.[12]

Decolonization took place rapidly and generally with little preparation. Except for the former Portuguese colonies, the process was largely completed in about ten years. In contrast to the colonial period in India, where the Indian Civil Service had a long history of indigenous administration, and Ceylon (Sri Lanka), where the British had steadily localized their colonial administration, few of the colonial governments made extensive efforts to prepare their African colonies for self-governance at independence. Nigeria had probably the highest percentage of upper level positions filled by Africans at independence: 15 percent.[13] In general, the new countries were faced with the choice of retaining expatriate capacity or living with the consequences of rapid change in administrative staff, as the civil services were quickly localized.

The new governments embarked on institutional reform and expansion in keeping with the prevailing idea that governments needed to be the catalysts, if not the engines, of their country's transformation. Public employment expanded to meet the new responsibilities and the political imperative that the new governments reward their supporters with jobs. In Ghana, employment in the public sector expanded by 15 percent a year from 1975 to 1983. Nigeria's federal civil service employment and Tanzania's public employment tripled in a little more than a decade.[14]

At first, in most countries, the civil service enjoyed an elevated status and was relatively well paid by local standards. A government worker in Kenya in the early 1970s earned an average of 11–16 percent more than an equivalent employee in the private sector, while in Tanzania, public sector employees earned about 14 percent more.[15] By the 1970s, however, as the post–World War II commodity price boom wound down, it became evident that there were fiscal limits to the advances African states could make.[16] Government after government found it increasingly difficult to meet payroll obligations on time, let alone implement the ambitious developmental goals proclaimed by its leaders.

Although relatively high salaries continued to hold for countries in the Communauté Financière Africaine (CFA) zone (until devaluation in 1994), low civil service salaries in the rest of Africa had become a serious problem by the early 1980s, well before the International Monetary Fund and World Bank austerity programs froze aggregate wage bills (see Table 1). Inflation and drops in revenue meant that by 1983, university graduates in the Nigerian civil service were making only 38 percent of their 1975 salaries, while by 1988 university graduates hired as new assistant directors in the Ugandan civil service were paid $16.99 a month, in real terms about 3 percent of the value of salaries in January 1975.[17] Wage increases for lower level civil servants were more likely to keep pace with inflation than those for upper levels, leading to significantly compressed wage scales. In Ghana in 1984, permanent secretaries at the head of ministries earned just over twice the amount earned by a messenger.[18] Low salaries and abysmal working conditions translated into minimal performance, as civil servants hustled to make ends meet in the informal sector. Many of the most skilled managers simply gave up their Sisyphean struggle. A recent U.N. study estimated that between 1986 and 1990, some 50,000 to 60,000 middle and high-level managers emigrated from Africa.[19] Crisis eroded what little legitimacy and authority many governments had possessed.

By 1989, the World Bank echoed the frustrations of many observers inside and outside Africa in its declaration that Africa's problems were founded in a "crisis of governance," compounded by corruption, indiscipline, general incompetence, and failed leadership.[20] Others contested this analysis, placing the blame for rising corruption more on economic desperation than on lack of political will. The Ugandan Public Service Salaries Review Commission noted in 1982 that, "The civil servant had either to survive by lowering his standards of ethics, performance, and dutifulness or [to] remain upright and perish. He chose to survive."[21] With economic crisis, corruption grew even in Botswana and Tanzania, both countries with strong normative traditions against bureaucratic malfeasance. By the mid-1990s, African state capacity appeared to be at its nadir.

Although some have sought to lay the blame for these problems on Africa's "all-powerful" state,[22] the problem had to do much more with weakness than with power. These weaknesses were reflected in the consistent inability of governments to generate revenue, to link budgeting with planning, to collect information on their own debts, and to audit their internal accounts. At the close of the twentieth century, state capacity remains inadequate for the task at hand: the effective promotion of economic renewal. First, the essential technical tools required to promote development—statistical services, topographical units, meteorological and hydrological services, agricultural research services, soil conservation institutions, and financial institutions for mobilizing

TABLE 1: TRENDS IN REAL BASIC STARTING SALARIES IN THE PUBLIC SECTOR, 1970–83 (1975 = 100)

Country and Grade	1970	1975	1980	1983
Ghana				
Principal secretary	—	100[a]	41.4	11.0
Officer/administrator III	—	100[a]	49.5	15.3
Messenger	—	100[a]	94.8	39.7
Malawi				
Undersecretary	—	100	84.0	64.5
University graduate	—	100	96.2	73.9
Unskilled labor	—	100	92.2	85.2
Nigeria				
Permanent secretary	85.9[b]	100	47.0	30.1
University graduate	82.1[b]	100	50.1	38.1
Unskilled laborer	69.2[b]	100	76.5	63.8
Senegal				
University graduate	—	100[c]	106.5[d]	73.8[e]
Secondary school diploma	—	100[c]	114.3[d]	84.7[e]
No diploma	—	100[c]	128.5[d]	112.7[e]
Sierra Leone				
Deputy secretary	122.0	100	62.2	—
Technical officer	119.0	100	70.2	—
Messenger	111.0	100	103.2	—
Sudan				
Deputy undersecretary	151.8	100	59.6	28.7
Secondary school	167.1	100	66.5	32.0
Unskilled worker	153.3	100	72.7	35.0
Uganda				
Permanent secretary	—	100	7.7[d]	5.0[f]
Entry—university graduate	—	100	9.1[d]	5.9[f]
Group employee	—	100	23.7[d]	15.4[f]
Zambia				
Permanent secretary	131.6[g]	100	68.2	44.9
Entry—university graduate	105.7[g]	100	63.0	40.9
Laborer	95.8[g]	100	85.2	87.7

Note: — Not available.

[a] 1977.

[b] 1972.

[c] 1976.

[d] 1981.

[e] 1984.

[f] 1975–82.

[g] 1971.

Source: David L. Lindauer, Oey Astra Meesook, and Parita Suebsaeng, "Government Wage Policy in Africa: Some Findings and Policy Issues," *World Bank Research Observer* Vol. 3, No. 1 (January 1988), p. 8.

domestic resources—are weak or nonexistent. Most African countries lack a complete data base on public sector employment, and auditing and accounting are poorly developed. Second, regulatory capacity is weak. Laws often remain unrevised, uncompiled, and uncodified, and regulations are inadequate for newly liberalized financial and economic activities. Third, extractive capacity is poorly developed in most countries, with revenues falling short of expenditures and tax collection dependent on a narrow base of trade taxes. Finally, administrative capacity is hampered by many factors, starting with irregularly paid salaries that are too low to compete with the private sector. The fundamentals of rational-legal management practices are still not institutionalized. The civil service requires clear job descriptions and effective sanctions in order to limit employment to properly qualified personnel. It also requires a stable and clear set of rules to support, but also limit, authority and to regulate predictably the behavior of persons inside and outside the state.

What affects capacity? Why are Africa's states weak? One basic problem lies with the nature of African political regimes. Leaders and followers are both ensnared by the politics of patronage, and society currently offers few countervailing forces. As long as leaders make arbitrary policy decisions not based on careful analysis and rule mainly through patrimonial ties rather than rational-legal norms, there will be little demand at the top for analytical capacity, technical skills, and good management in public administration. Rapid expansion, frequent "shuffling" of personnel, and political instability have hampered the managerial and technical learning process and thwarted efforts to develop a bureaucratic culture and to institutionalize professional values and norms.[23] In contrast, stability of ministers and other high-level personnel was the norm in the high-performing economies of East Asia and also in some of the countries that have done relatively well in Africa. In Côte d'Ivoire between 1957 and 1980, ministers remained in office for 7.5 years on average.[24] Botswana has also emphasized continuity, with only two finance ministers in the first two decades of independence.[25] Finally, many if not most African leaders have little basis for legitimacy among their societies, lacking the required foundation of traditional, charismatic, or constitutional authority. This may change as the post-1989 democratic transitions become consolidated.

Committed leadership *is* probably necessary for effectively modernizing the state.[26] The desultory development of the Republic of Korea under the leadership of Syngmon Rhee and its robust growth under the post-1960 leadership of Park Chung-hee illustrates the dramatic differences that can result from a change in top leadership and the subsequent imposition of new rules and sanctions within the bureaucracy. Leaders exert a strong influence over attitudes concerning the nature and function of civil service. Côte d'Ivoire's relatively strong capacity to manage development has been due in part to strong leadership. As one observer notes, "The patrimonial elements in the system have . . . not been allowed to override the *commitment set from the top* to legal-rational forms of control, effective role performance, and the implementation of an economic programme" (emphasis added).[27] Another observer echoed this in the case of Kenya: "High standards in the civil service are very sensitive to the appointment and promotion practices of the head of state."[28] Yet the focus on leadership obscures the gnarly political and historical roots of the problem of weak capacity. As Joel Migdal has argued,

> Scholars and aid officials alike have singled out bureaucrats in the Third World for their slothfulness, lack of will, and absence of commitment to reform. These scholars have paid scant attention to the calculus of pressures these bureaucrats have faced that have made them so "lazy" or "uncommitted." Success for public policies neither waits around the corner in a "new breed" of implementor, nor will it be found in an exclusive focus on new management techniques. In fact, the politics of administration in weak states lies at the heart of problems with policy implementation.[29]

African states' low levels of capacity have historical as well as political roots. Most of today's countries were totally new states at independence in the 1960s, and they were given (or won) the mantle of statehood without, in most cases, first building a unified nation. These new states had only a short period of time in which to learn how to manage complex bureaucracies before economic crises beginning in the middle to late 1970s caused a virtual breakdown of the public sector. Although leadership matters, even the finest leaders can do little without the proper tools and resources, information, managerial and technical expertise, appropriate policy instruments, and finance. Additionally, building capacity is a learning process. It grows with experience, both of individuals and organizations, and is aided by the institutionalization of bureaucratic values. State capacity is also shaped by capacity in society and by societal linkages, including policy networks that draw on private sector expertise and other institutions that allow for the embedding or inclusion of societal capacity in the state. Finally, the problem has been exacerbated by the unintended consequences of extensive dependence on foreign aid.

FOREIGN AID: WHAT HAS BEEN DONE TO BUILD CAPACITY AND WHY IT HAS NOT WORKED

Concern with capacity-building is not new in Africa. In the first post-independence decade, African leaders and funding agencies realized that capacity-building would be crucial for the new African states. As Sierra Leone president Siaka Stevens commented in 1971, "If there is anything that Africa is short of, it is administrative and managerial capacity for present-day tasks."[30] Aid agencies echoed these sentiments, but their approach to capacity-building had little impact on state capacity, and other aspects of foreign assistance inhibited institutional development. The following sections explore in more detail three popular vehicles for assistance: training and higher education, technical cooperation, and pay and employment reforms.

Training and Higher Education

The base of technical skills and expertise in Africa is much lower than elsewhere in the developing world, although it has been growing. During the colonial period, only some six universities were established in Sub-Saharan Africa, and by 1960 the enrollment ratios at the postsecondary level were only about one-sixtieth of those in Asia and Latin America.[31] Education was one of the top priorities of the first post-independence decade of the 1960s. A number of new universities were established (often with foundation assistance), and university enrollment accelerated sharply. Between 1960 and 1980, tertiary enrollment rose at an annual rate of 15 percent, from approximately 21,000 students to 337,000, rising to almost half a million by 1989.[32] Yet these increases, while impressive, must be seen in comparative perspective. By 1992, Sub-Saharan Africa had a tertiary enrollment rate of only 4 percent of the age group, while Latin America, a region with a slightly smaller population, had at least three times as many universities and a tertiary enrollment rate of 18 percent.[33] Furthermore, much of the training in African schools and universities was focused on liberal arts, and shortages of skills were particularly evident in science and engineering. In 1985, for example, while middle-income South American countries averaged 306 natural science and engineering enrollments per 100,000 population and countries in the OECD (Organisation for Economic Co-operation and Development) averaged 583, a sample of African countries for which data existed averaged only 23 per 100,000 population (see Table 2).[34] The situation is similar with regard to trained accountants. Table 3 indicates that out of 20 African countries in a recent study, 12 had fewer than 50 qualified accountants in the pub-

TABLE 2. SCIENCE AND TECHNOLOGY POSTSECONDARY ENROLLMENT IN AFRICAN, SOUTH AMERICAN, AND OECD COUNTRIES, 1985 (enrollment per 100,000 population)

Country	Total Enrollment	Natural Sciences	Engineering	Medical Science
Botswana	142.40	19.27	0.00	0.00
Burundi	62.95	4.68	4.39	5.93
Ethiopia	81.17	12.32	6.99	4.11
Ghana	12.11	2.52	0.00	2.65
Guinea	170.00	56.26	20.94	8.85
Kenya	115.82	7.65	45.16	6.03
Mozambique	10.83	0.52	4.06	1.22
Rwanda	34.86	6.39	1.75	2.89
Senegal	201.25	37.18	3.28	39.36
Sudan	164.19	6.24	12.67	9.88
Tanzania	19.70	1.21	3.29	2.03
Uganda	69.08	6.39	9.62	3.19
Zimbabwe	74.98	11.05	8.72	4.84
Average, Africa	89.18	13.36	9.30	7.00
Average, middle-income South America	1,467.86	74.55	230.86	151.73
Average, OECD countries	2,392.51	214.19	369.25	260.73

Source: Manuel Zymelman, *Science, Education, and Development in Sub-Saharan Africa,* Technical Paper 124 (Washington, DC: World Bank, 1990), p. 27.

lic sector, with perhaps twice that in the private sector.[35] By contrast, South Africa had about 15,000 qualified accountants in the public and private sectors. Thus, although more and more Africans have enjoyed access to secondary and tertiary education since independence, enrollment is still very low by world standards, and the skill base is weak. This contributes to low levels of technical capacity in the state.

Foreign donors have given substantial support to African education and training programs. During the 1960s, donors financed construction and staffed more than 40 Institutes of Administration in Africa. From 1981 to 1983, aid for education and training amounted to some $618 million a year—about 11 percent of total external aid—and paid for about 17 percent of African governments' education budgets.[36] Yet in many cases, although university and other training benefited the individuals concerned, it failed to build lasting capacity in the state. In Kenya, for example, a Canadian project trained 70 economists, planners, and financial managers from the Ministry of Planning and National Development between 1970 and 1981. Follow-up studies showed that by 1982, 35 percent had left the ministry, citing frustration with

TABLE 3. ACCOUNTANTS IN THE PUBLIC SECTOR, 1990			
Country	Fully Qualified Accountants	Accounting Technicians	Bookkeepers
Benin	75	190	199
Botswana	125	155	470
Burkina Faso	90	120	350
Burundi	1	—	—
Cameroon	25	450	700
Gambia, The	9	—	—
Ghana	86	—	—
Kenya	87	19,000	20,000
Lesotho	11	16	72
Malawi	39	100	2,001
Mali	6	152	34
Mauritania	52	110	160
Mauritius	25	335	1,000
Niger	109	473	372
Nigeria	827	—	—
Rwanda	15	150	150
Sierra Leone	17	49	300
Swaziland	6	16	—
Togo	86	162	4,734
Uganda	10	—	—

Notes: — Not available. Numbers are not precise figures, but rather orders of magnitude.

Source: Judy Makanda, "Accounting and Auditing Standards in Sub-Saharan Africa" (Capacity Building and Implementation Division, Africa Technical Department, World Bank, Washington, DC, January 1995), p. 27.

low salaries, poor working environment, and lack of upward mobility in the public sector; only four of these individuals remained in 1992.[37]

Training support outside the education sector, amounting to about a third of the total, was tied to project-related skills, through short-term, local programs run by contractors. In most instances, training was a much smaller portion of foreign aid spending than the other favored vehicle for building capacity: technical assistance. During the 1981–83 period, for example, 17 percent of education aid was spent on fellowships for study abroad and 44 percent on foreign experts.[38]

Expatriate Technical Assistance

After some three decades of foreign aid in Africa, the use of expatriate technical assistance remains quite high. In some countries—Botswana and Côte d'Ivoire, for example—expatriates still hold line positions within ministries. In others, line positions are filled by local staff, and expatriates serve formally as "advisers," although the distinction is blurred in practice. Kenya, a country with relatively high domestic capacity, still had 650 expatriates in its public sector (including universities) midway through the 1980s; the Ministry of Planning and National Development alone had 46 resident expatriate advisers.[39]

Whether obtained through a grant or a loan, foreign expertise is not cheap: the annual cost can be up to $300,000 a year per expert.[40] Housing, vehicles, and offices must be supplied, and salaries for foreign experts can be up to 100 times as high as their local counterparts, creating a situation ripe for resentment. In 1985, foreign experts resident in Equatorial Guinea were paid an amount nearly triple the total government public sector wage bill.[41] Commonly, technical assistants introduce innovations that collapse after their departure. The problems with the transfer of skills are complex. Among the more important are the time pressures felt by aid agencies caught in the project cycle, the seeming indifference of African governments that fail to provide counterparts in a timely manner or at all, and the inevitable shift of ownership and responsibility to foreigners, who bring both resources and expertise.[42] Reforming the system has proven to be difficult, in part because technical assistance has ballooned into a growth industry for western consulting firms and professionals who have a vested interest in its survival. Strategies to build a more capable state will need to tackle the dependency created by foreign experts, while finding a way to tap the skills many of them possess.

Technical assistance tends to work better with activities involving specific skills that can be learned—airplane maintenance or hybrid seed production—than with efforts to pass on general problem-solving or management skills.[43] In the indigenous private sector, African firms have identified and hired foreign technical assistants through private sector channels, and in many instances this approach has a better record of meeting the client's needs. This points to one of the problems with technical assistance and, by extension, other donor-initiated efforts to build capacity. Technical assistance in the public sector in Africa tends too often to be driven by supply rather than by demand and to be supplied when an aid agency defines a need. African governments accept the technical assistance for the sake of the accompanying resources. Shifting to a demand-driven model akin to that practiced by private firms is likely to result in assistance that meets specific learning needs in a short-term, sustainable fashion.

Pay and Employment Reforms: Trimming and Toning the State

Economic crisis weakened the fragile institutions built up in the first two post-independence decades. Rapidly declining salaries and work conditions easily devastate a professional civil service. These losses have been extremely difficult to reverse. Even in Africa's "model reformer" Ghana, by 1988 civil servants were still being paid only 28 to 41 percent of private sector equivalents, and by 1994 capacity was still weak. For example, the Office of the Accountant General had only four qualified accountants on its 4,500-person staff.[44] One study maintains that a correlation exists between those countries that have protected civil servants' pay and those that have superior public management. Yet even in a country like Malawi, cited by this study for "the competence and professionalism of its civil service" with "one of Africa's highest ratios of senior civil service pay to GDP [gross domestic product] per capita," civil servants are paid only a fifth of the level prevailing in the private sector.[45] The problem is part severe wage compression, with salary levels too low to retain qualified people, and part overall employment levels that are too high for African governments' limited budgets.

Under these assumptions, civil service pay and employment reform became a primary aim of many structural adjustment programs, beginning in the early 1980s. This new generation of reforms focused overwhelmingly on trimming the state: "The primary objective of most reforms was to reduce the aggregate wage bill."[46] Even with inadequate salaries, the large numbers of people employed by the government meant that the total wage bill had become unsustainably large in many countries. In 1981, for example, the Central African Republic was spending 86 percent of its budgetary receipts on its civil service wage bill alone. But in comparison with other developing regions, African countries did not tend to allocate a disproportionately larger percentage of central government expenditures to wages and salaries. In 1983, wages and salaries in Asia, Africa, and Latin America and the Caribbean averaged 22, 26, and 27 percent, respectively; by 1993, averages in all regions had crept up, but African countries—at 29 percent—were still between Asia (24 percent) and Latin America and the Caribbean (30 percent).[47]

Despite the emphasis on reducing staff and restructuring wages and salaries, these reform programs were unable significantly to reduce the wage bill: 10 out of 14 countries in one study actually increased their wage bill during reforms.[48] Little progress was made in decompressing wages, and pay increases awarded to counteract wage erosion generally wiped out the retrenchment savings, even in the more "successful" adjusters, the Gambia and Ghana.[49] Eliminating "ghost" workers and reducing the number of redundant positions at the lower levels of the civil service may have had some effect on cost without compromising efficiency. Other ways of reducing the civil service, such as offering early retirement, may have been counterproductive, because older public servants also have more experience and may have absorbed more of the ethos of public service from the earlier days of post-independence governance. The positive measures introduced to raise the effectiveness of the remaining staff had little impact. A civil service reform project in Guinea introduced merit exams as a requirement for employment. The tests were costly and criticized for being "unable to measure important job attributes."[50] The ministries concerned also failed to implement the results, suggesting that they did not place much value in the exercise. Overall, these reforms did little to increase state capacity: "Improved government performance," admitted one evaluation, "proved the most elusive of the reform goals."[51]

FOREIGN AID AND STATE CAPACITY

Despite all the external effort and funding directed to reforming and rebuilding the state, the results have been discouraging. Technical cooperation has been "of no avail to sustainable institutional development," an authoritative U.N. study concluded.[52] World Bank public management analysts admitted that under Africa's structural adjustment programs, "anecdotal reports do not suggest significantly more efficient civil services, even in the most successful reform cases."[53] Other aid agencies have found it equally difficult to find an effective way to improve African government capacity. A recent review of the efforts of the U.S. Agency for International Development (USAID) lamented the "failure of [USAID's traditional] techniques to build capacity within the public sector in Africa."[54] There are still far more questions than answers in this field. Political scientist David Leonard, who has long studied the issue of government performance in Africa, admitted that, "We certainly have no knowledge of what reforms might be used to improve the performance of Africa's public organizations."[55]

Furthermore, much of the effort expended by foreign aid to promote African development has, by its nature, undermined rather than supported institution-building. In the 1950s and early 1960s, aid helped build strong national agricultural institutions in India and strengthened economic planning bureaus in Korea and Taiwan.[56] However, "by the time development assistance . . . reached Africa, the wave of enthusiasm for institution-building was on the wane."[57] Responding to the trend, international funding agencies shifted their attention in the early 1970s to a well-intentioned but ultimately ineffective effort to channel assistance more directly toward the rural poor. A 1979 critique of USAID's "New Direction" charged that,

> As a result, projects intended to build the institutions or infrastructure of developing countries are now under-

> taken surreptitiously, if at all. Advocates of strengthening the skilled, high-level manpower base or of helping develop universities . . . are accused of being elitists or persistent adherents to the old "trickle-down" approach to development. . . . Reacting to the pressure, AID has deemphasized the two most effective tools: strong local training and research facilities and a supply of well-trained, indigenous manpower.[58]

This shift away from institution-building was compounded by the increasing tendency of aid agencies to avoid working directly within African government ministries because of their inability to follow through with promises made during project negotiations. Frustrated funding agencies developed a more "efficient" (in the short term) vehicle for project implementation, the by-pass project management unit, a nominally governmental institution staffed and managed by project personnel, strategically positioned outside the direct reach of the state. When projects managed in this way still failed the test of sustainability, attention turned to reforming policy and reducing the scope of the state (structural adjustment) by passing on some of its workload to the private sector and to private development organizations (NGOs or private voluntary organizations) and by decentralizing its operations.[59] None of these efforts has resulted in a significantly more capable state.

In many ways, foreign aid efforts have directly and indirectly contributed to African governments' institutional weaknesses. This occurs in part through aid program requirements for well-trained local staff, in part through the unique institutional demands that aid makes on African governments, and in part through the substitution of aid receipts for domestic taxation. First, as one observer noted in Kenya, "Despite their current complaints about ineffective capacity and institution-building by advisory projects, it is primarily the donors who are poaching economists whose skill levels have been effectively raised through the counterpart training and education programmes of the MPND's [Ministry of Planning and National Development's] technical assistance projects."[60] Under local pressure to offer international-level salaries for internationally trained Kenyans working on foreign-funded projects, aid agencies and local consulting firms offered Kenyan economists with master's degrees five times the starting salary (plus benefits) they would have earned in the civil service. In addition, many of the traditional measures used by foreign aid agencies to maintain the morale and commitment of government staff on their projects, such as paying extra for work that should be performed in the course of an employee's job, offering higher salaries for "enclave" employees, and so forth, are arguably counterproductive for institution-building, because they create disincentives for the individuals who do not have access to such perks. Likewise, increased support for local NGOs creates incentives for civil servants to leave the government. Studies have noted that the staff of new development NGOs often simply shifted from public sector jobs in related ministries.[61]

Second, foreign aid imposes a uniquely twentieth-century burden on African governments trying to modernize their countries. One reason why African governments tend to default on their implementation commitments is the strain of meeting the requirements of more than 82 different organizations that currently provide assistance and, in return, demand participation in project preparation, counterparts, quarterly reports, evaluations, and so forth. In commenting on the "institutional destruction" resulting from this cycle, one observer gave the example of Malawi, which in the early 1980s was "managing" 188 projects funded by 50 different agencies:

> If one asks whether Malawi's capacities to run its own affairs and establish its own policies have been increased by the donor onslaught, the answer is far [from] certain. Indeed, it appears more likely that donor and project proliferation have diverted the attention of the Malawi authorities from attempting to determine their own policies to simply trying to please their donors.[62]

Third, foreign aid has historically substituted for domestic savings and foreign exchange. Yet, as argued above, the ability to stimulate savings and extract resources locally to fund government goals is one of the most basic elements of capacity. In European history, the requirement of raising funds to fight wars of defense and conquest stimulated the development of a host of government institutions, from revenue bureaus to legislatures, as princes bargained with property owners over the size and disposition of their tax burden. Foreign aid undercuts the development of capacity-building and accountability through its supply of resources to countries that have not yet built up a capacity to stimulate savings and to extract revenues domestically through taxation. In many African countries, foreign aid is a very significant proportion of national income. In 1993, for example, net disbursements of development assistance accounted for 25 percent of GNP in Malawi and 40 percent of GNP in Tanzania.[63] This makes the dialogue over how to use those resources naturally a dialogue between rulers and foreign aid donors, rather than between rulers and citizens, quite possibly undercutting the institutional development that occurs when rulers need to stimulate both greater (taxable) production and when citizens push for greater accountability for their tax monies.[64]

There is no magic formula for capacity-building, other than the historical pattern of dual pressures for better governance from elites and leaders at the top and citizens and clients at the bottom. There is broad agreement on the failure of both the old practices of project-linked training and technical assistance and by-pass project management units and the more recent efforts to reduce, reorganize, and reenergize reluctant ministries. As political scientist Thomas Callaghy argues, "In much of the current policy work on the development of state capacity in Third World countries . . . there is a strong voluntarist or architectonic streak that argues that state capacity can be 'built' as part of a policy imperative. The historical record belies this assumption."[65] Yet the pattern of assistance to Africa continues to assume that outsiders can build state capacity despite the lack of effective internal demand for more capable governments. If the overall environment is hostile to good public administration, then aid-supplied technical assistance is like "driving a nail into a rotten piece of wood."[66] All too often demands for capacity-building come primarily from the donors. One of the key challenges for African capacity-building lies in reversing this situation by returning ownership of reforms to African governments and reinforcing *their* initiatives.

For donor agencies, this means reforming the supply side of capacity-building efforts. The foreign aid system in which both donors and African governments are deeply enmeshed needs to adjust enough to allow African governments to retake responsibility and initiative for their own capacity-building efforts.[67] As long as aid agencies continue to supply the funding, the ideas, and the personnel for reforms, local governments will have little incentive (or time) to implement their own reform programs. Donor agencies can best assist by withdrawing from an active role in public sector reform efforts and by phasing out donor-driven project funding for expatriate technical assistance and short-term resident experts.

With the resources saved from the phasing out of current, profoundly flawed modes of assistance, donors can better support local ownership either by using a selective, performance-based approach in which governments are reimbursed for reforms on an ex post basis or by developing regional funds or foundations that, for example, respond to funding proposals for projects and programs to improve technical and managerial skills, establish more effective judicial and regulatory systems, experiment with incentive systems, or expand an engineering department or a technical education center. The act of developing and presenting the funding proposal on a competitive basis would ensure local ownership of the process. Furthermore, a fund-based mechanism could easily respond to requests for developing capacity outside the public sector, thus expanding the cadre of professional engineers, lawyers, accountants, and business managers.

STRATEGIES FOR REBUILDING STATE CAPACITY

Despite ample research on the design and implementation of stabilization and liberalization reforms, the intellectual consensus on how to rebuild state capacity remains quite weak. When government elites are clearly committed to better governance and reinforced by societal demand for more effective performance, as has been the case in Asia and in some African countries such as Botswana, the strategy may be fairly straightforward, even if it takes quite some time to achieve. First, leaders who are convinced of the need to build a more capable state should establish and endeavor to enforce consistently a set of rules (which may already exist on paper) underpinning the kind of professional, properly compensated, merit-oriented government service required for economic renewal. Second, the extractive capacity of government—its ability to raise the revenues to fund its programs—is a clear priority for early reform. Third, because most governments will continue to require patronage opportunities, a realistic strategy is to accept this and to concentrate reforms in a few critical agencies first. Agencies critical for economic stability and the rule of law will perform better if they can be insulated from patronage pressures and short-term political demands. Fourth, capacity outside the central government—particularly in professional associations, professional schools, and local government—can serve both as a source of information and expertise and as a source of demand, reinforcing an increasingly accountable and capable state. Strategic training opportunities and long-term foreign expertise can all be part of the program of building up technical, administrative, extractive, and regulatory capacity, but the initiative and the plan *must* come from the government, not the donors.

Get the Basics Right

Nothing in the twentieth century has proven Weber wrong on his basic framework. Rational-legal bureaucracies are still the best organizational form for state-promoted development.[68] Building professionalism involves meritocratic recruitment of a properly compensated civil service with a common esprit de corps. It also requires clear rules and procedures, with accountability achieved through review procedures that enforce the rules. Finally, bureaucrats need incentives to ensure congruence between their personal goals and their agency's goal. These incentives, which are likely to be culturally specific, can be as simple as giving staff more influence, recognition, status, and a sense of shared mission.[69] In other parts of the world, building effective bureaucracies has been a very slow process, dependent on consistent political support and requiring, quite possibly, decades or even generations to be institutionalized. Regulatory capacity—the ability to establish and enforce the rule of law—is critical here. As Weber suggested, rules with sanctions will, over time, shape bureaucratic behavior. Governments also need to emphasize stability and continuity, rather than continual reorganization, and allow individuals and government bureaus to learn and institutionalize the norms of office.

Deepen Extractive Capacity

Extraction is in some ways the most fundamental dimension of capacity, both because it pays for the other dimensions and because improving capacity here may stimulate improvements in the critical areas of regulation and administration. African governments are largely dependent on indirect taxes such as tariffs and export taxes that take less capacity to collect. The ability to raise revenues from a variety of sources divides more from less capable states. African governments make little use of property taxes, value added or consumption taxes, sales taxes, or entertainment taxes, and income taxes are generally undercollected. Income taxes burden citizens directly and are considered to be one of the responsibilities they bear for the rights and privileges they receive. As the discussion of European institutional development pointed out, taxation and disputes over the use of revenues stimulated the development of greater citizen rights and privileges, with democratic institutions reinforcing accountability and greater transparency in expenditures. For these and also for purely revenue reasons, reforms of Africa's taxation capacity should be a priority for African governments.

Aid was never intended to substitute indefinitely for a country's ability to raise its own resources, and indeed in the Republic of Korea and Taiwan, economic aid was terminated in the 1960s once those economies were started on what appeared to be a sustainable path. In Europe, war-making and defense stimulated the development and improvement of systems of taxation. In Africa, the debt crisis and the economic turmoil that followed have created the stimulus for greater efficiency in the government's generation of revenue. In this regard, it would be useful to study, and to monitor the sustainability of, the World

Bank-sponsored reforms of national revenue services in the Gambia, Ghana, Zambia, and other countries.

Concentrate Reforms in Strategic Agencies

Even in countries such as Korea, which enjoys a high degree of government capacity, not all of the government has been effective. President Park Chung-hee allowed the domestic ministries such as agriculture and home affairs to continue as vehicles for patronage and clientelism, and as a result, they were much less efficient than the fiscal ministries (trade and industry, economic planning board, finance) that he held to much higher standards of performance.[70] Following this model, a realistic leader would begin by reforming and building technical and administrative capacity in one or more key agencies, which could then serve as sources of high standards and meritocratic norms to be diffused gradually throughout the government.

Which parts of the state should be upgraded first? Leonard's case studies of successful public institutions in Kenya pinpointed political demand for their services as critical for success.[71] The success of Ghana's reformed National Revenue Service depended in part on its "recognized strategic character . . . clear accountability for performance, [and] high-quality leadership."[72] Agencies with a political demand for their services and a recognized strategic character might include the central bank, customs bureau, and judiciary, although, depending on the country, veterinary services or tree crop extension might also be good candidates. These strategic agencies might be given special dispensation to experiment with ways in which to stimulate better performance.[73] It may be necessary to insulate these agencies from the patronage pressures faced by government bureaus in general. Life-time tenure for judges and governors of central banks can help ensure their independence, insulating the judiciary and the central bank from short-sighted political interference. Here, again, the establishment of successful strategic agencies of expertise depends critically on a committed leadership and a high level of domestic demand. Many examples exist of African institutions with skilled and expert staff who are ignored by their central governments and of "autonomous" central banks and "insulated" planning bureaus that are easily manipulated by patrimonial leaders.[74] This has clear implication for donors. Outside support for strategic agencies should always be a follow-on to a plan conceived and initiated by local leaders and should be for very specific, time-bound assistance that is not available locally. Without this demand, donor support for strategic agencies risks becoming another dead end: the by-pass project management unit of the twenty-first century.

Build Capacity and Professionalism Outside Central Government

Most of the previous discussion focused on building capacity in the central government, but equally important may be building capacity in nongovernmental entities. This entails capacity that central governments can tap as needed through consultancies, that can be drawn in for critical policy-relevant discussion, or that can serve as a pressure point to build political demand for better government performance. Experience in countries as diverse as Brazil and China points to demands by organized users and client groups as an important factor in enhancing the capacity of government agencies to deliver services and improve quality. Likewise, recent work on the East Asian newly industrialized economies suggests that their economic performance depended in part on close links between the private sector and economic bureaucracies.[75] To be effective, however, these linkages and demands need institutional channels.

One channel consists of professional associations, development NGOs, business associations, and producer groups like the tea farmers in Kenya or cotton producers in Mali. Although these groups will tend to support the interests of their membership above those of society as a whole, they can support accountability and developmentalism and reinforce the persons within the state who press for better governance. To do so, however, they must be able to present their own analyses of the costs and benefits of proposed policies and to offer cogent, alternative policies.

Professional associations can contribute to more capable and effective governance by reinforcing professional standards, values, and norms. These values were difficult to maintain in many post-independence governments, because bureaucracies expanded rapidly and were reshaped to meet the political needs of the new leaders.[76] When a "pocket of excellence" exists in the public sector, it seems to be supported not only by political demand but also by "*a professional group sustaining its values*" (emphasis added).[77] Short-term project-related training does little to develop the kind of professional values important for professionalization. Instead, as David Leonard suggests, governments should continue to support training in medicine, engineering, accounting, and law, all "rigorous . . . professional discipline(s) [with] clear minimum training requirements for membership . . . [and] ethical and technical standards."[78] Support for strong local and regional professional schools at African universities would provide opportunities for groups of people to train together, developing an esprit de corps and adding annually to a growing cadre of locally based professionals. Local professional associations that reinforce these values can be better linked with their international counterparts, and donors can assist these linkages through forums and workshops. These professionals, and the associations to which they belong, can become strong forces exerting pressure for greater accountability in government.

FINANCING IMPROVEMENTS IN STATE CAPACITY

How can capacity-building efforts be financed? States committed to steady support for bureaucratic development face the dilemma that while resources to support well-remunerated higher level officials must be found, these resources will most likely be found in the overstaffed, but often politically protected, lower levels of the bureaucracy. Attrition and the elimination of "ghost" employees may release some funds, but this dilemma is not going to be easily resolved. However these difficult decisions are made, they must be made by African governments themselves. Externally driven efforts to reduce the size of the civil service have rarely achieved their goal and may be counterproductive through the instability they engender. Debt relief, particularly on debt owed to multilateral creditors, would reduce the strain on government budgets in many African countries, where accumulated interest payments increasingly crowd out other government budget categories.

Many of the necessary reforms are not expensive, but involve making more effective use of existing resources. Ample sources exist for technical and managerial advice at reasonable costs that can be met from local resources.[79] The United Nations Development Programme, which already supports technical cooperation between developing countries, could help to reduce information and search costs for countries determined to find good advice, but with the reminder that long before the United Nations existed, countries (such as Japan, Prussia, and Russia) found ways to identify and hire foreign expertise for their own state capacity-building programs. Finally, the demand-based funds or foundation-style assistance discussed above could provide financing for capacity-building programs conceived and implemented by Africans inside and outside government.

CONCLUSIONS

Africa's efforts to build better governance are going to take time, just as they have in other parts of the world. Economic renewal can be enhanced by rebuilding four mutually reinforcing components of state capacity: extractive capacity, administrative capacity, regulatory capacity, and technical capacity. Committed leadership is critical in this regard, and to support local ownership, aid should always be subsidiary to programs conceived locally. Fund- or foundation-based mechanisms relying on a competitive application process can help to ensure that local ownership does exist; ex post funding of programs already begun is another way to support local initiatives.

History demonstrates that rules and norms can change behavior over time; rules require systems of accountability for enforcement; enforcement depends on leadership commitment. Committed leaders can work within the kind of state-society linkages found in patrimonial governance systems, if they concentrate first on reforming a small number of critical agencies, such as the central bank, the internal revenue service, or the judiciary. Because they help to finance other aspects of capacity, while building demand among citizens more directly for effective governance, the internal revenue service and extractive capacity are a particularly critical area to rebuild. Finally, professional schools and associations outside the state can help to create demand for a more capable and effective state, while reinforcing core professional values in both state and society. Ultimately, shifting from patrimonial to effective bureaucracies depends on local learning, experience, political leadership, effective social pressure, and *time*.

Notes

I would like to thank David Gordon, David Hirschmann, Mick Moore, Barbara Nunberg, Nicolas van de Walle, and Ernest Wilson, all of whom read an earlier draft of this chapter and tried to put me straight and who should not be blamed where I failed to follow their good suggestions. Thanks also to my class on Governance, Democracy, and Development, and particularly to Johana Ayers, Jeffrey Courtemanche, Sarah DeBolt, Abdoulaye Essy, Tobin Hickman, Jordana Newman, and Anja Robakowski. David Helevy, Charles Kenny, and David Pechevsky provided excellent research assistance.

[1] Arnold Rivkin, *Nations by Design: Institution Building in Africa,* Colloquium on Institution Building and the African Development Process, University of California, Los Angeles (New York: Anchor Books, 1968), pp. xii–xiii.

[2] Samuel Stephen Mushi, "Strengthening Local Government in Africa: Organizational and Structural Aspects," in United Nations Department of Economic and Social Development, *Seminar on Decentralization in African Countries: Proceedings and Recommendations*, Banjul, July 27–31, 1992 (New York: United Nations, 1993), p. 26.

[3] This figure is cited in the African Capacity Building Foundation's undated promotional brochure. The figure of $4 billion is also cited by Elliot J. Berg, *Rethinking Technical Cooperation: Reforms for Capacity Building in Africa* (New York: United Nations Development Programme, 1993), p. 245.

[4] This discussion of capacity builds on the work of Theda Skocpol, "Bringing the State Back In: Strategies of Analysis in Current Research," and Dietrich Rueschemeyer and Peter B. Evans, "The State and Economic Transformation: Toward an Analysis of the Conditions Underlying Effective Intervention," which both appear in Peter B. Evans, Dietrich Rueschemeyer, and Theda Skocpol, eds., *Bringing the State Back In* (Cambridge: Cambridge University Press, 1985); David Leonard, "The Political Realities of African Management," *World Development*, Vol. 15, No. 7 (1987), pp. 899–900; Joel S. Migdal, *Strong Societies and Weak*

States: State-Society Relations and State Capabilities in the Third World (Princeton, NJ: Princeton University Press, 1988); and Merilee Grindle, *Challenging the State: Crisis and Innovation in Latin America and Africa* (Cambridge: Cambridge University Press, forthcoming).

[5] Skocpol, op. cit., p. 17.

[6] Robert Putnam suggests some of these indicators in his recent book, *Making Democracy Work: Civic Traditions in Modern Italy* (Princeton, NJ: Princeton University Press, 1993), pp. 67–8.

[7] Charles Tilly, "War Making and State Making as Organized Crime," in Evans, Rueschemeyer, and Skocpol, *Bringing the State Back In*, op. cit., pp. 169–91.

[8] Leonard, "Political Realities of African Management," op. cit., p. 905.

[9] Robin Theobald, *Corruption, Development, and Underdevelopment* (Durham, NC: Duke University Press, 1990), p. 27.

[10] Sadig Rasheed, "Promoting Ethics and Accountability in the African Civil Services," in *Development Management in Africa: Toward Dynamism, Empowerment, and Entrepreneurship*, ed. David F. Luke and Sadig Rasheed (Boulder, CO: Westview Press, 1995).

[11] Basil Davidson, *Modern Africa* (London: Longman, 1983), p. 81; World Bank, *Education in Sub-Saharan Africa: Policies for Adjustment, Revitalization, and Expansion* (Washington, DC: World Bank, 1988), p. 12.

[12] Deborah Brautigam, "What Can Africa Learn From Taiwan?" *Journal of Modern African Studies*, Vol. 32, No. 1 (1994), p. 114.

[13] Gelase Mutahaba, Rweikiza Baguma, and Mohamed Halfani, *Vitalizing African Public Administration for Recovery and Development* (Hartford, CT: Kumarian Press in cooperation with the United Nations, 1993), p. 82.

[14] David L. Lindauer, Oey Astra Meesook, and Parita Suebsaeng, "Government Wage Policy in Africa: Some Findings and Policy Issues," *World Bank Research Observer* Vol. 3, No. 1 (January 1988), p. 2; and Mike Stevens, "Public Expenditure and Civil Service Reform in Tanzania," in *Rehabilitating Government: Pay and Employment Reform in Africa*, ed. David L. Lindauer and Barbara Nunberg (Washington, DC: World Bank, 1994), p. 66. This acceleration was a reflection of primary education and primary health campaigns and of the creation of new states in Nigeria.

[15] David Lindauer and Richard H. Sabot, "The Public/Private Wage Differential in a Poor Urban Economy," *Journal of Development Economics* Vol. 12 (February/April 1983), pp. 137-52; G. E. Johnson, "The Determination of Individual Hourly Earnings in Urban Kenya," Discussion Paper 115 (Institute for Development Studies, University of Nairobi, 1971). Both papers are cited in David Lindauer, "Government Pay and Employment Policies and Economic Performance," in Lindauer and Nunberg, op. cit., p. 30.

[16] I am grateful to Mick Moore, who referred me to Crawford Young's work on this point. See Crawford Young, *The African Colonial State in Comparative Perspective* (New Haven, CT: Yale University Press, 1994).

[17] Lindauer, Meesook, and Suebsaeng, op. cit., p. 8; and David C. E. Chew, "Internal Adjustments to Falling Civil Service Salaries: Insights from Uganda," *World Development*, Vol. 18, No. 7 (1990), p. 1004.

[18] Louis de Merode with Charles S. Thomas, "Implementing Civil Service Pay and Employment Reform in Africa: The Experiences of Ghana, the Gambia, and Guinea," in Lindauer and Nunberg, eds., *Rehabilitating Government*, op. cit., p. 161.

[19] J. Bossuyt, G. Lapotre, and F. van Hoek, *New Avenues for Technical Cooperation in Africa: Improving the Record in Terms of Capacity Building* (Maastricht, Netherlands: European Center for Development Policy Management, 1992), p. 16.

[20] World Bank, *Sub-Saharan Africa: From Crisis to Sustainable Growth* (Washington, DC: World Bank, 1989), p. 60.

[21] Republic of Uganda, *Report of the Public Service Salaries Review Commission 1980–82* (Kampala, 1982), cited in Lindauer, "Government Pay," op. cit., p. 21.

[22] World Bank, *Sub-Saharan Africa*, op. cit., p. 61.

[23] As political scientist Joel Migdal has noted, African leaders in weak states tended to shuffle their cabinet-level personnel regularly so as to thwart the buildup of independent power centers. See Migdal, op. cit., p. 240.

[24] Richard Crook, "Patrimonialism, Administrative Effectiveness, and Economic Development in Côte d'Ivoire," *African Affairs* Vol. 88 (1989), p. 220.

[25] Ravi Gulhati, "Who Makes Economic Policy in Africa and How?" *World Development* Vol. 18, No. 8 (1990), p. 1159.

[26] This point is made in Richard Sandbrook, "Hobbled Leviathans: Constraints on State Formation in Africa," *International Journal*, Vol. 41 (Fall 1986), p. 707. See also Ladipo Adamolekun, "Political Leadership in Sub-Saharan Africa: From Giants to Dwarfs," *International Political Science Review* ,Vol. 9, No. 2 (1988), pp. 95–106.

[27] Crook, op. cit., p. 225.

[28] David Leonard, *African Successes: Four Public Managers of Kenyan Rural Development* (Berkeley: University of California Press, 1991), p. 300.

[29] Migdal, op. cit., p. 242.

[30] Stevens's speech was cited in W. N. Wamalwa, "An Address," in *Economic Restructuring and African Public Administration: Issues, Actions, and Future Choices*, ed. M. Jide Balogun and Gelase Mutahaba (Hartford, CT: Kumarian Press for the African Association for Public Administration and Management, 1989), p. xxvii.

[31] Mutahaba, Baguma, and Halfani, op. cit., p. 82; World Bank, *Education in Sub-Saharan Africa*, op. cit., p. 12. Unless otherwise noted, all statistics in the rest of this section come from the World Bank source. These figures exclude South Africa.

[32] World Bank, *Education in Sub-Saharan Africa*, op. cit., p. 133.

[33] World Bank, *World Development Report 1995* (New York: Oxford University Press, 1995), pp. 216–17.

[34] Manuel Zymelman, *Science, Education, and Development in Sub-Saharan Africa*, Technical Paper 124 (Washington, DC: World Bank, 1990), p. 39. "Graduates" are upper level graduates who have at least four or five years of postsecondary education. The countries in the sample were Ethiopia, Ghana, Malawi, Rwanda, and Uganda.

[35] Having appropriate skills does not always mean that those skills are well used. Nigeria, with more than 800 qualified public sector accountants, "has not produced audited public accounts since 1982." Judy Makanda, "Accounting and Auditing Standards in Sub-Saharan Africa" (Capacity Building and Implementation Division, Africa Technical Department, World Bank, Washington, DC, January 1995), p. 31.

[36] World Bank, *Education in Sub-Saharan Africa*, p. 102.

[37] John Cohen, "Foreign Advisors and Capacity Building: The Case of Kenya," *Public Administration and Development*, Vol. 12 (1992), p. 499. Perhaps unfortunately for public institution-building in Kenya, there were many opportunities for trained economists and financial managers outside the public sector, and the government failed to enforce a bond system to ensure that individuals who received training returned to the ministry for a period.

[38] World Bank, *Education in Sub-Saharan Africa*, op. cit., p. 105.

[39] Cohen, op. cit., note 19, p. 504.

[40] Berg, op. cit., p. 244.

[41] Robert Klitgaard, "Incentive Myopia," *World Development*, Vol. 17, No. 4 (1989), p. 449.

[42] See David Hirschmann, "Institutional Development in the Era of Economic Policy Reform: Concerns, Contradictions, and Illustrations from Malawi," *Public Administration and Development*, Vol. 13, No. 2 (1993), pp. 113-28.

[43] See Arturo Israel, *Institutional Development: Incentives to Performance* (Baltimore, MD: Johns Hopkins University Press, 1987).

[44] de Merode with Thomas, op. cit., p. 164; Makanda, op. cit., p. 30.

[45] Lindauer, "Government Pay," op. cit., p. 28; Hirschmann, op. cit., p. 121.

[46] Barbara Nunberg, "Experience with Civil Service Pay and Employment Reform: An Overview," in Lindauer and Nunberg, op. cit., p. 153.

[47] International Monetary Fund, *Government Finance Statistics Yearbook* (Washington, DC: International Monetary Fund, 1983 and 1993).

[48] Nunberg, op. cit., p. 153.

[49] Nunberg, op. cit.; and de Merode with Thomas, op. cit.

[50] de Merode with Thomas, op. cit., p. 172.

[51] Ibid.

[52] Bossuyt, Lapotre, and van Hoek, op. cit., p. 58.

[53] Barbara Nunberg and David L. Lindauer, "Conclusion: The Political Economy of Civil Service Pay and Employment Reform," in Lindauer and Nunberg, eds., op. cit., p. 239.

[54] Louis Picard and Michele Garrity, "Improving Management Performance in Africa: Collaborative Intervention Models," in *Policy Reform for Sustainable Development in Africa: The Institutional Imperative*, ed. Louis Picard and Michele Garrity (Boulder, CO: Lynne Rienner Press, 1994), p. 138.

[55] Leonard, "Political Realities of African Management," op. cit., p. 906.

[56] See, for example, Arthur A. Goldsmith, *Building Agricultural Institutions: Transferring the Land-Grant Model to India and Nigeria* (Boulder, CO: Westview Press, 1990).

[57] Elliot R. Morss, "Institutional Destruction Resulting from Donor and Project Proliferation in Sub-Saharan African Countries," *World Development*, Vol. 12, No. 4 (1984), p. 468.

[58] William R. Cotter, "How AID Fails to Aid Africa," *Foreign Policy*, No. 34 (Spring 1979), p. 107.

[59] On decentralization, see the critical review offered by James S. Wunsch, "Institutional Analysis and Decentralization: Developing an Analytical Framework for Effective Third World Administrative Reform," *Public Administration and Development*, Vol. 11 (1991), p. 433.

[60] Cohen, op. cit., p. 500.

[61] Carrie A. Meyer, "A Step Back as Donors Shift Institution Building from the Public to the 'Private' Sector," *World Development*, Vol. 20, No. 8 (1992), p. 1121.

[62] Morss, op. cit., note 4, p. 468.

[63] World Bank, *World Development Report 1995*, op. cit., p. 198.

[64] See Deborah Brautigam, "Governance, Economy, and Foreign Aid," *Studies in Comparative International Development*, No. 27, No. 3 (1992), pp. 3-25.

[65] Thomas Callaghy, "Toward State Capability and Embedded Liberalism in the Third World: Lessons for Adjustment," in *Fragile Coalitions: The Politics of Economic Adjustment*, ed. Joan M. Nelson, U.S.-Third World Policy Perspectives No. 12 (New Brunswick, NJ: Transaction Publishers in cooperation with ODC, 1989), p. 117.

[66] Bossuyt, Lapotre, and van Hoek, op. cit., p. 15.

[67] David Hirschmann made this point quite well in his article, op. cit.

[68] Rueschemeyer and Evans, op. cit., p. 50.

[69] Barbara Geddes, "Building 'State' Autonomy in Brazil, 1930-1964," *Comparative Politics*, Vol. 22, No. 2, p. 231.

[70] David C. Kang, "South Korean and Taiwanese Development and the New Institutional Economics," *International Organization*, Vol. 49, No. 3 (Summer 1995), p. 575.

[71] Leonard, *African Successes*, op. cit., p. 300.

[72] De Merode with Thomas, op. cit., p. 188.

[73] See Klitgaard, op. cit.

[74] In the 1970s, both Nigeria and Ghana established high-level "policy analysis units"; Côte d'Ivoire, Ethiopia, Tanzania, and Zimbabwe set up "semi-autonomous policy research institutions," all of which lacked political demand and found their work ignored by policymakers. Mutahaba, Baguma, and Halfani, op. cit., p. 50. The World Bank also promoted this approach in the 1980s, concentrating primarily on ministries of finance and central banks. Although there have been some successes, the failure of this approach in other cases (Nigeria, for example) can be traced to its external origin and lack of effective internal commitment.

[75] Peter Evans, *Embedded Autonomy: States and Industrial Transformation* (Princeton, NJ: Princeton University Press, 1995).

[76] Crook, p. 222.

[77] Leonard, "Political Realities of African Management,"op. cit., p. 300.

[78] Ibid., p. 273.

[79] Consultants can be hired from local or regional institutions and universities or from other developing countries that have made greater progress in developing effective bureaucracies: Korea, Taiwan, or Indonesia, for example. They can also be hired from regional institutes such as the Indian Institute of Public Administration.

Chapter Three

Enhancing Human Capacities in Africa

Simon Appleton and John Mackinnon

INTRODUCTION

Despite marked improvements in the last 30 years, Africa remains disadvantaged in health and education.[1] Low levels of health and education are often seen as inevitable consequences of poverty, either because they are consumer goods with a positive income elasticity of demand, or because there are low returns at low levels of income. This paper, however, takes a different view. Both health care and education are partly investments in human capital and can help a country escape poverty as well as save lives. Because of the low levels of health and education, the marginal returns to further investments (of the right kind) are almost certainly higher in Africa than in developed countries. Although poverty certainly plays a part, low levels of attainment of health and education reflect pervasive market and state failure. Private markets in both education and health care operate imperfectly, and public-sector decisions on health and education spending are highly inequitable and may be very inefficient as well. As a result, Africa's performance is worse than it could and should be, and worse than other regions' at similar income levels.

To improve Africa's performance in health and education, this chapter recommends a central role for a reformed public sector. It begins by surveying the existing state of health and educational outcomes in Africa and considers the channels through which public policy affects educational and health achievements, as well as the returns to those achievements. It then turns to the causes of market failure, arguing that these failures are quite fundamental to Africa's poor performance compared to other regions. Finally, the chapter considers policy responses, first to financing issues and then to public provision and relations with the private sector. There is some hope that the situation may be improving.

THE CURRENT SITUATION IN AFRICA

The State of Education

The rapid post-independence expansion in educational provision in Africa was a remarkable achievement. The proportion of children in primary school doubled over two decades while the proportion in secondary school increased by a factor of five or more. But the 1980s brought a halt to these rapid gains. Averaged across countries, primary enrollment ratios remained constant during the last decade, while secondary enrollment ratios continued to rise, but at a much slower rate (Table 1). This aggregate slowdown masks great variation across countries. While primary school enrollment ratios fell in at least 16 countries, they increased in 19 other countries; secondary school enrollment ratios are reported to have fallen in seven countries.

The 1980s left African countries with a wide diversity of educational access. A few countries have almost universal primary schooling, although dropouts remain a problem. In others, particularly in Sahelian countries, most children do not attend school. Typically, however, pri-

TABLE 1: GROSS SCHOOL ENROLLMENT RATIOS IN A SAMPLE OF AFRICAN COUNTRIES (percent)

	Primary (All)		Primary (Female)		Secondary (All)	
Year	Mean	Median	Mean	Median	Mean	Median
1960	36	38	27	25	3	2
1970	51	41	40	30	8	7
1980	70	68	61	51	15	14
1990	69	69	62	63	19	16

Notes: Sample size is 35. Due to lack of data, the 35 countries are all Sub-Saharan and also exclude Angola, the Congo, Gabon, Namibia, and South Africa, together with all countries with a population below 0.5 million. Where figures were not available for 1990, the nearest year for which they were available was used. Means are for countries, unweighted by population.

Source: World Bank Stars data set; and World Bank, *Education in Sub-Saharan Africa: Policies for Adjustment, Revitalization, and Expansion* (Washington, DC: World Bank, 1988).

mary school enrollment is substantial though far from universal; only a relatively small number of children go to secondary school; and tertiary enrollment rates seldom exceed 3 percent. By contrast, primary school enrollment ratios in the rest of the developing world average around 100 percent, and most people receive some secondary schooling.

Adult literacy rates suggest the effect of past school enrollment on current capacities. Only about half of African adults are believed to be literate. In all African countries women bear the brunt of illiteracy, with three out of five women being unable to read.

In addition to the comparatively lower enrollment rates, Africa has also experienced a reduction in the *quality* of education due to falling real educational expenditure per capita and possibly even the earlier quantitative expansion.[2] Indicators of what students have learned are not systematically gathered and publicized across Africa, whether because of difficulty or sensitivity, and what evidence does exist is not encouraging.[3] Instead, quality is most often measured indirectly by inputs. Averaging over all non-Arabic African countries, the primary student-teacher ratio was 37 in 1990; for developing countries as a whole the figure was 28. At least 11 Sub-Saharan African countries still have primary student-teacher ratios of over 50. Research, however, has not established a clear link between class size and primary school performance. Research on student performance suggests that the proportion of expenditure devoted to teaching materials is a better guide to quality. In Africa, this proportion is relatively small; the median share of teaching materials was only 1.1 percent in 1983 for 20 countries with data. In the 1980s, the shares seem to have fallen further for 12 countries with data, leaving student-textbook ratios of between 10 and 20 in some countries.[4]

Measures of internal efficiency—repetition and dropout rates—are sometimes taken as quality indicators. In the least developed countries in Africa, the mean percentage of primary school students who were repeating grades was 19 percent in 1991. In more than half of the countries with available data, most primary school students will not complete the course.

The State of Health

Health may be measured in terms of outcomes or inputs. Outcomes are clearly of more fundamental importance; measures include anthropometric status, morbidity, and mortality. We focus here on mortality because of its great intrinsic importance and because it does not raise the difficult issues of intercontinental comparison raised by the other measures. Life expectancy is low in Africa and mortality is high, even by comparison with countries elsewhere at similar income levels, as Table 2 demonstrates. Even the best performers in Africa, such as Kenya, have life expectancy no higher than the norm for countries of other continents at the same level, and most African countries perform worse than the norm.[5] A similar story emerges for adult mortality; in 1990 the adult mortality rate (aged 15–59) was between 300 and 500 per thousand in most African countries compared to under 200 in China and around 250 for India. The relatively high prevalence of HIV in Africa almost certainly implies that Africa's relative performance for this indicator is worsening.

It might be thought that this relatively poor performance reflects a fundamentally more hostile environment. However, historical experience suggests that there is no reason to be defeatist. Life expectancy has risen in Africa since 1945, even though some countries such as Uganda and Zambia did not share in this progress. The levels of mortality now observed in Africa are shocking to modern observers, but they would not have seemed high to observers from other continents in previous centuries.

Mortality is almost universally higher in rural areas than in urban areas in contemporary Africa, a striking contrast to the historical experience of early industrialization in previous centuries. This is probably because the advantages that urban areas potentially have in terms of the provision of services are more powerful in the twentieth century, both because modern medicine can achieve much more and because the state has usually provided medical services to urban areas. In previous centuries, urban areas' sanitary disadvantages often outweighed any advantage they might have in the availability of medical services.

The better performance of urban over rural areas is widely observed across continents, but Africa is more distinctive in its pattern of illness by gender. In general girls do not seem to do worse than boys, in strong contrast to South Asia. Education is powerfully related to health performance, a theme we return to when we discuss the determinants of health.

The diseases that cause mortality vary across countries; however, it is very often observed that children are in particular danger soon after birth because of neonatal tetanus, and during weaning, whether because of the loss of immunity conferred by the mother, the increased risk of infection as children learn to crawl, or a drop in nutritional intake relative to requirements. Major killers include diarrhoea, respiratory infection, and malaria, as well as measles and other illnesses for which there are vaccines. For the argument of this chapter, it is important to note that most of the causes of death among African children are treatable or preventable and that most relate to communicable disease.

TABLE 2: HEALTH INDICATORS IN AFRICA AND COMPARABLE COUNTRIES, 1993

Countries	GNP Per Capita (dollars)	Life Expectancy (years)	Infant Mortality Rate (per 1,000 live births)	
			1970	1993
African				
Mozambique	90	46	171	146
Tanzania	90	52	129	84
Ethiopia	100	48	159	117
Sierra Leone	150	39	197	164
Burundi	180	50	138	102
Uganda	180	45	117	114
Malawi	200	45	193	142
Chad	210	48	171	120
Madagascar	220	57	181	93
Guinea-Bissau	240	44	185	138
Kenya	270	58	102	61
Mali	270	45	204	157
Niger	270	47	171	122
Burkina Faso	300	47	178	129
Nigeria	300	51	114	83
Togo	340	55	134	83
Gambia	350	45	185	130
Zambia	380	48	106	103
Central African Republic	400	50	139	101
Benin	430	48	146	85
Ghana	430	56	111	79
Guinea	500	45	181	132
Mauritania	500	52	148	99
Zimbabwe	520	53	96	67
Côte d'Ivoire	630	51	135	91
Lesotho	650	61	134	77
Namibia	1820	59	118	59
Non-African				
Vietnam	170	66	111	41
Nepal	190	54	157	96
Bangladesh	220	56	140	106
Laos	280	52	146	95
India	300	61	137	80
Albania	340	72	66	29
Pakistan	430	62	142	88
China	490	69	69	30
Sri Lanka	600	72	197	164

Notes: The quality of data is likely to vary across countries, depending on frequency of censuses and demographic surveys. Detailed information on child mortality is available in United Nations, *Child Mortality Since the 1960s: A Database for Developing Countries* (New York: United Nations, 1992), which suggests that there is a shortage of good data on African countries and confirms some of the pessimistic findings, for instance the stagnation of mortality in Uganda.

Source: World Bank, *World Development Report 1995* (New York: Oxford University Press, 1995).

Crucial illnesses that cause adult mortality include malaria, tuberculosis, problems associated with birth, and HIV. Tuberculosis and most maternal risk can be treated, though they both require careful handling. HIV is an exception in that mortality cannot usually be prevented by medical treatment, though it can be delayed. Strategies for prevention of HIV, however, are feasible and include attempts to change sexual habits, promotion of the use of condoms, and—an avenue of great potential importance—the quick treatment of other sexually transmitted diseases that make the risk of infection from any single encounter much greater.

International measures of health inputs (such as doctors per head) tell only a partial story, because they tend to ignore quality and distribution. The performance of health services varies very widely across the continent and has been much affected by civil disorder. In Uganda, for instance, a relatively strong system fell apart during the period from 1973 to 1986 and is only now recovering.

DETERMINANTS OF AND RETURNS TO HUMAN CAPACITIES AT AN INDIVIDUAL LEVEL

Although much research finds economic returns to investments in education and health, the evidence is limited because it is typically nonexperimental[6] and almost always concerned with private, as opposed to social, returns. Consequently, the state of knowledge does not provide overall quantifications of the gains from public investments in human resources. Nevertheless, the balance of existing evidence does suggest that both education and health services can save lives and bring sizable economic returns.

Determinants of Educational Status

Studies of the determinants of educational status in Africa are rather scarce. One positive indicator for the future is the likely existence of "ratchet effects," such as the fact that parents seldom wish their children to be less educated than they are themselves. The relationship with socioeconomic status is less clear and appears to vary by country.[7] It has been argued that school factors such as teaching materials and teacher quality are more important in educational achievement in developing countries than in the West. Primary school enrollment is often determined by demand, although the availability of local schools also has some effect. Post-primary public schooling is typically rationed, and at this level access often depends more on academic performance than demand. Consequently, girls' low educational status may be directly due to demand factors (via nonenrollment in or dropping out of primary school) or due to underachievement in primary and secondary leaving examinations.[8]

Determinants of Health Status

The main clinical causes of death and disease in Africa were surveyed above. Most mortality is caused by communicable disease, much of which is both preventable and treatable at fairly low cost. Sometimes, as with diarrhoea, treatment does not require interventions by medical professionals if parents are well equipped and informed. Socioeconomic factors, however, are considerably harder to establish. We focus here on two issues of direct importance for policy: the role of public health interventions and the role of informational factors.

Where data are available, public health interventions are often found to make a difference, although the evidence is rather fragmentary.[9] One study of a water-supply project found that the main benefits arose from an increase in the public awareness of health.[10] There are good a priori reasons to expect some actions such as the provision of immunization to have a dramatic effect. There is, however, a need for research that proves this.

At the level of the household, health is affected by both 1) the resources available to the household, including its command over food, housing, and access to services; and 2) informational or attitudinal factors. The difference between the two is critical because markets are often better at allocating resources than transmitting information. The discussion below, while not disputing the important part played by resources, examines the role of information.

In evaluating how information affects health, two kinds of evidence apply. First, much research examines the relations between health and education. Parental education is associated with reduced child mortality, probably causally. Some evidence suggests that female education is particularly important; however, this is less clear in Africa than elsewhere, perhaps because men are sometimes responsible for financing child health. Other studies find no benefits from the early years of primary education, and still other studies find that the relation between education and health outcomes is strongly convex. The link with education is clearer for mortality than for anthropometric status; reported child morbidity, by contrast, is sometimes positively related to parental education, suggesting that more educated parents are better than less educated ones at recognizing medical problems in their children. Some studies find that education and public services interact, sometimes as complements, sometimes as substitutes. In Kenya and Côte d'Ivoire, for example, parental education increases usage of health services. It should be noted, however, that we know much less about the determinants of adult health than of child health, and it seems likely that resources play a more central role in adult health.[11]

An important aspect of this kind of evidence is that one cannot always isolate the informational or attitudinal effects of education. Education may affect mortality by increasing income or affect the control of resources by women or the returns to child health. A few studies do, however, relate health outcomes directly to information, suggesting that information is indeed important. In Brazil, education is found to affect health partly by influencing the ways mothers gather information, for instance whether they listen to a radio or buy a newspaper. In Uganda, recent work finds that parental beliefs about the causation of illness have a significant effect on child mortality, even when education is included as a factor.[12]

A second kind of evidence, mostly collected by doctors or anthropologists, documents informational failures likely to affect health. For example, newborn babies in some parts of Sudan are fed potentially lethal juice from acacia bark. In one area of Mali, children with diarrhoea are forbidden water, contributing to dehydration, and the under-five mortality rates for children of aristocrats approaches 50 percent (higher than for others because of differences in childrearing practices). In parts of Uganda, children with swollen gums are often operated on by painful and occasionally lethal excisions of parts of the gum (the swollen gums may be due to nutritional deficiencies and the excisions are likely to be of no medical benefit). Studies of traditional medical beliefs are numerous; in some cases the beliefs recorded are clearly potentially harmful. Few studies relate these beliefs to actual health outcomes, but work in Papua New Guinea found that mothers who did not believe child faeces were dirty and who did not regularly sweep their compound were much more likely to have children suffering from diarrhoea than other mothers. It seems, therefore, that the harm done by traditional beliefs can be very specifically identified and related to specific medical conditions, if adequately refined data are collected.[13]

For some purposes, information needs to be distinguished from attitudinal factors, although they affect each other; for example, an attitude of fatalism may reflect a belief that medical treatments are ineffective. The distinction matters because some argue that public informational campaigns will make little difference without the changes in attitude that only education can cause, but this issue has not been empirically resolved.[14]

Overall, the evidence that information is a major factor in health seems strong, especially considering the scarcity of directly relevant data and the intrinsic difficulty of clearly distinguishing information from other factors. Our judgment that information is crucial plays an important part in the policy discussion that follows. The point, to which we return below, is that where consumers are ill-informed, markets may give very bad outcomes.

Returns to Education

Education has cognitive and noncognitive effects on productivity and other determinants of welfare such as health and fertility. Noncognitive effects may include the instillation of the discipline appropriate to industrialization. It can also take a more liberating form, raising students' ambitions and making them more receptive to new ideas.

It is natural to want to quantify these effects and use the results to set priorities for policy. However, such an exercise must be undertaken with caution for two reasons. First, as we argue in the next section, high returns to education do not in themselves imply the need for public funding; additional arguments are necessary. For example, one must explain why the returns would not be realized privately. We offer several such explanations later, but here it should be noted that these tend to imply that some returns to education are of greater importance for policy than others. For example, parents may be well aware of the higher wages their sons may acquire from secondary schooling but do not realize that educating their daughters will improve the health of future grandchildren. The second problem with basing policy on rates-of-return estimates is that the most commonly used estimates are much less reliable than sometimes thought.

Rates of return to education are most frequently estimated from earnings in employment. Reviewing the evidence for Africa, George Psacharopoulos of the World Bank has concluded that the social rates of return to education are 24 percent for primary schooling, 18 percent for secondary schooling, and 11 percent for tertiary schooling. These figures are widely cited, both to support public funding of education and to give priority to primary education in particular. Paul Bennell of the Institute of Development Studies, however, has shown that the evidence used in the original Psacharopoulos study is ambiguous; only in four of twelve countries did differences between primary and secondary rates of return exceed two percentage points. The data used were often based on government salary scales, and in some cases assumptions about earnings were little more than guesswork. Moreover, most of the studies reviewed by Psacharopoulos were pre-1980s, and the results may no longer hold. More recent studies of Côte d'Ivoire, Ethiopia, Ghana, Kenya, South Africa, and Uganda tend to indicate that secondary schooling may have fairly high wage returns, whereas those to primary schooling are low.[15]

Several factors explain why returns to primary schooling may have fallen while those to secondary schooling have been maintained. Technological advances may have increased skill requirements. Quality may have fallen, increasing the amount of schooling needed to attain any given level of competence. Finally, the increased supply of primary education will have reduced its power as a signal of ability.

Rates of return based on wage data are sometimes questioned on methodological grounds. Here recent research has made some progress in addressing these concerns. For example, one source of scepticism is the possibility that higher wages may not imply higher productivity. This hypothesis has been directly tested (and rejected) for the first time in Africa in a study by Tracy Jones of the Centre for the Study of African Economies in Oxford. Using data on Ghanaian manufacturing firms and their workers, she finds comparable estimates of returns to education in both firm productivity and worker pay.[16] Another source of doubt is that any higher productivity associated with education may reflect pre-existing ability rather than education per se. This possibility was first tested and rejected for Kenya and Tanzania. Subsequent studies of Ghana and Morocco have also found cognitive skills more important in determining remuneration than measures of pre-existing ability.[17] If education benefits productivity through conveying cognitive skills, quality as well as quantity should matter, but evidence on this is scarce and tentative. There are many alternative possible measures of school quality, but it is difficult to identify the characteristics of the schools that workers attended in their childhood. However, positive links have been found in Ghana, South Africa, Tunisia, and several non-African countries.[18]

Perhaps a more important problem with rates of return based on wages is that most Africans—particularly the poorest—are not in wage employment, and there is relatively little research on monetary returns to education in Africa outside of employment. One widely cited conclusion from surveying 37 studies on farm productivity in developing countries is that four years of primary education increases output by around 7 percent.[19] However, the studies included only two from Africa and both found no returns to education. More recent African evidence suggests positive returns, but it is still hard to draw confident conclusions. Initial impressions suggest that these returns can be large but are not found in all countries; they may also accrue more to primary schooling than post-primary schooling.[20] Even less work has been done on estimating the returns to nonagricultural self-employment, although studies in Ethiopia and Côte d'Ivoire have found positive returns.[21]

The combined monetary returns to education from wages and other activities can be estimated by analyzing total income. Using household data, the effects are typically positive. Poverty profiles for Africa typically find the poor to be less educated. A multivariate study of the determinants of poverty in Uganda found positive effects of education in all regions and at all income levels. However, even this may not be uniform across the continent; one study found no significant benefits of education on household incomes in rural Côte d'Ivoire. An analysis for Mauritania found significant returns only for wage-earning households.[22]

The relation between education and total income can also be studied using macroeconomic data, as in the "growth accounting" studies. Unlike the use of household data, this approach should incorporate external (though not distributional) benefits of education. Some early studies found large effects of education, but some more recent work found virtually no effect in Africa. This should not be surprising. Through the 1960s and 1970s, Africa experienced a large educational expansion but fairly stagnant growth. The effect of education may have been suppressed by bad economic policies. Conversely, a complementary effect of good policies may explain why the returns to education appear to have been so high in East Asia.[23] Differences in quality of education may also account for the mixed findings on returns to quantitative expansions.

Education confers non-market benefits as well. The effects of parental education on child schooling and health were discussed above. Education can reduce fertility by increasing the monetary costs of children and the opportunity costs of time spent rearing them, and by reducing parents' dependency on their children in old age. A contrary effect is that education may reduce the time spent breast-feeding, a natural contraceptive. Evidence supports the negative relationship, particularly for secondary schooling.[24]

Returns to Health

Here we consider the returns to health per se rather than to health services, which were discussed above among the determinants of health. The direct effects of health on welfare are central but difficult to quantify, so here the discussion is limited to the effects of health on labor supply and savings.

The effects of health on productivity have been extensively studied. One approach focuses on nutritional status. Workers with better nutritional status may be expected to produce more, but the reverse causation from productivity to income and nutrition needs to be properly accounted for. A recent careful survey by economist Jere Behrman of the University of Pennsylvania examines two types of studies: experimental, where different groups of workers are given different kinds of nutritional supplement; and socioeconomic, which examine the effects of anthropometric status on productivity.[25] The effects of nutrition on health are often substantial, and as Behrman points out, some very dramatic conditions are directly related to specific nutritional failures, such as blindness due to vitamin A deficiency. And even though the economic costs have not been satisfactorily measured in this case, the costs of blindness to the individual are clearly large.

The second approach to studying the effects of health on productivity focuses on episodes of disease, which affect labor supply in several ways: the number of days of work lost to illness (both directly and indirectly through the time of caretakers), the length of the working life, the quality of the labor supplied, and the predictability of supply. Quantification of these effects, however, is not easy because the absolute number of days lost to ill health no doubt varies considerably across countries, and survey-base estimates are hard to come by. Data from Côte d'Ivoire suggest that during any four-week period one-third of the population is ill, losing an average of a quarter of their time. This implies that a twelfth of labor time is lost due to illness.[26]

The effects of ill health on savings and investment—and hence on economic growth—have been less studied. In the long run, by increasing the variability of income, a higher incidence of illness will induce a larger holding of liquid assets. The effects on the volume of total savings are ambiguous, because the dissaving of the sick may be balanced by the precautionary saving of the currently well. A very important case is the impact of AIDS, the diagnosis of which reduces life expectancy and therefore may induce dissaving, depending on what arrangements individuals are making for their children. Some regions of Uganda where AIDS has struck particularly hard are characterized by households swollen by orphans and a visible decline in the quality of coffee plantations.[27] Because no one foresaw AIDS, precautionary saving actions were impossible; hence, its effects on investment will almost certainly be negative and may be very significant.

Conceptual Concerns: Private and Social Returns

The above discussion considered all returns as internal to the household, which raises three problems. First, the concept of a "private rate of return" becomes ambiguous where there are differences of interest between different members of the same household. The education decisions made by parents may reflect expected returns to parents, rather than returns to the children themselves. This is an important part of the justification for subsidy or even compulsion in these areas.

Second, social and private rates of returns will differ if the government's social welfare function places a higher weight on the income of the poor than of the rich. For instance, tertiary education increases the income of the relatively well-off. Consequently, the case for public funding has to rest on externalities rather than on the benefits to students themselves.

Third, public policy should be guided by the returns to public investment in an activity, rather than the returns to the activity itself. If public funding is simply substituting for private activity, then the high returns to the activity do not provide a case for public support.

MARKET FAILURE IN HEALTH AND EDUCATION

There are strong a priori grounds for believing that without public action, investments in human resources will be inequitable and inefficient. In Africa various forms of market failure are pervasive, reducing levels of health and education below what would be possible and desirable given the resources available to the economies concerned. Therefore, some actions with high social returns simply cannot be left to the market. Public action is justified on a number of grounds: extensive information failure, externalities, secondary market failure, and distributional objectives (both inter- and intra-household).

Informational Failures

GENERAL INFORMATIONAL FAILURE. Profit-making agents have little incentive to spread better information about health. In particular, preventive measures tend to reduce revenue to medical firms from curative sales. It is also typically more profitable to sell technology than information: Compare the profits from selling sachets of oral rehydration salts to those from educating mothers in the necessary proportions of sugar and salt in the solutions. Sometimes, private producers even have an incentive to misinform consumers, as with the effects of infant milk and tobacco. Furthermore, the main technologies for spreading information in Africa are not easy to charge for. Broadcasting, for instance, can be used cheaply to spread these messages, but it is difficult to make listeners pay. Contrast this with the markets for popular health literature in developed countries. In this sense, general medical information has some of the properties of a public good.

In the case of education, many argue that individuals in developing countries underestimate non-marketed returns. Evidence on parental perceptions of returns is fragmentary, but several studies show that some societies do perceive non-marketed benefits of education. For example, mothers in Ethiopia value education because it encourages cleanliness; in Uganda, because it will make their daughters better mothers; and in South India, because of its benefits to social competence rather than productivity.[28] However, uneducated parents may not fully perceive the benefits of education—for example, that it may improve the health of any future grandchildren. Such informational failures imply government subsidies may be justified.

Public-good arguments apply also to the need for research. African countries are probably in a better position to free ride on foreign technological developments in health than in agriculture, because the relevant biology is less location-specific. Where research does need to be done inside the individual countries is in the socioeconomic area; if resources are to be devoted to disseminating health messages, it is vital to find out what misconceptions are actually damaging people's health, and these are highly location-specific. And hand-in-hand with location-specific research, there is also a desperate need for international support for research on illnesses that disproportionately affect Africa, including malaria and AIDS.

INDIVIDUAL- OR LOCALITY-SPECIFIC INFORMATIONAL FAILURE. Informational failure can occur on an individual or locality-specific basis as well. Education and health care involve the sale of expertise that has to be taken on trust, and therefore a lack of trust between patient and clinician can radically compromise the value of advice given. In some countries, clinicians faced by a secular decline in wages have resorted to imposing illegal charges or diverting drugs to private sale. Moreover, physicians paid per visit (rather than by a capitation fee) have incentives to exaggerate the amount of treatment actually needed. This may be one reason for the problem of "polypharmacy"—the excessive prescription of drugs—which is very widely reported in Africa. Another possibility is that if drugs are given, the patient has no way of knowing what physicians are charging for their time. Mistrust is probably one reason why failures in the market for drugs are so serious in Africa.

In education, consumer ignorance may remove the incentive for teachers to improve quality. Hence improvements may need to be imposed top-down by changes in the curriculum, but curriculum reforms can be effective only when teacher-training accompanies the new material.

Externalities

"Externalities" are the effects of one agent's action on others; they include both monetary externalities, which operate through the effect of the action on market prices, and direct externalities, which do not operate through prices. Where direct externalities exist, market outcomes are not usually efficient. Technical externalities in health include the risk to others constituted by a person's having a communicable disease—and the reduction in this risk when the disease is successfully treated—and the effects of the use of drugs on future resistance of the disease. For instance, full courses of antibiotics are advised not necessarily because the patient needs them but because incomplete courses can encourage the development of resistant strains of germs. Resistance to antibiotics and anti-malarials is a major problem in many African countries, because unlike in many developed countries where antibiotics are available only on a doctor's prescription, in most African countries self-prescription is standard practice, often resulting in incomplete courses of antibiotics.[29] Another externality is that private medical advice to one person may enable that person later to advise someone else who has a similar condition. In this sense, figures quoted on the "share of preventive care" in government spending are misleading if the medical service is functioning well; all care is partly preventive and has positive externalities.

For education, externalities between households are of two main forms. One is that education affects skills relevant to social interaction (e.g., literacy, numeracy, and competence in a national language) and increases ability to pass on innovations to others. This may be particularly pertinent during democratization (just as the introduction of mass education in Great Britain was closely associated with the extension of the franchise in the Second Reform Act). Second, some skills have *much higher social than private returns* because, although they are marketed, the shadow wage is above the market wage. In this case, distributional considerations may cause the authorities to prefer to subsidize training rather than to pay the shadow wage. For instance, the impact on GDP of a senior civil servant involved in economic policy reform might be very large and could not be internalized through any conceivable wage. Similarly, in the private sector, the training of qualified people (particularly in the traded sector) may increase the demand for less qualified labor, with beneficial distributional effects.

Increasing Returns and Monopoly

Transport constraints and scattered populations in rural areas of Africa can make education and health care natural monopolies; if profits are maximized and there is no price discrimination, price will be above marginal cost and consumption will be suboptimal.[30] There are also economies of scale to specialized tertiary institutions such as universities and training hospitals.[31]

Secondary Market Failure

Education spending depends on credit markets, which in Africa are often very weak. Possible sources of credit market failure include: the impossibility of creditors taking possession of human capital, the impossibility of contracting formal liabilities as a child, the difficulty of locating and prosecuting defaulters, the difficulty of identifying individuals for whom returns to education will be high, and the lack of collateral. Some education may be effectively financed by parental lending in that educated children feel more obligation to remit money to their parents than those who were not educated.[32]

Health spending, on the other hand, depends on insurance markets. Formal insurance markets do exist in Africa, but mostly serve the relatively affluent and operate only in urban areas, essentially because of the cost of monitoring and adverse selection. Informal insurance mechanisms have been widely documented in Africa. Some groups provide mutual support during acute illnesses; remittances from urban areas may also be a source of funds. However, the need for large medical expenditure can occur with great suddenness and can be completely unforeseen; for instance, the time scale within which a course of antibiotics is needed is far shorter than the time scale over which a food stock declines. Hence it would be surprising if informal networks were completely effective in substituting for a formal market. Research on the Bamako Initiative in Botswana uncovered several ways of financing health care; the two most reported were borrowing from friends and selling produce. A study of a rural area of Zaire, before the introduction of a prepayment scheme, found that patients sometimes delayed for several days between being referred to a hospital and actually being admitted in order to find enough money. The extent of effective informal insurance, however, is a subject for further research.[33]

Distribution Objectives

In most African countries, cash transfers to poor people are administratively difficult to implement, raise incentive problems, and often do not command a political consensus. Health and education may therefore be better vehicles for reaching the poor. The extent to which this is true varies by level of service: Tertiary health and education facilities typically benefit the more affluent, whereas primary facilities are often of equal benefit to different socioeconomic groups. This is true of public sector clinics in Uganda, which are cheaper but seen as lower quality. The poor are less likely to seek treatment when ill, but if they do fall ill they are more likely to go to the public sector. Similarly, poor households in Uganda have lower primary enrollment ratios but have more children. These two factors roughly balance out, so that the proportion of people in school is similar among the poor and the better-off.[34] Public intervention may also affect the distribution of wealth within the household; targeting health and education at girls and women is likely to be more effective than targeting generalized transfers.[35]

Manifestations of Market Failure

Although more research is needed comparing the roles of public and private sectors in different countries, the following impressionistic picture is probably accurate. Formal private clinics and pharmacies are mainly found in urban centers. They are very often seen, rightly or wrongly, as superior to the public sector. In villages, people rely mainly on public-sector clinics, drugs sold by unqualified shop owners, and treatment by traditional healers. (Treatment by traditional healers is widespread in Africa, although it is usually under-reported in surveys and of varying quality.) The quality of medical advice available from the private sector in rural areas is low. In education, the pattern varies enormously across countries. The private sector has a significant role in some countries, and sometimes it specializes in the provision of religious education, which, it has been argued, does not deliver benefits comparable to modern secular education.[36] More importantly, we are not aware of any country where the private sector alone has achieved good levels of literacy and life expectancy in rural areas. Therefore, if the state does not act, these goals will not be achieved.

PRIVATE AND PUBLIC FINANCING OF EDUCATION AND HEALTH

Once the need for public action in education and health is established, the question becomes how best to finance it. Most existing work suggests that economic returns to schooling compare well with those in other sectors, whereas rates of return on health projects raise serious conceptual problems, particularly concerning the value of life. It seems more satisfactory to argue that preventable mortality is an evil that should be reduced and then to quantify the numbers of lives that given interventions can save. Indeed, this approach—cost-effectiveness rather than cost-benefit—is most widely adopted by the medical profession. Without reliable quantification of social benefits, the question cannot be settled once and for all, but significant improvements in education and health are achievable with commitments of resources that are not prohibitive for most African countries. For example, the experience of other regions suggests that child mortality rates of 20 percent can be at least halved by a combination of basic education and health measures. (Table 2 shows that infant mortality rates have fallen as low as 3 percent in China and just over 4 percent in Vietnam, which is a very poor country.) The exact contribution of different kinds of measures is unknown, but a firm commitment to a package of such measures can produce a transformation in child survival, as in China. For many countries, a commitment of 20 percent of the recurrent budget to the right kinds of health and education spending could probably achieve this objective.

Priorities for Public Finance of Education

Although, as we have seen, the evidence on primary education is less clear than is often thought, the case remains strong in terms of equity, external, and non-wage benefits. Feasibility varies across countries because both governments' fiscal positions and the costs per pupil differ greatly across countries. Universal primary education is not immediately achievable everywhere. Economic theory suggests that public funding will encourage over-consumption, but this fear does not seem to be justified in the case of primary education. Universal primary education would be very beneficial in most African contexts. There is also good reason to think that where education is privately funded, girls will benefit less than boys and that this differential is costly. Demand for education, like demand for health care, is self-limiting because it consumes the person's time; hence, free provision will not elicit infinite demand. This is important because it means that free provision need not imply rationing.

For those African countries with near universal primary school enrollments, the key questions for educational policy concern secondary schooling. We noted the recent evidence that, unlike primary schooling, secondary schooling brings high wage returns. Since these gains go to the recipient, altruistic parents are likely to be willing to pay at least some of the costs of secondary schooling. This is indeed observed in Africa, where secondary school fees—even in state schools—are large relative to household incomes. Given the constraints on public finance, there is some justification for mobilizing this private funding, both through a permissive attitude to private education and through some cost recovery in state secondary schooling. This case is particularly strong if fees are retained locally to be used to improve school quality. More work is needed to quantify the relative external benefits of secondary schooling as opposed to primary schooling. For example, it is clear that secondary schooling has more effect in reducing fertility, but there is no consensus on which is more effective in reducing child mortality. Although quantifying these benefits is difficult, it is clear that they warrant some public funding of secondary schooling, perhaps especially for girls. Credit market failures also imply that relying solely on private finance is likely to be suboptimal, both in terms of efficiency and equity. Here some targeting of subsidies to the poor would be desirable, perhaps through scholarships for able students from disadvantaged backgrounds.

Because the private returns to tertiary education go overwhelmingly to those who are already relatively well-off, public funding should therefore be given only if three conditions are met: 1) there must be positive externalities from the activities that education makes possible (e.g., medical services, policymaking, manufactured goods expansion, and artistic endeavor); 2) there must be a significant response of demand to charges (e.g., charges can reduce the quality of students, which may matter very much if the quality of students in turn affects the external benefits generated); and 3) students who are financed must be likely to stay in the country. It should be noted with this third condition, however, that bonding to a specific job or institution may prevent students from making the best use of their skills and may even encourage emigration. Graduates of master's programs are often frustrated by their employer's failure to use their skills and need to move to find rewarding work. The best thing seems to be to establish an environment in which young, well-qualified people find their skills appreciated in the most important government departments. In some countries, such as Ethiopia, the flight of human capital is a major problem that needs serious attention.

Where any of these conditions are not met, public funding is hard to justify, but the state may still want to help with the problem of secondary market failure. By the late 1980s, 30 developing countries had established student loan schemes. Christopher Colclough of the Institute of Development Studies, in reviewing the experience of these countries, concluded that loan schemes can be workable but are subject to limitation because they do not generate large resources quickly; are never self-financing; have high administrative costs, especially where the banking system is under-developed; and need to be supported by means-tested scholarships.[37]

Consequently, graduate income taxes seem an attractive alternative on several grounds. They are distributionally preferable; are not likely to pose as severe a deterrent to tertiary study as loans (this is beneficial in efficiency grounds in the absence of an insurance market); and are probably simpler to administer than loan schemes, especially where structures for the collection of income tax already exist or many graduates receive salaries from the government. They may also be politically more acceptable than loans, since they could be levied on employers.

Priorities for Public Finance of Health Care

Some have argued for targeting services that have particularly high externalities or public good elements such as environmental action against malaria. However, market failure and externalities are pervasive in the health sector, even in the case of "private goods" such as drug therapy. In addition to its distributional advantages, a well-funded public system, with established trust between patient and physician, is more likely to produce efficient outcomes than a private sector riddled with informational failure. Different kinds of health care should come as a package; in local health centers, informational and technological roles are inextricably linked. Moreover, given the existing pattern of private care, the fear that public funding will simply be substituting for a well-functioning private sector seems wildly misplaced.

Consequently, the state should aim at funding a package of health services that are to be made available to those who need them. There is no merit in providing public financing for expensive methods of treatment that could not feasibly be extended to the majority of the population needing them. The goal of policy should be to make some selected methods of treatment universally available and to restrict subsidy to these services. The services provided should be selected according to their cost-effectiveness, measured in terms of lives saved or quality-adjusted years of life. Often, the differences between the cost-effectiveness of different treatments are so vast that any two sensible indicators will give the same ranking. However, the severe externalities that an adult's death imposes on the surviving children suggest that adult health should be valued more than children's; existing measures, by focusing on length of life, value it less.[38] Subject to this caveat, recent work by Dean Jamison of the World Bank and others makes a major contribution to the assessment of cost-effectiveness of different health interventions and their estimates should be extremely useful.[39] Using this work, the World Bank has suggested that prenatal and delivery care, family planning, management of sick children, and treatment of tuberculosis and of sexually transmitted diseases all have high priority; antibiotic therapy for acute bacterial infections such as meningitis and pneumonia and, where relevant, treatment of malaria are also obvious candidates. But the particular components of the purchase are beyond the scope of the paper (and its authors' competence). Often, the package could be administered in a decentralized fashion by equipping clinics with the appropriate package of drugs and implementing clear guidelines about their use.

The need for tertiary structures, i.e., hospitals, in this package is controversial. One valuable piece of information is often unknown—the extent to which a referral hospital serves people referred from rural areas rather than the smaller urban population. Even so, there is much agreement that at least some existing tertiary services should not be included in such a package.

As discussed earlier in this chapter, the relative role of "technological" and "informational" factors in generating health and mortality remains uncertain. This is mirrored in an uncertainty about the relative efficacy of technological and informational interventions. For instance, Jamison and his colleagues are very informative on the relative efficacy of different curative treatments, whereas their evidence on the importance of spreading information about disease is scanty.[40] And although the costs of both kinds of interventions are likely to vary greatly across countries, some suggestions can be made.

First, China's great progress in reducing mortality was achieved by village health workers who were trained to stress the importance of a hygienic environment, enhanced by public awareness campaigns.[41] These techniques are potentially cheap and are at the heart of achieving reductions in mortality. Some nongovernmental organizations (NGOs) are involved in similar campaigns in Africa, and AIDS, in particular, has been the target of public awareness campaigns in several countries.[42]

Second, suppliers of health care should have both training and incentives that encourage them to move flexibly between technological and informational approaches at a local level. Physicians need to be trained to see communication as the most fundamental part of their job. They should be prepared to send a patient away with some good advice and no pills if that is appropriate.

Third, cost-effectiveness can also be applied to interventions that save lives in other areas of public policy, such as education. If education saves more lives per dollar than a form of health care, it is clearly preferred since education has other benefits as well. While an economist at the World Bank, Lawrence Summers, in a widely discussed article, suggested that this may be the case.[43] Although it is welcome that the issue has been made so prominent, Summers' estimates are admittedly superficial. For instance, they assume that education saves lives without incurring intervening medical costs and that the medical alternatives considered (interventions in dangerous childbirth) are highly expensive ones. Further research in this area would be valuable.

The free universal provision of a basket of primary care may be prohibitive in some countries. Cost estimates were included in the World Bank's 1993 *World Development Report,* which outlines a package that could be provided for $12 per head in developing countries, but these costs are likely to vary significantly between countries. In most countries, important improvements in public health could be achieved by better prioritization of spending in the health ministries. At the same time, when health spending constitutes only 5 percent of government spending, a large increase in the health budget (e.g., to 8 percent) implies only a small proportional cut in other budgetary items.

User Charges

The introduction of user charges for public services has been one of the most controversial features of structural adjustment in many African countries. As a means to help finance health and education, user fees have both positive and negative aspects. The issues are extremely complex, but the following major considerations apply.

Advice on policy depends on the agency being advised. It would be quite consistent for example, to advise the central government that it should fund universal free primary health care, but to advise the health ministry that, given the central government's unfortunate budgetary priorities, the best results can be achieved within the ministry's current budget by charging for health services. The Bamako Initiative of the late 1980s, under which several African countries introduced user fees for some aspects of primary health care, was an initiative of health ministers.

However, if user fees are justified on the grounds of underfunding by the central government, one must consider whether the central government will further reduce its support in response. One study of five African countries that have adopted some local user charges reports no apparent tendency for the government to cut resources to the health sector, but the issue needs further research.[44]

Similarly, donors should not push for user charges in primary health care or primary education without simultaneously arguing for an increase in the share of government spending on these items. The missionary zeal of some writings in favor of user charges would be better devoted to persuading governments of the value of public spending. And both donors and recipients must keep in mind that market failure in

Africa is so pervasive that there is no compelling efficiency case for charging for primary health services. One exception may be where services are actually malfunctioning because of unnecessarily trivial causes of demand; for example, some African hospitals have in effect become huge primary clinics. The main argument concerns revenue raising.

The distributional properties of health and education charges do not make them attractive where services are being universally provided; they are distributionally regressive and become a tax on families with many children, which tend to be relatively poor. Distributional effects can be mitigated by targeted exemptions. Sometimes, widespread exemptions for user charges for health have been resisted. For instance, people in Benin preferred to limit exemptions to very well-defined groups such as abandoned women and victims of natural disasters. On the other hand, exemptions are reported to be popular in nongovernment facilities in Tanzania.[45] Scholarships for talented children from poor families are common for higher education, but extending them to primary and secondary schooling would be problematic due to the much greater numbers of potential students from poor households.

There may be indirect ways of targeting the poor by directing the charges to those who can better afford to pay them. One method is geographic, imposing higher charges in urban areas and exempting very backward regions. This would also contribute toward the goals of expanding health spending and coverage, levying higher charges in areas of excess demand and giving special assistance to backward areas. Targeting by location is constrained by the possibility of outsiders sending their children or sick to poorer areas to take advantage of greater subsidies. As such it may be most suitable for primary services, where the subsidies per individual are modest.

User charges may improve services by changing the attitudes of providers and users of education and health services, motivating students, and making suppliers more accountable. Some observers believe that user charges make medical staff treat patients more courteously.[46] If true, this is a strong argument in favor of user charges, because good communication between medical staff and patients is vital for the diffusion of medical understanding. However, the effect is only likely to be strong if the revenue raised matters to the health staff, which is an argument for the local retention of user fees. In addition, in some countries illegal charges are frequent. If official user fees substitute for the illegal ones, they may be beneficial. However, they may simply be additional.

User charges can avoid the problems of secondary market failure. In the case of health, the appropriate device is prepayment schemes. Some evidence is quite encouraging: For example, a prepayment scheme in rural Zaire achieved 63 percent registration within a few years of starting. Naturally, there is some concern about the 35 percent or so who did not register. One study found that the households not registering included both relatively poor households and relatively affluent ones. Sometimes communities collectively buy a stock of drugs or provide labor in building a clinic. A tradition of rotating funds for drugs is reported in Guinea.[47]

Many critics of user charges have noted that there is a significant response of demand. The evidence for this is strong and unsurprising; the elasticity of demand is not zero and often it may be higher than is commonly asserted.[48] This is an argument against user charges given the arguments above that purchases will be sub-optimal if people are charged the marginal cost.

User charges may encourage misallocation in the prescription of drugs. First, patients who have paid for a consultation often feel unfairly treated if they do not receive a prescription, making it harder for doctors to refuse to prescribe unnecessary drugs. Second, people who are paying for drugs can often afford only a day's antibiotics. And third, user fees encourage people to bypass the medical profession and go straight to pharmacies, potentially lowering the quality of information and raising incentive problems.

Overall, user fees on primary services are not justified as means of raising revenue for the central government or for trying to avoid the public funding of primary services. However, where primary services are underfunded by central government, consumers may prefer a local arrangement under which they pay something and get better services. One study of Rwanda found that 90 percent of rural people were willing to pay charges if they resulted in an improvement in quality.[49] If this argument is valid, it may be found that the introduction of user charges, combined with quality improvements, can lead to increases in use, which would be a good test for whether introduction of user fees has been a success. But, even then, the interests (and use) of richer and poorer consumers may diverge.

If a local community decides to impose user fees, the following conditions should be met. The money should stay at the local level, without a consequent reduction in central funding; user fees should be formally administered by a committee (not an individual); receipts should be provided; local communities should be involved in designing the scheme; and the interests of the poor should receive explicit attention. Given the inequalities of power that exist in most communities, attention to the interests of the poor is not guaranteed simply by "community management," but the more people involved, the likelier it is that the needs of the poor will be addressed.

Existing Spending: Patterns, Reasons, and Prospects

The priorities advocated above are consistent with most contemporary advice, but contrast sharply with the existing pattern of spending. Government spending can be viewed in terms of ratios: the ratio of government spending to GDP, of education and health spending to government spending, and of primary education and health to total education and health spending.[50] All these ratios vary widely among different countries, but some generalizations are useful (Table 3). Where data exist, the median share of education in African government budgets is 15 percent; this is roughly comparable to the shares for industrialized countries such as the United States and the United Kingdom (18 and 11 percent, respectively). However, the median African share of health expenditure is only 5 percent; very low by comparison to the United States and the United Kingdom (14 and 10 percent, respectively).[51] The degree of commitment to social sectors varies enormously between countries; shares in the most "pro-social sector" half of the sample are around twice as high as shares in the other countries.[52]

Except in a few countries such as Botswana, real public spending per capita on education and health in Africa fell in the 1980s.[53] However, this reflected stagnant government spending and a growing population, rather than a change in priorities. In 11 of the 15 countries with data, the share of health spending rose. The number of countries with increasing and with decreasing education shares are equal. Strong economic growth makes it easier to increase social sector spending (witness Botswana, Cameroon, and Ghana), but such increases are also possible without marked growth (as in Burkina Faso, Kenya, and Zimbabwe).

The existing data suggest a bias toward tertiary facilities (although there are definitional problems in some cases, other evidence supports this as well). Public primary health spending is rarely over 2 percent and sometimes as little as 0.5 percent of GDP. Primary schooling typically takes most educational expenditures, followed by secondary education. But secondary and tertiary students receive more resources per capita. A study using 1983 data found expenditures per student in secondary schools were typically four times those in primary education; in higher education, students received over 60 times as much as primary school pupils. Moreover, students bear a greater share of costs in primary education than they do in higher education. Estimates by the World Bank put the proportion of cost recovered from primary schooling at 6 percent in East Africa and 11 percent in West Africa. In both areas, cost recovery was estimated at only 3 percent in higher education. These inequalities are higher than in other regions. Encour-

TABLE 3: CENTRAL GOVERNMENT EDUCATION AND HEALTH SPENDING (percent)

Country	Year	Central Government Spending as Share of GDP	Education as Share of Central Government Spending	Pre-primary Primary, and Secondary Share of Education	Health as Share of Central Government Spending	Non-Hospital as Share of Health Spending[a]
Botswana	1990	35	21	67	5	40
Burkina Faso	1986	15	18	—	5	—
Burundi	1977	21	21	—	5	—
Cameroon	1985	21	14	73	5	86
Chad	1976	15	14	71	3	89
Ethiopia	1990	39	10	77	3	53
Gambia	1990	25	11	63	6	63
Ghana	1992	17	24	—	8	—
Guinea Bissau	1987	53	5	—	5	—
Kenya	1992	30	19	—	5	—
Lesotho	1991	59	22	79	11	26
Liberia	1988	24	11	71	5	31
Madagascar	1991	—	17	69	7	—
Malawi	1988	28	12	55	7	13
Mali	1988	—	9	61	2	—
Mauritania	1979	36	10	78	3	53
Mauritius	1991	25	15	—	9	—
Namibia	1990	—	21	63	11	89
Niger	1980	19	18	—	4	—
Nigeria	1987	22	3	—	1	—
Rwanda	1980	14	19	60	5	—
Sierra Leone	1990	10	13	—	10	—
Somalia	1978	—	8	79	3	—
Sudan	1982	14	6	24	1	—

TABLE 3, CONTINUED: CENTRAL GOVERNMENT EDUCATION AND HEALTH SPENDING (percent)

Country	Year	Central Government Spending as Share of GDP	Education as Share of Central Government Spending	Pre-primary Primary, and Secondary Share of Education	Health as Share of Central Government Spending	Non-Hospital as Share of Health Spending[a]
Swaziland	1989	22	24	—	8	—
Togo	1987	31	20	—	5	12
Uganda	1986	13	15	—	2	—
Tanzania	1985	22	8	38	6	20
Zaire	1982	13	16	—	3	—
Zambia	1988	38	9	63	7	38
Zimbabwe	1989	41	23	75	8	16

[a]In Chad and Mauritania, the "non-hospital share" refers to health spending not on "hospitals and clinics."

Notes: — indicates not available. Data in this table refer only to central government spending (with the exception of Malawi). Local government spending is omitted, because in some countries such as Kenya, local government spending is relatively small, while in others such as Nigeria, it is very large, making cross-continent comparison difficult. The figures for the United States and the United Kingdom refer to shares in total government spending (in these countries education is mainly financed by local and state government).

Source: International Monetary Fund, *Government Finance Statistics Yearbook* (Washington, DC: IMF, various issues).

agingly, there are signs of reform; one study of 22 Sub-Saharan countries found the share of primary education in total educational spending rose in 15 cases and fell in only five,[54] and stayed the same in the remaining two.

Having identified the pro-tertiary bias of public spending, it is necessary to ask why it occurs. Several reasons can be suggested:

■ *Recipient bias.* Favored groups might be defined in terms of income (the better-off), class (the middle and upper classes), geographical location (urban dwellers), gender (male), age (adults), religion or ethnicity (country-specific).

■ *Provider interest.* Rewards to tertiary suppliers are typically higher than those to primary ones.

■ *Prestige and visibility.* The decay of existing tertiary institutions is more conspicuous than the absence of new primary ones. This factor also helps to explain the overemphasis on physical rather than human capital that has often been observed in public spending.

■ *Budgetary inertia.* For instance, a structure inherited from the colonial period cannot change very fast if budgeting is incremental.

■ *Donor pressure.* Knowing that donors tend to want to fund primary services, recipients might believe that their own spending on such services will tend to crowd out donor support.

■ *Policymaker skepticism, either about the effectiveness of primary services or about the need to finance them.* Some African leaders argue strongly that health and education will solve themselves if economic growth occurs. If our arguments about market failure are right, they need to be disseminated widely.

■ *Disequilibrium.* Policymakers may foresee a change in future spending levels and be unwilling, for instance, to shut institutions that will become viable in the future. This may relate to bargaining between the spending ministry and the treasury.

■ *Preference for fast returns.* Primary education gives relatively slow returns, partly because primary graduates may go into secondary education. In addition, there is a delay before they are likely to become heads of households where their education is likely to become most effective.

■ *Demand from competing public goods such as military spending.* While this does not explain the pro-tertiary bias as such, it does help to explain the scarcity of funds for human resources, which tends to exacerbate the other factors.

These reasons represent a research agenda rather than a state of knowledge; too little is understood about the desperately important question of why primary services are underfunded in so many countries.

Some mechanisms suggested are likely to have led to a bias against other forms of government spending: rural roads may fall victim to urban bias; agricultural extension and research to urban bias or short-termism. Even so, there are some hopeful signs. In some countries democratization has redressed the urban bias of some policies, such as the taxation of export crops. Decentralization is fashionable and may be one means of reducing the bias toward spending in the capital cities, although it can also be used as an excuse for central authorities to shed unwelcome but important responsibilities, leading to renewed urban bias at a lower level.[55] The effects in Africa, where subsidiary urban centers tend to be small, may be different from the effects in other regions, but it is too early to judge the effect of the decentralizations started in countries such as Uganda and Ethiopia. Privatization now seems a politically feasible option for removing the burden of some prestigious institutions from the health and education budgets without actually closing them. Finally, donors have become considerably more aggressive about the sectoral pattern of spending, and the share of priority areas is the subject of conditionalities in some structural adjustment programs.

PROVISION OF EDUCATION AND HEALTH CARE

Public finance does not imply public provision, nor vice versa. In the provision of services, three major issues—the size of the public sector, the support and regulation of the private sector, and the improvement of public provision—must be considered.

Determining the Role of the State Sector

Currently, African governments are providing and financing some expensive services that we have argued should be privately financed. If the state does not intend to subsidize a service at all, then it should avoid managing it unless it is sure to make a profit. In general, privatization seems a preferable option in this case. Implicit subsidies are not always transparent in public accounts; for instance, the opportunity cost of public land may not be properly accounted for, and agents within the public sector may be more able to agitate for subsidy than those outside. As a result, the state may end up subsidizing services without having explicitly decided to do so. However, where the state can be sure to make a profit, activities should be considered. A good example is private beds in public hospitals. These are useful revenue-raisers in several countries and were introduced in parts of Africa during the 1980s. They may also enhance hospital standards.

Public subsidy need not preclude private provision. Privatization may increase technical efficiency, although market failure and public funding make this uncertain. Private hospitals that can simply reclaim costs from the government may have no incentive to reduce costs. Much depends on the regulatory structure and the extent and nature of competition. Possible modalities include contracting services out and voucher schemes where individual consumers choose the provider and costs are passed on to central government.

Even purely private health and education institutions are often run by people concerned with professional standards and social responsibility as much as personal enrichment. Moreover, purely nonprofit organizations also play a major role in Africa. If a major concern is the inefficiency of existing public services, then a transfer of funding to NGOs with good track records of performance is an attractive remedy.

Empirical evidence lends some support to the theoretical arguments for private provision. Several recent studies have examined the relative effectiveness of private and public schools. In Tanzania, students from private secondary schools were found to perform less well than those from state schools. However, private schools tend to cater to primary school leavers who have not performed well enough to enter the state sector. Controlling for this difference in the quality of school intake, private schools appear more effective in raising performance. Similar work outside Africa also suggests a private-sector advantage. But there are some counter-examples: One study in Kenya concluded that public schools brought higher returns in the labor market, even after controlling for differences in pupils' preexisting ability and selectivity.[56] Evidence on the quality of health provision is mixed. In Uganda, for instance, there are clear signs that the private sector is perceived as superior, but this perception may not be accurate. Even if private provision is thought better, the administrative and political costs involved in privatization and the risk of undervaluing public assets are serious considerations.

Regulation and Public-Private Interactions

The private sector plays a major role in health care and education in most of Africa. In the case of education, there are few grounds for regulation. Some countries, such as the Congo and Ethiopia, have tried to ban private schools on equity grounds. But while it is true that private schools may create a social elite, the price of preventing this may be too high. A study of East Africa suggested that restrictions on secondary school enrollments in Tanzania led to lower levels of education, cognitive skill formation, and formal sector productivity. Interestingly,

Kenya's more liberal and expansionary policy increased the equity of secondary schooling: Children's enrollment probabilities varied much less by parental background than in Tanzania's small exclusively state-run sector.[57] The withdrawal of the affluent from public to private schools can reduce political pressure for higher quality in the public sector, but it can also reduce the burden on the state sector and offer a possible standard.

Several African countries, including Tanzania, Mali, and Mozambique, liberalized private medical practice in the 1980s, but the benefits and costs of this policy have not been studied very much.[58] Sometimes private practitioners may be serving the poor, but in many cases they are primarily providing relatively expensive care for the better-off. An important question here is the effect of privatization on the supply of physicians to the public sector. These effects can go either way. Private-sector work may pull people from the public sector, or it may pull people from abroad, some of whom may work in the state sector as well. One option would be to make the right to open a private clinic conditional either on some services in the public sector or on the provision of some low cost services for poorer patients. In addition, the movement of drugs between private and public clinics needs to be monitored (for instance, by dual-key systems for drug cupboards), and working hours in public clinics, reasonably remunerated, need to be enforced.

The public sector can support private medicine in several ways. One is to talk to traditional healers, who, in many African countries, are the most important health providers in rural areas and are much more likely to be used by the poor than modern facilities. Some African countries have used traditional healers as a way of distributing health messages. For instance, healers are distributing condoms in Zambia, and traditional birth attendants have been trained in several countries, although opinions on the effectiveness of the training are mixed. Another approach is to offer training to those private medical practitioners providing high-priority services. For instance, private pharmacists are often playing the role of medical consultants and should have basic diagnostic and communication skills (it would be unrealistic to end this role).[59]

Regulation of the private sector is potentially justified in health by the informational failures discussed above, but effective interventions are not easy to administer. The certification of suppliers and the provision of information about performance are potentially valuable; however, it is not yet clear that consumers in Africa can use the information. Often the sectors are not sufficiently developed to make regulation feasible. For instance, many people in Africa buy their drugs from local general stores rather than from trained pharmacists, and it would be difficult to train every shopkeeper in the sale of drugs. In principle, the state should seem more trustworthy than a profit-maximizing individual, but in Africa this is not always true. For instance, there has been much public discussion about the integrity of public examination systems in some African countries. And where the main rival to the state is a religious organization, people may be more inclined to believe in the integrity of the officials of the religious organization than those of the state. Moreover, in most African societies, there are multiple forms of authority; traditional healers are believed to have expertise, and patients often differentiate between which diseases are suitable for the modern clinic and which are for the traditional healer.

One area where regulation is urgently needed is in the sale of industrial products that affect health, most notably drugs and food. Tobacco is going to kill many individuals in Africa in the next 30 years, and because the effects of smoking are delayed, the epidemic of lung cancer has only just begun. Smoking-related deaths can be reduced by prohibiting cigarette advertisement, banning smoking in public places, taxing cigarettes, controlling their importation, or even banning tobacco altogether. In some countries, because relatively few people are addicted, these measures would be relatively painless, and libertarian arguments become less persuasive when so many people do not know the dangers associated with smoking.

Alcohol raises some of the same issues, particularly if drunkenness is strongly associated with domestic violence. For instance, some women's groups in India have campaigned against the sale of alcohol in villages.[60]

Medical drugs raise an extreme case of market failure. The World Bank estimates that if drugs were used efficiently, Sub-Saharan Africa could spend only 12 percent of what they now spend on drugs and achieve the same therapeutic benefit.[61] There are many symptoms of this. There is extensive over-prescription, often an average of more than three treatments per visit, when the optimum number for some conditions is zero. Druggists are publicly mistrusted. Some courses of drugs are dangerously brief, as in the case of Benin, where antibiotics are often prescribed just for one day. Incomplete courses of treatment for tuberculosis not only may fail to cure the patient but may also make subsequent treatment much harder, as resistance to commonly used drugs such as chloroquine is spreading. There are also wide price differentials between brand-name and generic versions of the same drug; reliance on over-priced brand-name drugs currently costs Africa eight times what is should. And in addition to market failure, there is also state failure. Publicly provided drugs can be diverted to private sale, and high-level corruption can block the adoption of essential drug policies.[62]

To be effective, medical drug reform should have the following elements. Public purchases of drugs should be restricted to those on a list of essential drugs and should be purchased as cheaply as possible (if the government wishes to protect high-cost domestic industries, the pharmaceutical sector is a poor one to choose). Public distribution should be controlled by using drug kits, by management of drugs by local heath committees, and by monitoring health clinics' prescription practices. Private imports of these drugs should also be encouraged and possibly even subsidized at the point of entry. This may be more effective than public distribution of drugs where there is an incentive for diversion; however, this depends on the particular circumstances. Lastly, and most controversially, we suggest prohibiting the private import of nonessential drugs because of the extensive exploitation of poorly informed consumers through the sale of expensive or ineffective drugs. Tariffs would not solve this problem, and prohibition is probably easier to enforce than taxation in this case.

Reform of Public Provision

Public provision of health care and education could be improved in a variety of ways. The current mix of inputs may be suboptimal, and, more generally, there should be pay-offs to reforms that try to attain some of the benefits in terms of incentives, decentralization, and competition traditionally associated with the private sector.

INPUTS. One area where there can be substantial improvements in public provision is inputs. To this end, governments should make the following changes.

■ *Increase spending on educational materials.* Textbooks are almost invariably found to raise student performance, yet African countries often spend negligible fractions of their education budgets on educational materials even though increases in spending on these materials may actually pay for themselves. An experimental study in Northeast Brazil found that increased school spending on materials improved student performance, thus reducing dropouts and repetition. The lowered amount of schooling required to produce school graduates and the savings from this more than justified the initial outlays on educational materials.[63] Higher spending on educational materials is likely to be justified even at the expense of cuts in labor costs.

■ *Realign teacher salaries.* Relative to national living standards, teacher salaries vary markedly between African countries. In the mid-1980s, average teacher salaries as a multiple of GNP per capita ranged from a low of 2.3 in Botswana to the high of 13.7 for Mali and Mauritania.[64] Although appropriate salaries must be determined with reference to local labor market conditions, both extremes probably represent severe misalignment of teacher salaries. On average, primary school teachers in Africa receive around five times GNP per capita. In countries where the proportion is markedly higher, policymakers should consider whether it is warranted. Conversely, in some countries teacher salaries may be so low that absenteeism, poor morale, and poor quality recruits seriously impede student learning.

■ *Raise student-teacher ratios.* This adjustment is another possible means of making large savings in the education budget. In particular, extensive research on the determinants of student achievement in many countries almost invariably finds pupil-teacher ratios to be unimportant. This work is confined to countries where pupil-teacher ratios are fairly reasonable compared to some African countries and may not be valid for ratios over 50.[65] However, increases for ratios below 50 could save large amounts of money in many countries at apparently no cost to student performance.

INCENTIVES AND COMPETITION. More generally, the public sector can sometimes suffer from lack of incentives and competition. Another approach to reform is to consider measures to rectify this:

■ *Establish clear terms of reference for managers of the particular institutions.* Medical services in Africa do not always carry out the services they are intended to; for instance, many national hospitals are performing a large amount of primary care that could be more cheaply provided elsewhere. Setting targets for objectives may also be useful, especially when the activities with high social returns are not prestigious or attractive to the providers.

■ *Carefully monitor and assess individual public institutions.* This allows best practice to be identified and recommended. Even better, more successful managers could be used either as "trouble-shooters" or allowed to "take over" under-performing institutions. Head teachers of successful public schools are often assigned to unsuccessful ones. This practice might be more effective if the successful head teachers retained control of their old schools, allowing them to increase their organizations until further expansions no longer brought gains.

■ *Establish performance-related pay.* Applied to managers, this would give extra weight to assessments of institutions. With individual workers, giving managers some discretion over pay increases might improve incentives. Public-sector wages are often very low in Africa, and selective increases in pay may be a more effective way for managers to reform their organizations than wholesale retrenchment or across-the-board salary increases. Managerial discretion, however, can be abused, and the efficacy of this measure will depend on context.

■ *Reduce job security of public-sector employees.* At present it is often difficult to remove poor teachers and head teachers unless they are grossly incompetent (though politically inspired dismissals, which do sometimes occur, are to be deplored).

■ *Introduce capitation fees.* Financing institutions according to the number of students or patients served can create competitive pressures to provide the services that people want. Correspondingly, rules that limit the range of public institutions that people can use—for example, restrictions on school catchment areas—stifle such competitive pressures.

■ *Decentralize control and prescription.* Less central control will encourage innovation and responsiveness to local needs and conditions. Hence, measures to transfer control over spending to local managers (e.g., head teachers) should be considered. Allowing schools to follow different curricula might also be desirable, although national requirements such as basic literacy, numeracy, and health education are likely to be appropriate. Variety in provision can be justified either by the diversity of consumer preferences or by the returns to experimentation. In the health sector, however, many existing staff would need substantial training before further independence could be justified.

In general, all these suggestions place some burden on the administrative or political capacities of the administration. They also rely to a greater or lesser extent on the integrity and impartiality of those involved. Because both administrative capacity and the integrity of public service vary, the implementation of any of these suggestions depends on local conditions. The large size of the public sector provides a relatively neglected opportunity for experimentation. Reforms can be pilot tested in selected areas, so that the costs of implementation and the risks of failure are not imposed on the wider population. In addition, policymakers should aim to identify the lessons from the natural experiments provided both by nongovernmental provision within their own countries and by the practices of those in other countries. For financially constrained governments, qualitative reform should be an attractive means of enhancing human development and one which complements the case for increased public funding made above.

SUMMARY AND CONCLUSIONS

The economic analysis of government policy seeks to identify the most valuable place to spend public resources. It is now generally agreed that states in Africa are highly constrained and therefore should avoid doing things that the private sector can do as well. In education and health, private provision is profoundly flawed. In primary education, public involvement can achieve some degree of equity in the distribution of a fundamental asset. In the case of health, the current very high levels of mortality in Africa are substantially due to the intrinsic problems of private markets in this area, combined with a failure of public action. There is simply no substitute for public action.

We would like to be able to buttress this argument with quantitative comparisons of rates of return, but existing estimates of rates of returns in primary education are often badly flawed. In the case of health, the whole exercise raises profound conceptual problems. Nevertheless, the evidence that African countries would gain by a higher priority for these sectors is extremely strong.

The forms that public action should take, however, remain quite fluid. Although informational interventions are important, the successful design of such interventions—and their importance relative to more technological approaches—needs more research. The common sense approach of studying success stories elsewhere could be very fruitful. The relative returns to different forms of education and the role of education in promoting development in agricultural societies remain unclear.

The most hopeful sign is that these issues are being discussed in many African countries more openly than before. Informed public debate will be needed if the gap between actual and potential achievment is to be bridged.

Notes

We would like to thank Tim Besley, Ravi Kanbur, Glen MacGee, Germano Mwabu, and the editors for useful suggestions in the course of work on this paper. Responsibility for all errors rests with the authors.

[1] Unless otherwise stated, Africa refers to Sub-Saharan Africa.

[2] Bruce Fuller, "Is Primary School Quality Eroding in the Third World?" *Comparative Education,* Vol. 30 (1986), pp. 491–507.

[3] See Table C-5 in World Bank, *Education in Sub-Saharan Africa: Policies for Adjustment, Revitalisation, and Expansion* (Washington, DC: World Bank, 1988).

[4] According to UNESCO data, the proportion of education budgets spent on educational and instructional materials in Africa is half the level of Europe's expenditure. For example, for Western Europe the proportion is around 2 percent (but with notable intercountry variations). For data on inputs, see World Bank, *Education in Sub-Saharan Africa,* op. cit.; and UNESCO, *The 1995 Statistical Yearbook* (New York: UNESCO, 1995).

[5] Although international comparisons of GDP involve certain problems, it seems likely that similar patterns would be observed even using purchasing power parity (PPP)-adjusted GDP.

[6] In experimental data, researchers are able to control the value of explanatory variables. This is not the case with nonexperimental data.

[7] For example, for Uganda there is evidence that neither enrollment nor performance at primary school depends strongly on socioeconomic status. See Margaret Kakande and Rose Nalwadda, "A Report on a Study of Factors Influencing Access to and Attendance of

Primary Education in Uganda," *PAPSCA Report* (Kampala, Uganda: Ministry of Finance and Economic Planning, 1993); and Stephen Heyneman, "Why Do Impoverished Children Do Well in Ugandan Schools?" *Comparative Education,* Vol. 15 (1979), pp. 175–85.

[8] See Simon Appleton, *Exam Performance in Kenyan Primary Schools: Determinants and Gender Differences* (Washington, DC: World Bank, 1995); and "The Interaction Between Poverty and Gender in Human Capital Accumulation: The Case of the Primary Leaving Examinations in the Côte d'Ivoire," *Journal of African Economies,* Vol. 4, No. 3 (1995) pp. 192–224.

[9] See John Strauss, "Households, Communities, and Preschool Children's Nutrition Outcomes: Evidence from Rural Cote d'Ivoire," *Economic Development and Cultural Change,* Vol. 38, No. 2 (1990), pp. 231–62; Kofi Benefo and T. Paul Schultz, "Determinants of Fertility and Child Mortality in Côte d'Ivoire and Ghana," Living Standards Measurement Working Paper, No. 103 (Washington, DC: World Bank, 1988); and John Mackinnon, "Health as an Informational Good: The Determinants of Child Malnutrition and Mortality During Political and Economic Recovery in Uganda," Centre for the Study of African Economies Working Paper, No. 95-9 (Oxford: University of Oxford, 1995).

[10] P. Lindskog and J. Lundqvist, "Why Poor Children Stay Sick: The Human Ecology of Child Health and Welfare in Rural Malawi," Research Report No. 85 (Uppsala: Scandinavian Institute of African Studies).

[11] See, among others: Mackinnon, op. cit; Strauss, op. cit.; John Hobcroft, "Women's Education, Child Welfare, and Child Survival: A Review of the Evidence," *Health Transition Review,* Vol. 3, No. 2 (1993); Simon Appleton, "The Impact of Public Services on Health Care and Morbidity: Evidence from Kenya," Centre for the Study of African Economies Working Paper (Oxford: University of Oxford, 1995).

[12] John Mackinnon, op. cit.; Duncan Thomas, John Strauss, and Maria-Helena Henriques, "How Does Mother's Education Affect Child Height?" *Journal of Human Resources,* Vol. 26, No. 2 (1991), pp. 183–211.

[13] K. Hilderbrand, A. Hill, S. Randall, and M. L. van den Eerenbeemt, "Child Mortality and Care of Children in Rural Mali," in *Population, Health, and Nutrition in the Sahel,* ed. A. Hill (London: Routledge and Kegan Paul, 1985); H. el Bushra, N. Tigerua, and A. el Tom, "Perceived Causes and Traditional Treatment of Diarrhoea by Mothers in Eastern Sudan," *Annals of Tropical Paediatrics,* Vol. 8, No. 3 (1988), pp. 135–40; G. Bukenya, R. Kaser, and N. Nukoloo, "The Relationship of Mothers' Perception of Babies' Faeces and Other Factors to Childhood Diarrhoea in an Urban Settlement of Papua New Guinea," *Annals of Tropical Paediatrics,* Vol. 10, No. 2 (1990), pp. 185–9.

[14] See John C. Caldwell, "Routes to Low Mortality in Poor Countries," *Population and Development Review,* Vol. 12, No. 2 (1986), pp. 171–220.

[15] See George Psacharopoulos, "Returns to Investment in Education: A Global Update," *World Development,* Vol. 22, No. 9 (1994), pp. 1325–44; Paul Bennell, "Rates of Return to Education: Does the Conventional Pattern Prevail in Sub-Saharan Africa?" Institute of Development Studies Working Paper No. 10 (Brighton, UK: University of Sussex); John Knight, Richard Sabot, and D. Hovey, "Is the Rate of Return to Primary Schooling Really 26%?" *Journal of African Economies,* Vol. 1, No. 2 (1992), pp. 192–205; Simon Appleton, John Hoddinott, Pramila Krishnan, and Kerry Max, "Gender Differences in the Returns to Schooling in Three African Countries," background paper for the *World Development Report 1995 on Labour Markets,* (Washington, DC: World Bank, 1995); Paul Glewwe, "Schooling, Skills, and the Returns to Government in Education: An Exploration Using Data from Ghana," LSMS Working Paper, No. 76 (Washington, DC: World Bank, 1991); Tracy Jones, "Are Manufacturing Workers Really Worth their Pay?" Centre for the Study of African Economies Working Paper, No. 94-2 (Oxford: Oxford University Press, 1994); and Peter Moll, "Quality of Education and the Rise in Returns to Schooling in South Africa 1975–85," *Economics of Education Review,* Vol. 11 (1991), pp. 1–10.

[16] See Jones, op. cit.

[17] M. Boissiere, J. Knight, and R. Sabot, "Earnings, Schooling, Ability and Cognitive Skills," *American Economic Review,* Vol. 75, No. 2 (1985), pp. 1016–30; Victor Lavy, J. Spratt, and N. Leboucher, "Incidence, Patterns of Change and Correlates of Illiteracy in Morocco" (Washington, DC: World Bank, 1992, mimeo); Glewwe, op. cit.

[18] See Glewwe, op. cit.; Moll, op. cit.: and M. Carnoy, R. Sack, and H. Thias "Determinants and Effects of School Performance: Secondary Education in Tunisia" (Washington, DC: World Bank, 1977).

[19] Dean Jamison and Lawrence Lau, *Farmer Education and Farm Efficiency* (Baltimore, MD: Johns Hopkins University Press, 1982).

[20] A survey of the African literature is included in Simon Appleton and Arsene Balihuta "Education and Agricultural Productivity in Uganda," *Journal of International Development* (forthcoming 1996).

[21] See P. Krishnan, "Family Background, Education and Employment in Urban Ethiopia," Centre for the Study of African Economies Working Paper, No. 94-8 (Oxford: Oxford University Press, 1994); and Wim Vijverberg, "Profits from Self-employment: A Case Study of Côte d'Ivoire" LSMS Working Paper, No. 34 (Washington, DC: World Bank, 1988).

[22] See Appleton et al., op. cit.; Simon Appleton, "'The Rich are Just Like Us, Only Richer': Poverty Functions or Consumption Functions?" Centre for the Study of African Economies Working Paper (Oxford: Oxford University Press, 1995); Paul Glewwe, "Investigating the Determinants of Household Welfare in Côte d'Ivoire," *Journal of Development Economics,* Vol. 35 (1992), pp. 307–37; Harold Coulombe and Andrew MacKay, "Modelling the Determinants of Poverty in Mauritania" (Department of Economics, University of Nottingham, mimeo).

[23] For early studies, see George Psacharopoulos, "The Contribution of Education to Economic Growth: International Comparisons," in *International Comparisons of Productivity and Causes of the Slowdown,* ed. John W. Kendrick (Cambridge, MA: Ballinger, 1984). For more pessimistic later results, see Lawrence Lau and Dean Jamison, op. cit.; F. Louat, "Education and Productivity in Developing Countries: an Aggregate Production Function Approach," Policy, Research and External Affairs Working Paper, No. 612 (Washington, DC: World Bank, 1991); Martin Weale, "Education, Externalities, Fertility and Economic Growth," World Bank Working Paper Series 1039 (Washington, DC: World Bank, 1992); and Lant Pritchett, "Where Has All the Education Gone?" (Washington, DC: World Bank, 1995, mimeo).

[24] See Simon Appleton, "How Does Female Education Affect Fertility? A Structural Model for the Côte d'Ivoire," *Oxford Bulletin of Economics and Statistics,* Vol. 58 (1996); United Nations, "Relationships Between Fertility and Education: A Comparative Analysis of World Fertility Survey Data for 22 Developing Countries" (New York: United Nations, 1983); Demographic and Health Surveys, "Women's Education—Findings from Demographic and Health Surveys," paper presented for the World Conference on Education for All, Bangkok, Thailand, 1990.

[25] Jere Behrman, "The Economic Rationale for Investing in Nutrition in Developing Countries," *World Development,* Vol. 21, No. 1 (1993), pp. 1745–72.

[26] Paul Gertler and Jacques van der Gaag, *The Willingness to Pay for Medical Care: Evidence from Two Developing Countries* (Baltimore, MD: Johns Hopkins University Press, 1990).

[27] Ishmael Magona, *The Economic Impact of AIDS in Rural Uganda* (master's thesis, Makerere University, Kampala, Uganda, 1992).

[28] Helen Pankhurst, *Gender, Development and Identity: An Ethiopian Study* (London: Zed Books, 1992); Abby Nalwanga-Sebina and E. R. Natakunda, "Uganda Women's Needs Assessment Survey" (Kampala, Uganda: Makerere University, 1988, mimeo); and John C. Caldwell, P. H. Reddy, and Pat Caldwell, "Educational Transition in Rural South India," *Population and Development Review,* Vol. 11, No. 1 (1985), pp. 29–52.

[29] For some alarming case studies, see Susan Reynolds Whyte, "Medicines and Self-Help: The Privatization of Health Care in Eastern Uganda," in *Changing Uganda,* ed. Holger Bernt Hansen and Michael Twaddle (London: James Currey, 1991), pp. 130–48.

[30] Sara Bennett and Innocent Modisaotsile, "The Costs and Financing of Selected Primary Health Care Activities in Botswana," Bamako Initiative Technical Report, No. 6 (Geneva: WHO, 1991).

[31] George Psacharopoulos, "The Economics of Higher Education in Developing Countries," *Comparative Education,* Vol. 26 (1982), pp. 139–59.

[32] John Hoddinott, "Modelling Remittance Flows in Kenya," *Journal of African Economies,* Vol. 1, No. 2 (1992), pp. 206–32.

[33] Ronald Vogel, "Health Insurance in Sub-Saharan Africa: A Survey and Analysis," World Bank Working Paper, No. 476 (Washington, DC: World Bank, 1990); F. Moens, "Design, Implementation, and Evaluation of a Community Financing Scheme for Hospital Care in Developing Countries: A Pre-paid Health Plan in the Bwamanda Health Zone, Zaire," *Social Science and Medicine,* Vol. 30, No. 12 (1990), pp. 1319–27.

[34] Simon Appleton and John Mackinnon, "Poverty in Uganda: Characteristics, Causes, and Constraints," (Oxford: Oxford University, 1995, mimeo).

[35] See Simon Appleton and Paul Collier, "On Gender Targeting," in *Public Spending and the Poor: Theory and Evidence,* ed. Dominique van de Walle (Baltimore, MD: Johns Hopkins University Press, forthcoming 1995).

[36] Caldwell, "Routes to Low Mortality," op. cit.

[37] Christopher Colclough, "Education and the Market: Which Parts of the Neo-Liberal Solution Are Correct?" Innocenti Occasional Paper Economic Policy Series, No. 36 (New York: UNICEF, 1993).

[38] M. Over, R. Ellis, J. Huber, and O. Solon, "The Consequences of Adult Ill-Health," in *The Health of Adults in the Developing World,* ed. R. Feachem, T. Kjellstrom, C. Murray, M. Over, and M. Phillips (Oxford: Oxford University Press, 1992), ch. 4.

[39] Dean T. Jamison, W. Henry Mosley, Anthony H. Measham, and Jose Luis Bobadilla, *Disease Control Priorities in Developing Countries* (Oxford: Oxford Medical Publications, 1993); World Bank, *Investing in Health: World Development Report 1993* (Washington, DC: World Bank, 1993); and Samuel H. Preston, "Review of the *1993 World Development Report,*" *Population and Development Review,* Vol. 20, No. 2 (1994), pp. 464–7.

[40] For instance, Jamison et al., op. cit, p. 101, report that there are few attempts to quantify the effects of informational interventions on diarrhoea, and those that were identified deal mainly with handwashing, which may not be the main issue.

[41] See W. de Geyndt, X. Zhao, and S. Liu, "From Barefoot Doctor to Village Doctor in Rural China," World Bank Technical Paper, No. 187 (Washington, DC: World Bank, 1992); L. Chen, "Coping with Economic Crisis: Policy Development in China and India," *Health Policy and Planning,* Vol. 2, No. 2 (1987), pp. 138–49.

[42] de Geyndt et al., op. cit.; Caldwell, "Routes to Low Mortality," op. cit.

[43] Lawrence H. Summers, "The Most Influential Investment," *Scientific American,* No. 267 (1992).

[44] Barbara McPake, Kara Hanson, and Anne Mills, "Implementing the Bamako Initiative in Africa: A Review and Five Case Studies," Department of Public Health Policy Paper, DPHP No. 8 (London: London School of Hygiene and Tropical Medicine, 1992).

[45] Ibid.; and P. Mujinja and R. Mabala, "Charging for Services in Non-governmental Health Services in Tanzania," Bamako Initiative Technical Report Series, No. 7 (Geneva: WHO, 1991).

[46] C. Waddington and K. Enyimayew, "A Price to Pay: The Impact of User Charges in Ashanti-Akim District, Ghana," *International Journal of Health Planning and Management,* Vol. 4, No. 1 (1989), pp. 17–48.

[47] Moens, op. cit.; McPake et al., op. cit.

[48] See A. Bekele and M. Lewis, "Financing Health Care in the Sudan: Some Recent Experiments in the Central Region," *International Journal of Health Planning and Management,* Vol. 1, No. 2 (1986), pp. 117–27; Waddington and Enyimayew, op. cit.; R. Yoder, "Are People Willing and Able to Pay for Medical Services?" *Social Science and Medicine,* Vol. 29, No. 1 (1989), pp. 35–42; Keith Hinchliffe, "Economic Austerity, Structural Adjustment, and Education: The Case of Nigeria," *IDS Bulletin,* Vol. 20, No. 1 (1989), pp. 5–10; Frances Stewart, "Education and Adjustment: The Experience of the 1980s and Lessons for the 1990s" (London: Commonwealth Secretariat, 1990, mimeo); K. Savadogo and C. Wetta, "The Impact of Self-Imposed Adjustment: The Case of Burkina Faso, 1983–1989," in *Africa's Recovery in the 1990s,* ed. G. Cornia, R. van der Hoeven, and T. Mkandawire (Oxford: St. Martin's Press, 1993); U. Kann, *Problems with Equity in the Education System: The Provision of Basic Education in Botswana* (Gaberone: Macmillan, 1984).

[49] D. Shepard, G. Carrin, and P. Nyandagazi, "Household Participation in Financing of Health Care at Government Health Centres in Rwanda," in *Health System Decentralisation: Concepts, Issues, and Country Experience,* ed. A. Mills, J. Vaughan, D. Smith, and I. Tabinzzadeh (Geneva: WHO, 1990), ch. 6.

[50] This approach was suggested in the United Nations Development Programme, *Human Development Report 1991* (New York: Oxford University Press, 1991).

[51] Care must be taken in assessing the figures in Table 3 since they refer to central government spending only (with the exception of Malawi). The figures for the United States and the United Kingdom refer to shares in total government spending (in these countries education is mainly financed by local and state government).

[52] The most pro-social-sector half of the sample are defined as the top 50 percent, ranked by shares of government spending going to health and education.

[53] David Sahn, "Public Expenditure in Sub-Saharan Africa During a Period of Economic Reforms," *World Development,* Vol. 20, No. 5 (1992), pp. 673–93; Beth Ebel, "Patterns of Government Expenditure in Developing Countries During the 1980s: The Impact on Social Services," Innocenti Occasional Papers Economic Policy Series, No. 18 (New York: UNICEF, 1991).

[54] World Bank, *Financing Education in Developing Countries: An Exploration of Policy Options* (Washington, DC: World Bank, 1986); World Bank, *Education in Sub-Saharan Africa,* op. cit.; D. Berstecher and R. Carr-Hill, *Primary Education and Economic Recession in the Developing World Since 1950* (Paris: UNESCO, 1990).

[55] See Ebel, op. cit.

[56] Emanuel Jimenez and D. Cox , "The Relative Effectiveness of Private and Public Schools," *Journal of Development Economics,* Vol. 33, No. 3 (1990), pp. 99–122; George Psacharopoulos, "Public Versus Private Schools in Developing Countries: Evidence from Colombia and Tanzania," *International Journal of Educational Development,* Vol. 7 (1990), pp. 59–67; Emanuel Jimenez, Marianne Lockheed, and N. Wattarawaha, "The Relative Efficiency of Private and Public Schools: The Case of Thailand," *World Bank Economic Review,* Vol. 2 (1988), pp. 139–64; Emanuel Jimenez, V. Paqueo, and M. de Vera, "Student Performance and Schools' Costs in Private and Public High Schools in the Philippines," World Bank PPR Working Paper, No. 61 (Washington, DC: World Bank, 1988); J. Armitage and Richard Sabot, "Socio-Economic Background and the Returns to Schooling in Two Low-Income Economies," *Economica,* Vol. 54 (1987), pp. 103–108; Emanuel Jimenez, Marianne Lockheed, E. Luna, and V. Paqueo, "School Effects and Costs for Private and Public Schools in the Dominican Republic," World Bank PPR Working Paper, No. 288 (Washington, DC: World Bank, 1989).

[57] John Knight and Richard Sabot, *Education, Productivity, and Inequality: The East African Natural Experiment* (Oxford: Oxford University Press, 1990). Similarly, Pakistan's decision in 1979 to permit private schools appears to have encouraged a significant increase in the numbers going to school. Emanuel Jimenez and J. P. Tan, "Decentralised and Private Education: The Case of Pakistan," *Comparative Education,* Vol. 23, No. 2 (1987), pp. 173–90.

[58] P. Mandl and S. Ofosu-Amaah with R. Knippenberg, R. Niimi, K. Jarr, and M. Topping, "Community Financing Experiences for Local Health Services in Africa," UNICEF Staff Working Paper, No. 2 (New York: UNICEF, 1988); A. Koita and J. Brunet-Joilly, "Mali," *Recurrent Costs in the Health Sector,* ed. B. Abel-Smith and A. Creese, WHO/SAS/NHP/89.8 (Geneva: WHO, 1989), ch. 2; U. Camen, "Macroeconomic Evolution and the Health Sector: Mozambique Country Paper" (Geneva: WHO, 1992, mimeo).

[59] World Bank, Africa Technical Department, Human Resources and Poverty Division, "Better Health in Africa," World Bank Technical Working Paper, No. 4 (Washington, DC: World Bank, 1993); J. McGuire and Barry Popkin, "Helping Women Improve Nutrition in the Developing World: Breaking the Zero Sum Game," World Bank Technical Paper, No. 114 (Washington, DC: World Bank, 1990).

[60] J. Price, "Who Determines Need? A Case Study of a Women's Organisation in North India," *IDS Bulletin,* Vol. 23, No. 1 (1992), pp. 50–7.

[61] World Bank, "Better Health in Africa," op. cit.

[62] See McPake et al., op. cit.; D. Bradley, "Malaria," in *Disease and Mortality in Sub-Saharan Africa,* ed. Richard Feachem and Dean Jamison (Oxford: Oxford University Press, 1991), ch. 12; Waddington and Enyimayew, op. cit.; Susan Foster, "Economic Aspects of the Production and Use of Pharmaceuticals: Evidence and Gaps in Research," in *Health Economics Research in Developing Countries,* ed. Anne Mills and Kenneth Lee (Oxford: Oxford University Press, 1993), ch. 12.

[63] R. W. Harbinson and E. A Hanushek, *Educational Performance of the Poor: Lessons from Rural Northeast Brazil* (Oxford: Oxford University Press, 1992).

[64] Marianne Lockheed and Adrian Verspoor, *Improving Primary Education in Developing Countries* (Oxford: Oxford University Press, 1991).

[65] Bruce Fuller, "What Factors Raise Achievement in the Third World?" *Review of Educational Research,* Vol. 57 (1987) pp. 255–92.

Chapter Four

Agricultural Transformation: The Key to Broad-Based Growth and Poverty Alleviation in Africa

Christopher L. Delgado

Agriculture is central to economic growth and the alleviation of poverty in Africa. In the average African country, agriculture accounts for 70 percent of total employment, 40 percent of merchandise exports, and one-third of GDP; these averages obscure an even greater role of agriculture in many countries of the region.[1] Primary agricultural commodities account for at least two-thirds of merchandise exports in the lower income countries of Africa and from one-third to one-half of exports in the better-off countries, excluding South Africa.[2]

It is therefore deeply disturbing that assistance by bilateral and multilateral donor agencies to fundamental investment in African agriculture has declined in both absolute and relative terms in recent years, and that funding by African governments themselves is also being reduced. This decline is part of a worldwide trend: Donor assistance to developing-country agriculture has declined from $11.7 billion in 1980 to $10.1 billion in 1990 (all dollar figures in this paragraph are in 1985 U.S. dollars), or from 22 percent of worldwide development assistance to 14 percent. U.S. bilateral assistance to agriculture in developing countries has declined in real terms from $1 billion in 1985 to $388 million in 1990.[3] Africa's share of a shrinking pie of agricultural assistance expanded from 22 percent in 1980 to 31 percent in 1990, but real donor assistance to agriculture in Africa today appears to be declining.

African governments have made serious efforts to invest in national institutions that support agricultural development, but they are trapped by the fiscal restrictions imposed by the need for structural adjustment. Some adjusting countries (such as Malawi and Burkina

Faso) are barely maintaining agriculture's share of government expenditure, while others are cutting it sharply. In Ghana, for example, government expenditure on agriculture fell from 12 percent of total government spending in 1980/81 to 4 percent in 1987/88.[4] Effective privatization of some agricultural functions undoubtedly accounted for some of the change, but not all of it.

Agricultural research, so central to the Green Revolution in Africa and elsewhere, provides an example of the trend away from financial support for agriculture. Although the number of scientists working in African national systems grew fourfold (sixfold if South Africa is excluded) in the last three decades, growth in the amount of research support per scientist tapered off in the 1970s and has been declining over the past decade. For a sample of 17 countries, operating and capital expenditures per researcher fell steadily from $53 to $45 over the 1986–1991 period (in constant 1985 dollars). Informed observers believe that the effectiveness of research workers has been jeopardized.[5]

Lethargy in policy circles with respect to African agricultural development, both outside and inside the continent, is fueled by three factors, all of which suggest a fundamental misunderstanding of the nature of the process at stake. First, it is fueled by complacency about food availability, brought about by a declining secular trend in world cereals prices. Second, a 60-percent decline over the 1980s in real prices for Africa's agricultural commodity exports has cooled enthusiasm for agriculture-led growth strategies.[6] Third, policy lethargy toward agriculture is undoubtedly fueled by fatigue from lack of a visible Green Revolution in Africa outside the maize-producing areas. Fourth, it is compounded by the belief—at least on the donor side—that the extensive and necessary market reforms going on in many African countries will somehow take care of the problem without further attention from public authorities.

This paper will argue that markets in African rural areas behave differently from rural markets in fully commercialized market economies. In commercialized economies, price signals quickly induce factor flows, including investment and technological change. A need for more food is quickly translated into production of either more food or more nonfood items whose sale can finance food imports; whether food or nonfood goods experience the increase in output depends upon comparative advantage. If the country in question has the potential to expand agriculture, market incentives will encourage both appropriate output mixes and investment inflows, and growth will occur.

A prolonged process of agricultural transformation is necessary to produce the conditions within which such a market response will occur. This paper argues that much of Africa has not yet gone through such a transformation, and that in fact it must be induced by a proactive policy stance. Public intervention is necessary even if virtually all the resources engaged directly in agricultural production and distribution are in the private sector. Specific government actions are needed to promote structural change. Many of these will require the commitment of substantial fiscal resources and a strategy to ensure proper sequencing and relative levels of support to different activities. Development of successful strategies must incorporate a better understanding of how agricultural transformation occurs in countries at early stages of economic development, and of the supply- and demand-side constraints on economic growth in the rural areas of such countries.

AGRICULTURAL TRANSFORMATION: WHAT IS IT AND WHY IS IT IMPORTANT?

Agricultural transformation is hard to define but easy to observe in those places where it is happening. It involves a change from one structural stage to another. This is typically manifested by increasing specialization in production, greater use of purchased inputs, greater resource inflows to farming from other sectors, and substantial cuts in unit costs of production due to technological change. Secular changes, such as population growth, affect these changes directly but also indirectly through changes in the structure of incentives perceived by farmers. Policies also affect these incentives, but how they do so is greatly influenced by the presence of market externalities. In early stages of development, the absence of even a basic road system can hinder producers' responses to price increases. In intermediate stages, farmers' responses to price changes will depend on the existence of complementary interventions on the input side, since credit markets, for example, will not function well without land markets to provide collateral. Policies toward credit, fertilizer, and other inputs will be necessary adjuncts to price policies. In later stages of development, overall production response probably works best when the role of government is limited to ensuring fair play. In sum, the nature of externalities changes across stages of development, specific agricultural policies work differently within different stages, and desirable policies for growth and equity are different at different stages.

Agricultural Transformation, Intensification, and Agricultural Productivity Trends

Peter Timmer, a professor at Harvard University's Kennedy School, defined four stages of the agricultural transformation and the differences in policy emphasis necessary for each stage.[7] In the first stage agricultural productivity per worker begins to rise; here significant public investment is necessary to produce and extend this productivity increase across geographic areas. In the second, the surplus resulting from rising labor productivity is tapped through taxes or rents, and significant public intervention is required to mobilize further resources for investment and to extend the gains. In the third stage, agriculture as a sector becomes increasingly integrated into the rest of the economy, and this integration facilitates intersectoral factor, input, and output flows. Efficient rural resource use becomes the main issue, and private market development is central to progress. Finally, agriculture begins to behave like any other industry. Issues of income distribution and environmental protection become more important to household and policy decisions affecting agriculture; independently, the potential contribution of agriculture to overall growth diminishes in relative terms.

Passage through these four stages is also typically characterized by increasing intensification of agriculture, which is central to achieving sustained growth in output wherever land is scarce. Intensification consists in increasing all other factors of production relative to the scarcest factor (with scarcity defined in terms of social opportunity cost). In land-constrained systems, this means increasing the use of purchased inputs (or capital) and labor per hectare of land.

Similarly, Derek Byerlee, a World Bank economist with many years field experience working with the International Center for the Improvement of Maize and Wheat (CIMMYT), distinguishes four stages of technical change in increasing the intensity of agriculture within land-constrained systems.[8] The "pre–Green Revolution" phase exhibits boosted productivity growth per unit of land. The Green Revolution itself is characterized by widespread adoption of the improved crop varieties that agricultural research has made available. A first "post–Green Revolution" phase sees continued growth in returns to land through increased inputs of chemicals (fertilizers, herbicides, and pesticides) and labor per hectare. In the second post–Green Revolution phase the use of these inputs remains high, and further gains in productivity depend largely increasing the efficiency of their use.

Each of these structural stages is associated with a quite different policy approach to the successful development of agriculture. It is self-defeating to adopt a third- or fourth-stage development strategy for countries in the first stage. Privatization, for example, is more likely to boost output if a road network is in place, and it is probably unrealistic in most African settings to expect privatization to induce the growth of a road network.

The Green Revolution, corresponding roughly to Timmer's first and second stages, is usually thought of as a process of policy-induced intensification of agricultural production.[9] In Asia, it involved massive expansion of irrigation—particularly in lowlands where prior investments in canal, road, and electrical infrastructure had occurred—for the cultivation of improved crop varieties that made more efficient use of chemical inputs such as inorganic fertilizers. In Latin America and parts of highland Africa there has also been considerable impact from the extension of improved varieties of maize responsive to increased use of chemical fertilizers, pesticides, and herbicides on upland areas. Although the general impact of Green Revolution technology has been land-augmenting in the sense of substituting fertilizer and labor for the extra land that would otherwise have been required to produce the extra outputs, there has also been considerable substitution among other inputs over time.

Timmer found that, from 1965 to 1973, African labor productivity rose faster than land productivity, and both did in fact grow.[10] From 1973 to 1984, however, both measures of productivity fell. This, Timmer points out, had not happened in other parts of the developing world. Thus agricultural transformation, as understood in developing countries elsewhere, had not occurred in most of Africa by 1984, on this account.

Block estimated total factor productivity growth and partial productivity ratios for each of five subregions of Africa from 1963 to 1988, using wheat equivalents instead of purchasing power parity to compare aggregate outputs across countries.[11] He found that whereas labor productivity fell for the continent as a whole from the early 1970s to the early 1980s, because of sharp falls in western and southern Africa, both land and labor productivity rose during the 1980s in all regions except the Sahel, where land productivity grew but labor productivity stagnated.

In all the subregions, total factor productivity—growth not explained by growth in individual factors—grew in the 1960s (by an average of 1.4 percent per year for Sub-Saharan Africa as a whole), stagnated from the early 1970s to the early 1980s, and began growing again in the mid- to late-1980s. Growth in the last period was more marked in western and central Africa than in eastern and southern Africa; for the continent as a whole it reached 1.6 percent per year. Although Block's total factor productivity results for western and central Africa in the 1980s give some cause for optimism, in contrast to the bleak conventional wisdom, the role of favorable weather in the second half of the decade and of one-shot incentive reforms suggests caution in interpreting Block's results as evidence of the beginnings of agricultural transformation.

Today most of Africa is clearly at the very early stages of the agricultural transformation and technical change, whereas large parts of Asia and Latin America are clearly in the late stages. This strongly suggests that the relevant issues for policy-led intensification of agriculture in most of Africa are quite different from those confronting the major developing regions that have made the transformation.

Agricultural Transformation and Commercialization in "Semi-Open" Economies

Why does so much of Africa remain at the initial stage of agricultural transformation and intensification? Although bad policy is partly to blame, especially if the role of donors in the policies actually pursued is acknowledged, it is grossly insufficient as an explanation. A complex of structural factors is also at work, including the effects of remoteness and lack of infrastructure, the comparative recency and abruptness with which rural Africa was opened to the outside world, low population densities, and a natural resource base that is relatively difficult to access and still incompletely understood.[12]

Most African countries today are in fact still only "semi-open." Like small, open economies, they must rely on comparative advantage as the key to growth, since scarcity of foreign exchange is a real constraint. However, as in closed economies, major sectors of these still largely rural economies consist of locally produced items that are typically not close substitutes for imports.[13] The prices of these items are therefore only weakly influenced by trade flows. Shocks to either domestic supply or demand in these semi-open economies are not easily dampened by the world market and thus can have more than transitory effects on relative domestic prices and macroeconomic balances.

African economies are semi-open because transport and other marketing costs for the bulky items in which they trade—including food staples and major exportables—end up doubling and tripling the price of exportables at the African dockside (the free-on-board, or f.o.b., price) relative to their price at the farm gate; a similar price rise occurs for importables between their delivery to an African port (the cost-plus-insurance-and-freight, or c.i.f., price) and the point of consumption. These price markups along the marketing channel are a function of poor infrastructure, large distances, and the low volume of production. Policies also play a role: Regulation of traders and taxation of spare parts for trucks are examples.[14]

These high transport costs explain why many major consumer items in Africa are nontradables as far as world markets are concerned, and often even with respect to regional markets. These nontradable goods differ from tradables only in that, at the point of production and consumption, their domestic equilibrium prices fall between widely separated import and export parity prices for the goods in question.[15]

Traditional food staples such as root crops and coarse grains are the most important consumer items in the region; they are also often nontradable, especially in landlocked parts of Africa. High transport costs are not the only reason for this. Importable food staples, such as wheat and rice, are surprisingly poor price substitutes in consumption for domestic starchy staples. At domestic prices they typically cost much more per calorie than do domestic staples such as millet and cassava. The implication is that it is expensive to switch to imported food; domestic food prices would need to rise significantly before poor consumers (who make up most of the population) would have an incentive to switch.[16] This in turn implies that increases in demand for food staples cannot easily be met by more grain imports. Instead, increased effective demand has to be met either by rising domestic relative prices for these items that choke off demand, or by increased local production, or both. Unless the supply of such goods is perfectly inelastic with respect to price, net increases in rural demand for these items will lead to net increases in agricultural producer incomes, through a sustained net increase in overall production levels, in addition to gains from higher prices.

Thus, the elasticity of supply of nontradables (such as local foods) takes on a key strategic role in the semi-open economy, since this elasticity determines whether success in stimulating household incomes in the tradable sectors, such as agricultural exports, will lead to further income growth in the nontradable sectors, or only to more price inflation for nontradables. If local foodstuffs are inelastic in supply, and if imported grains are not good substitutes, then increased demand for food will lead, *ceteris paribus,* to higher food prices relative to prices of agricultural exports. Higher prices for food are likely in turn to lead to higher wage demands, given the importance of food in African household budgets. This suggests that the competitiveness of exports will be hard to maintain under conditions of growth if the supply of domestic food staples is not elastic with respect to prices.

Conversely, the fact that large segments of rural economies in Africa consist of nontradables suggests the possibility that a significant share of rural primary resources can remain underused for long periods of time, even if macroeconomic and trade reform remove price distortions. Thus economic strategies for agricultural and rural development in Africa need to address the fact that much of the rural economy may be demand-constrained as a result of high transfer costs, lack of information, and general fragmentation.

Agricultural Transformation and the Prospects for Food Security

By 2020 Africa's population is likely to be two-and-one-half times its present size.[17] The World Bank projects that Africa will also see the biggest expansion of any region in its share of the world's absolute poor, from 19 percent to 27 percent as early as the year 2000. In that year more than half the African population is projected to be below the absolute poverty line, defined as a household income of less than one U.S. dollar a day. Rural areas account for 70 percent of Africa's population and 90 percent of Africa's poor.[18] Finally, population pressure on agricultural land is now becoming more widespread in Africa. African policymakers are justifiably worried about both rural employment growth and rural food security.

Africa is the only major world region where food production per capita has been falling over the past 20 years.[19] Even if real world food prices do not increase significantly over the next two decades, most African countries will need to find their way to a much more favorable growth path than they achieved over the last two decades, if they are to generate the foreign exchange needed to finance the vast quantity of imports that will be required. The value of cereal imports, including food aid, in Africa in 1990 was roughly $3 per capita, or less than 5 percent of per capita exports from the region.[20] The implication of a 3-percent population growth rate, static exports, and 50 million tons of cereal imports would be a rise in the cost of food imports at constant prices to more than $12 per capita, or 18 percent of exports, a level that no large region of the world has ever been able to sustain.

Apart from the national problem of generating foreign exchange to finance food imports, for households to purchase food even at constant domestic prices requires income. To the extent that the comparative advantage of much of Africa still lies in agricultural commodities, it is difficult to see where this household purchasing power will come from without widespread and sustained growth in smallholder agriculture.

Agricultural Transformation and Political Stability

Given the role of agricultural transformation in broadly improving rural incomes, it should come as no surprise that agricultural transformation is also tightly linked to political stability. In Africa as in South Asia, the rapid social changes associated with successful agricultural transformation can be profoundly destabilizing. This phenomenon is only now beginning to appear in the more densely populated parts of Africa, such as the parts of eastern and southern Africa with greater agricultural potential. If the underlying rural political issue is access to land, the absence of successful intensification policies for agriculture is likely to produce an even worse situation because more land will be required to sustain a growing population than would be the case if intensification occurred. Thus, lack of a strategy to achieve intensification in a sustainable fashion contributes to greater human misery and a worsening of class relations.

Failure to adopt policies that promote increased labor absorption in rural areas is a recipe for disaster. It will aggravate migration to major cities, with all the problems that brings. It will also eventually lead to quicker degradation of the natural resource base, since those who remain on the soil in stagnant agricultural systems have only farming as a source of income—and an increasingly meager one at that. As will be seen below, agricultural transformation is central to rural employment creation on and off the farm. In the long run, such employment creation is a *sine qua non* for both political stability and environmental sustainability.

There is widespread agreement in the literature that, in the medium run, agricultural transformation will improve the incomes of the African rural poor in absolute terms. Yet there is considerable disagreement about its impact on the distribution of rural incomes. There is some evidence from Latin America and India that higher income rural households, living in areas where the intensification of agriculture is progressing, tend to capture a larger share of the increased income from agricultural growth than do lower income households.[21] Yet some evidence from Africa indicates the opposite.[22]

Even if progression through the stages of agricultural transformation seems to be associated with wider disparities in rural incomes, it is difficult to make causal inferences, since too many of the related factors that would need to be taken into account are not included. An adequate assessment would require taking into account second-round and subsequent effects, and adequately assessing the counterfactual: What would have occurred in the absence of new technology?

Agricultural economists Christina David and Keijiro Otsuka examined the overall impact of Green Revolution technology for rice on income distribution in high- and low-potential agricultural areas of Asia. They clearly show that, in the higher potential areas where agriculture has become greatly intensified under Green Revolution technology, adoption of that technology was widespread across all classes of farmers.[23] Critical in promoting an equitable outcome were the strongly positive impact of agricultural intensification on labor use and the impact of lowering the cost of subsistence through lower food prices. The unresolved equity issue for Asian rice areas, according to David and

Otsuka, is the impact of differing rates of intensification across agro-ecological zones. Negative impacts on the lower potential areas were mitigated by labor migration and agricultural diversification.

The regional equity issue is of special relevance to Africa, since political boundaries often have ethnic factors associated with them, and the latter are often highly correlated with agro-ecological regions. Therefore the political sustainability of agricultural transformation policies in Africa will be particularly sensitive to how its impacts on regional equity are handled. Agricultural transformation strategies in Africa need to recognize that policies toward lower potential areas should differ from those toward higher potential areas, and that policies toward the former must try to build on the growth going on in the latter.

PROMOTION OF SMALLHOLDER AGRICULTURAL DEVELOPMENT ON THE SUPPLY SIDE

Diversity and the Emerging Consensus

The countries of Africa are extremely diverse—ethnically, politically, ecologically, to name but a few ways—and few countries outside Africa have undergone such rapid change in their fundamental development strategies since the early 1960s, when most of the African countries became independent from colonial rule. Agricultural development is a case in point. Africans themselves have had relatively little input into the design of strategies that affect how their countries grow and how wealth is distributed. Instead, shifting development fashions from outside the continent have influenced their strategies, with a preponderant role in intellectual affairs played by expatriates and foreign institutions.[24] External strategies have tended to focus on the supply side, shifting from more traditional support for production activities—state-led provision of research, extension, input supply, and so forth—up through the 1970s to an increased focus since 1981 on prices received by farmers.

Despite the largely foreign-financed and foreign-conceived search over many years for a "silver bullet" that would put the continent on the path of sustained agricultural development, Africa's challenges and uncertainties remain greater than ever. There may at least be an emerging consensus as to what those challenges and uncertainties are: how to raise rural productivity, how to lower astronomical transport and other transaction costs, how to promote increased rural employment, how to reintegrate remote and difficult areas into national growth strategies, and how to ensure a sense of ownership of national policy on the part of the political class.[25]

The premier supply-side constraint on African agriculture was—and in a few places still is—the anti-agriculture bias inherent in market, trade, and macroeconomic policies that promote urban and other special interests. The agricultural debate at present in most countries has largely moved on and concerns less the desirability of macroeconomic and subsidy reforms than what to do once they have been achieved. The central issue is one of setting priorities with fewer fiscal and aid resources.

Land Versus Labor Constraints

It is useful in this regard to distinguish the more land-constrained systems, which tend to predominate in eastern and southern Africa and in parts of the humid zones of western Africa, from the more labor-constrained systems, which still can be widely observed in western and central Africa, and less commonly in parts of eastern Africa. In the land-constrained systems the primary growth issue on the supply side appears to be how to implement or strengthen a policy-induced intensification of agriculture, for example in the maize-based systems of highland eastern and southern Africa. The scope for continued expansion of production by bringing new land under cultivation would appear small. The primary constraints to progress lie on the structural side—high transport costs and underfinanced research systems—and in the level of policy support for smallholder agriculture.

In the labor-constrained systems the clear challenge is to find both technologies and a policy environment that will permit rapid increases in labor productivity. Productivity per worker must rise substantially, to provide both an alternative to the flight of resources off the farm and to provide enough surplus over subsistence consumption to permit resource mobilization in rural areas. However, mechanical innovation that increases land-labor ratios will only be useful if it provides a means to alleviate binding seasonal labor constraints. Seasonality is a much sharper constraint in western Africa than elsewhere because virtually all annual rainfall in the savanna areas where most cereals are grown, as well as field crops such as cotton and peanuts, occurs in a narrow band of three to five months. Furthermore, soils in these zones typically do not hold water well. Under these conditions, cropping must follow a rigid, crop-specific calendar, and seasonal labor requirements are a determining factor in the uptake of agricultural technology.[26] The returns to a few weeks labor at peak periods, when added to rural nonfarm income, may not be enough in these systems to keep labor on the farm. This explains why in these zones out-migration is common, and remaining labor on the farm is intensely busy during a few bottleneck periods and underemployed during much of the year.

To the extent that seasonal labor is the scarce resource influencing allocation decisions, intensification in these systems will require policies and technology that induce substitution of nonpeak labor and capital for peak-season labor. The introduction of cash crops was an example of such an innovation in western Africa, because the cropping calendars of the new crops such as peanuts and cotton were sufficiently different from those for traditional cereals in much of the area. Farm power innovations such as animal traction—nearly ubiquitous in developing countries elsewhere but still relatively rare in large parts of Africa—are also more likely to be taken up where the presence of other new factors (such as the possibility of growing cotton and having access to fertilizer) permit the substitution of capital and nonpeak labor for peak-season labor.[27]

Thus, intensification issues in the land-constrained parts of Africa, although especially hard to resolve, are probably not fundamentally different from those encountered in land-constrained developing countries elsewhere, and the policy environment is central to eventual success. In the labor-constrained areas of Africa the same constraints apply, but the problems for both agricultural research and policy are even greater. On the research side, the seasonal labor demands of new technologies are critical to the types of technologies that are developed. It is not enough that they increase returns to labor—they also have to increase returns to labor during seasonal bottleneck periods. Some technologies, such as using oxen for plowing, may increase total labor productivity but decrease returns to labor in bottleneck periods. On the policy side, in addition to the concerns faced elsewhere, policy needs to create an environment that helps ease seasonal labor constraints in agriculture. The issues here primarily concern indirect support for the development of agricultural labor and credit markets where these do not now exist or function poorly.

Lack of Incentives for Intensification

Moving African smallholders to concentrate resources in farming will require incentive structures that spread some of the many risks of such concentration. Farmers in the labor-constrained rural areas tend to heavily diversify their sources of income outside farming.[28] Even though this typically increases farm income, it does not contribute to the intensification of agriculture, which calls for farmers to devote more of their nonpeak labor and capital to land improvements such as constructing earthen bunds, planting trees, and composting and manuring.

Given the historical yield and price variability of Africa's rainfed agricultural systems, it is hard to see how farmers could either risk concentrating their resources in agriculture or adopt conservation practices that might reduce expected short-run income, unless they are reasonably confident that public policy will help out in the event of massive crop failure.

Examples of supportive public policy in this regard would be maintenance of effective ceiling prices for grain and provision of a safety net through self-targeting mechanisms for drought relief, such as food-for-work schemes.[29] Such policies follow the logic—if not the end objective—of the agricultural development maxim of the 1960s in Africa that the primary way to encourage cash crop development (i.e., the commercialization of subsistence agriculture) was to ensure a stable, low price for staple grains in rural retail markets.[30]

ADDING BACK THE DEMAND SIDE: PROMOTING LABOR-INTENSIVE RURAL DEVELOPMENT THROUGH AGRICULTURAL TRANSFORMATION

Development theorizing in the 1950s and 1960s was heavily influenced by concerns over rural employment in Asia, perhaps because Malthus's gloomy predictions looked so pertinent at that time and for that place. These conditions promoted a neo-Keynesian view of rural economic issues in South Asia in particular. There were underemployed resources caught in a vicious circle of poverty. Labor had to find either employment off the land or increased employment on the land; neither could happen unless extra food were available to feed the workers, and they had incomes sufficient to purchase the extra food. An external intervention, such as technological change in agriculture that cut unit costs of production, was required to break the cycle.

Thankfully, the Green Revolution of the 1960s and 1970s in Asia undeniably boosted rural employment inside and outside agriculture. Increased use of labor within agriculture under the Green Revolution was demonstrated both by farm-level surveys of labor use and by the massive migration from nonirrigated areas into areas experiencing the Green Revolution.[31] Yet the impact of higher cereal productivity on labor absorption in Asia was also high outside agriculture, through the widespread development of services and small-scale manufacturing activities in Green Revolution zones. Studies of the impact of rising producer incomes in these zones have shown that an extra dollar of agricultural income was typically associated with a further 80 cents of nonagricultural income from local enterprises stimulated by the spending of farm households.[32]

This additional growth beyond the initial increase in agricultural production, a result of processes called "agricultural growth linkages," was due to the fact that, because of high transaction costs, the services and other nonfarm activities in question had little alternative outlet for their production other than the local rural area. The development of these activities, which are so widespread in Asia today, depended on the growth in local demand stemming from a steadily growing stream of farm income from selling crops outside the local region.

In Africa, on the other hand, the apparent abundance of land in much of the continent up through the 1970s appears to have contributed to complacency about rural employment issues. Furthermore, development theorizing in the late 1970s began to move away from its earlier neo-Keynesian preoccupation with demand constraints on output, to focus more on the role of incentives in inducing increased supply in agriculture. The new approach tended to neglect structural differences between areas of the world, or to reduce them to differences in the level and composition of "policy distortions." African countries were characterized as small, fully open price takers, like many of the countries in Latin America and Southeast Asia. Under these assumptions, the optimal labor intensity of growth paths producing the highest output was thought to be inevitably determined by the market and not a matter of policy, other than to resist the temptation to intervene.

Agricultural Growth Linkages in Africa

More recent work has begun to challenge this view as it applies to most of Africa's countries. Results from a series of large and detailed household studies from the mid-1980s to the early 1990s challenge the notion that most countries of Africa can be usefully thought of as fully open economies. Very large shares of household income in rural areas derive from, and very large shares of consumption are devoted to, items that are nontradables of the semi-open economy, such as services, bulky traditional starchy foodstuffs, perishables, and locally processed foods. This means that many people in rural areas can remain underemployed for long periods of time if effective local demand for what they can produce does not rise.

A study by the International Food Policy Research Institute (IFPRI), covering Burkina Faso, Niger, Senegal, and Zambia, investigated the implications of rural household income growth for rural employment, through agricultural growth linkages of the Asian type but allowing for the serious demand constraints facing many African rural commodities.[33] The results suggest that higher rural incomes, broadly spread, have great potential to stimulate further increases. Realizing this potential will require a proactive and sequenced strategy to promote agricultural transformation. In the countries studied, a one-dollar increase in rural household incomes—from, say, the sale of exportable agricultural commodities—was estimated to have the potential to lead to one to two dollars of additional income from new spending on nontradable rural goods, services, and intermediate inputs.

Local production of the nontraded goods and services that figure heavily in rural consumption patterns—perishable fruits and vegetables, perishable prepared foods, services of all kinds, local handicrafts, fresh meat and milk, and some bulky local starches—typically accounts for three-quarters of nonfarm employment and the majority of total household income in the rural areas studied. Profitable local production of these items requires rapidly expanding local demand backed by purchasing power generated from sales to points outside local areas.

Key Issues for Promoting Labor-Intensive Rural Growth in Africa

Because much of rural Africa has a large share of nontradable items in both consumption and production, the extreme positions in the debate about African agricultural development strategies in the early 1980s were and remain untenable. One side assumed away the possibility of an aggregate supply response of agricultural goods to price changes. The other assumed that all agricultural items are tradables faced by infinite world demand, such that a supply response would occur automatically once incentive policies were reformed. In fact, the persistence of high transport costs and other barriers to trade in rural Africa implies that rural primary resources such as labor and land can remain underused for long periods of time, even if policy reform programs act to remove major macroeconomic barriers to trade, such as overvalued currencies and parastatal marketing monopolies. Because so much of the rural economy is constrained by these high transport costs and other barriers, markets for local goods are thin. Sustained increases in local household incomes can stimulate local employment through net increases in production of farm and nonfarm goods and services that could not otherwise be sold.

New local income originating outside the local region, as might occur with the initiation of a cash crop project, brings new local income beyond that from export cropping itself, as cash crop producers spend export-generated income on local goods and services that would not otherwise have been sold. This is like the agricultural growth linkages that were found to be so prominent in boosting rural employment in Asia under the Green Revolution, except that they are fueled primarily by receipts from export cropping and livestock, rather than by technological change in the cultivation of starchy food staples.

Where a region has a comparative advantage in food production, as do the maize-producing areas of parts of southern Africa, something more directly comparable to historical experience with the Green Revolution in Asia might be observed. Elsewhere the main role of technological change in starchy food staples is as a vital second step in rural growth, providing the commodities that rural dwellers wish to buy more of, once their incomes go up. Unlike in Asia, technological change in staple food production in Africa is less likely to be the initial motor of rural growth, and more likely to be the handmaiden of growth, unless a change in comparative advantage from nonfood agriculture to food can be achieved through major technological progress.

As commercialization and transformation proceed, producers and consumers benefit from the efficiency gains of the division of labor, and overall regional income attains a higher equilibrium. Conversely, increased commercialization also implies that the scope for demand-led growth is diminishing, since demand constraints are now less of a problem. Thus, over time, income will grow with commercialization, but the multipliers arising from agricultural growth linkages will shrink. Decreasing potential for demand-side growth will be counterbalanced by increased potential for supply-side growth of the structural adjustment type.

Over time, all commodities enter a level playing field; technological change in food production that was previously nontradable now can be used to produce income from sales outside the local area. Where significant demand constraints still persist, policies aimed at supply-side incentives are not enough to promote labor-intensive growth, although they help set the scene for later overall growth.

The time frame for the transition from a rural growth strategy based on alleviating demand constraints to one based on improving incentives is highly variable across locations, and in any case does not involve abrupt shifts but rather a gradual change in emphasis. In any event, it seems probable that the potential for demand-led growth in, for example, Malaysia, where IFPRI, using data from the early 1970s, found high agricultural growth multipliers, is much smaller 20 years later. The potential for demand-led growth in employment in rural Africa is likely to remain high for the foreseeable future, especially in remote and lower potential areas, which are relatively abundant in the region.

Three Lessons for Promoting Employment Growth

The preceding analysis yields three important lessons for promoting employment growth in Africa. The first is that rural Africans need to have an agricultural market outside their local areas if local nonfarm activities are to develop. Even if rural dwellers get most of their income from the local nontraded sectors, there still needs to be a continued injection of income from outside the area, from the sale of tradables, in order for local employment in nontraded sectors to grow.

Second, there is only one feasible way to promote the major surge in consumer spending that will in turn stimulate production of consumer goods, and that is to achieve sustained and widely distributed growth in rural incomes from trade outside the local region. Since increased consumption is the driving force of employment growth in demand-constrained areas, unlike in fully open economies, a small amount of income, widely distributed, will have a more favorable impact on employment, other things equal, than a large amount concentrated among a few households. Growth in smallholder production of tradable agricultural commodities, such as export crops, livestock, and some cereals, appears to be the most feasible way to sustainably boost the incomes of large numbers of rural dwellers. Policy reforms that lower unit costs of distribution in rural areas can provide a one-time stimulus. Ultimately, however, sustained growth must come from investment in infrastructure that lowers the unit costs of distribution, and from continuing technological progress that lowers the unit costs of production in agriculture.

Third, translating potential growth linkages from the expansion of tradable agricultural commodities into actual income growth will require much more attention to making the supply of food and the other things that people in rural areas consume more responsive to prices. Household income growth in rural localities will soon lead to greatly increased rural demand for food staples and for improved diets; if this increased demand does not lead to increased production, the relative prices of these items will rise rapidly also. Rises in the cost of living would destroy the gains in competitiveness of African agricultural items that started the growth process off in the first place, either directly through higher prices for tradable items, or indirectly through higher production costs as rural dwellers adjust their sales to the rising cost of feeding their families. Once growth is reestablished in the export sectors, it is vital that growth in food supply follow rapidly. Technological change in food production and decreases in marketing costs for food are vital components of strategy at this point.

Integrating Rural Areas of Low Agricultural Potential into Development Strategies

Rural areas of high agricultural potential are defined as those able, by virtue of their resource endowment and integration with a broader economy, to achieve progressive intensification of production of agricultural tradables, in a manner consistent with growing yields, rising average productivity of labor, and the existence of a market for output. This definition covers not only irrigated areas with the potential for an Asian-type Green Revolution, which tend to be rare in Africa, but also the more favorably endowed of the rainfed areas in both Asia and Africa currently under intensified production. African examples of the latter include the cotton-producing areas of western Africa, the highland tea areas in eastern Africa, and the hybrid maize zones in the more favorable parts of southern Africa. There is a broad technical consensus about what to do for these areas.

Far less consensus exists about what to do in rural areas of lower agricultural potential, which are especially numerous in Africa. This issue is of special policy interest, for both humanitarian and political reasons. The lower potential areas tend to be remote and to support a disproportionately large share of the human population, suggesting that present problems of food insecurity in these areas will only grow worse over time.

National agricultural diversification should be at the heart of efforts to promote diversification in these areas. In an era when expensive subsidies and inefficient tax schemes are no longer feasible to promote regional redistribution, other alternatives to help lower potential regions benefit from growth in the higher potential regions must be considered. Policies that are commonly emphasized in periods of structural transformation, such as those aimed at developing infrastructure and facilitating the emergence of private marketing agents, can be designed in such a way as to contribute to regional equity goals, while retaining a focus on growth. This approach emphasizes that agricultural diversification in one area is often the counterpart to agricultural specialization in another, and that national agricultural diversification is compatible in some instances with regional specialization.

The impact of a growing comparative advantage in maize production in areas of higher potential, through declining unit costs of production under technological change, will be to greatly increase the amount of maize available for sale in the areas producing it. Since the opportunities for cereals exports are limited in most of Africa in most years, domestic maize prices are likely to fall. The only way out of this is to facilitate the marketing of maize to less favored areas not experiencing a maize-based Green Revolution.

Outside of drought years, attempts to strengthen marketing links between the more favorable and less favorable cereal areas have typically run afoul of marketing policies designed to maintain cereal production and cereal producer incomes in the less favored areas through restriction of cereals movements. Furthermore, if less favored areas are to import additional cereals from more favored areas, effective demand in the former must increase as well, which rarely happens in protected environments. The unfortunate results of such well-intentioned policies are twofold. First, they prevent the transfer to the less favored areas, through cheaper food, of the long-run benefits of the Green Revolution in the more favored areas. Second, they delay adjustments in production patterns in the lower potential areas—adjustments that are necessary to maintain economic viability in the long run.

Increased sales of maize from more favored to less favored areas will lower maize prices in the latter but will reinforce the latter's comparative advantage in providing other items to the more favored areas, whose households have high marginal propensities to consume items typically not traded on a large scale with the outside world, such as meat, fish, fruits, vegetables, local handicrafts, and services. In addition to promoting better market links, the focus of policy in such cases should be to enhance supply responsiveness in the less favored areas in those nontradable items most in demand in the more favored ones. Producers in the less favored areas will benefit both from increased sales of nongrain items and from lower subsistence costs.

The main difference where nonstaple cash crops are the most profitable product in the higher potential areas, as in the Malian cotton zone or the Kenya Tea Development Authority project areas in western Kenya, is that producers in the more favored area are less likely to be able to supply cheaper food to the less favored ones. Although it is likely that the increase in agricultural productivity within the more favored area will still include expanding food production, the area itself is likely to absorb a large share of the additional food produced, and food prices are less likely to decline in the nonfavored areas. The latter will retain a considerable incentive to remain in subsistence food production, leading, *ceteris paribus,* to lower net gains from diversification into nonfood, nontradable items for sale to the more favored areas.

In sum, because so much of rural Africa is semi-open, with domestic foodstuffs a very imperfect substitute in both production and consumption for fully tradable cereals, technological progress in tradable items for the higher potential areas will be particularly useful for inducing growth in the nonfavored areas, through trade between the two in a setting where many agricultural and nonagricultural commodities are largely protected from the world market by high transport costs.

This process cannot work, however, if policies attempt to protect the lower potential areas from progress in the higher potential ones through internal trade restrictions for cereals, as is often the case. Such restrictions divert demand in the lower potential areas away from trade with those with higher potential.

STRATEGIES FOR STRUCTURAL CHANGE

The picture developed here of a demand-constrained rural Africa is, on the whole, quite different from that of a fully commercialized economic sector, where inputs and outputs are allocated independently, in response to price signals generated by functioning markets for all inputs and outputs. Although Africa is probably also widely subject to supply constraints as well, as a whole the region is simply at a different stage of agricultural transformation than is most of the developing world. Although some parts of eastern and southern Africa resemble the areas of Asia and Latin America transformed by the Green Revolution, most of the rural areas of the continent do not.

It is hard to see how the vicious circle of rural fragmentation and poverty can be broken without a well-coordinated and sequenced series of actions capable of addressing the powerful constraints described above. Such a strategy should involve a series of closely related initiatives, beginning on the supply side, incorporating potential for growth on the demand side, and fully mobilizing local resources.

Investing in New Sources of Productivity Growth

First and foremost, people living in rural areas where agricultural transformation is in its early stages need the benefits of research and extension services to cut the unit costs of production of those items they produce for which they are likely to have a market. It does not greatly help at this point to promote nontradables, including services and micro-scale local manufactures, since these lack an expanding local market. Instead it seems more fruitful to focus on cutting costs of production for those items for which a broad market already exists and that can absorb production increases without large price declines. This means promoting agricultural and livestock exports, in most cases.

At early stages of agricultural transformation it is unrealistic to think that the private sector can replace public agencies in providing research and extension services. This will be possible later on, at the higher stages, particularly where benefits are capturable. In stage 3 and 4 zones, for example, markets for patented hybrid seed develop, and companies can recoup their development and marketing costs, since true seed must be purchased anew each year from certified seed producers. In the early stages the risks facing private commercial research and extension initiatives are too great and the returns too hard to capture. In a given country both systems can coexist, provided they do not try to do each other's job.

Finally, the debate will soon become moot between those who think there is a lot of unused agricultural technology on the shelf in Africa today and those who think that technology is not appropriate for local conditions. Reforms of policies that held back adoption of off-the-shelf technology have been under way for some time. Technologies that expand the supply of nontradables at existing prices will probably lead to oversupply, despite market reforms and despite being technically sound. This is because demand for these items is limited to local demand. On the other hand, demand for technologies that alleviate supply constraints for tradables will grow. It would be a travesty if the supply of such technologies and their extension were to dry up at just the point that they can be used.

Promotion of Market Development Through Investment in Transport

Freeing up the movement of goods and services in Africa is the second priority. Some of this can be accomplished by direct policy action, and some will require major infrastructural investment.

Village-level transport in Africa by cart or moped is a major local constraint on expansion of local production, and it is a major welfare issue for women who need to haul wood or water long distances. Yet this is an issue that market liberalization, by reducing local monopolies and taxes on vehicles and spare parts, can help solve.

Truck transport is a harder issue. Much can be accomplished here also by liberalization of transport industries, which has been slower to occur in Africa than other forms of liberalization. The abolition of 80 percent tariffs on spare parts, as in Senegal, or of high tolls charged by local police forces, as in the central corridor of western Africa, promises a significant reduction in agricultural transport costs, if the political will is there.[34] Beyond such initiatives there is little alternative to improving the central physical grid infrastructure, expensive though it is. This is one of the most appropriate areas for asset redistribution from the industrial to the developing countries, and it is distressing to hear well-meaning people in the former argue against it on the grounds that it does not help rural dwellers in the developing world.

Reduction of Other Transaction Costs Barriers

In the absence of major technological change in staple food production, an important means of developing smallholder agriculture is to promote production of higher value products on the farm. This is even more true when barriers to smallholder entry, such as agricultural dumping by the industrial countries and subsidization by distorted national economic policies of consumption of imported agricultural items, are being done away with through policy reform in both the North and in Africa. Yet it is not uncommon to find farmers reluctant to enter new, seemingly profitable activities, even where transport costs are not a major problem.

Most high-value products such as nontraditional agricultural exports and import substitutes such as dairy production and aquaculture in Africa are subject to especially high transaction costs. The following is a nonexhaustive list of the factors that give rise to these high costs: perishability; large differences in quality depending on handling and degree of transformation; lumpiness of initial investments (economies of scale) in production, processing, and marketing; inflexibility and lags in production plans; and seasonal variability in output.[35]

Supportive policies to lower the transaction costs facing smallholders wishing to become involved in these activities will require significant institutional innovation. In Africa's changing political and fiscal environment, many of these innovations will involve decentralization and privatization of functions once thought to be more appropriate to parastatal activity. In part they will involve grassroots producer organization, in part the emergence of trader associations. Such institutions will need to be able to function within market principles, yet also deal with the public-goods nature of some of the issues. They will need to facilitate the integration of the production, marketing, and retailing functions of the marketing chain.

National Agricultural Diversification in the Context of Subnational Specialization

The harsh international economic environment of the 1980s brought home to African countries the need to diversify their agricultural export base. Food and beverages typically account for well over half of merchandise exports in the non-oil-exporting countries of Africa, excluding South Africa, and the top three agricultural exports have historically accounted for more than 80 percent of agricultural export earnings in most African countries. In the mid-1980s, coffee and cocoa alone accounted for over half of total agricultural export earnings of Africa, if

South Africa is excluded.[36] This concentration of exports in a few agricultural products has led to considerable year-to-year instability in foreign exchange earnings.

Despite the concentration of exports at the national level, one of the distinguishing characteristics of African agriculture is its extreme diversity across countries, within villages, and even on individual farms. As in the case of income diversification examined earlier, crop and livestock diversification at the micro level in Africa is in large part a matter of risk management. At the farm level in Africa, as elsewhere, technological progress and commercialization will probably be associated with increased specialization of households, in addition to diversification across households. Similarly, one can foresee a time when farmers in dry areas will do better to concentrate their activities on livestock for trade, rather than spend most of their time producing food grains under difficult conditions. Better transport links between areas producing different types of commodities would help, but it is not enough.

To reap the growth benefits of the division of labor and to promote both commercialization and technological progress, public policy in countries at an early stage of agricultural transformation will need to find ways to reduce the risk of farm, village, or regional specialization. It would be irresponsible to advocate such specialization under current conditions of unpredictable food supplies, only partially liberalized markets, and arbitrary policy shifts. Yet it is important to remember that much of the success of previous regimes in introducing cash crops came from guaranteeing the availability of food. It is hard to see how agricultural transformation will occur in countries in the first stage, subject to the unpredictable annual variation in rainfall facing most of Africa, without some form of public agency sharing some food security risks with farmers.

Subnational specialization of production in most African countries will only be feasible from a food security standpoint if internal trade prospects are much improved. This would lead to growth from the division of labor and would also help alleviate demand constraints on output for some subzones. Finally, interventions that have the effect of increasing intravillage, intranational, and intraregional trade in rural Africa can generate important second-order growth linkages of the type examined previously.

Maximizing Growth Linkages Among Rural Areas

The key to increasing rural employment in Africa is to promote widespread and sustained income increases for large numbers of rural Africans from sources that do not depend on local demand. Increased smallholder production of tradable crops and livestock resulting from lower unit costs of production and distribution are the best bets to date for achieving this widespread impact. Once the engine of growth is in place, policy must facilitate the supply response of those things that rural dwellers wish to buy when their incomes rise, especially foodstuffs. This will help ensure that rural demand increases are translated into increased production rather than only into price rises.

Instead of regarding all of rural Africa as an undifferentiated, open playing field, as might be appropriate in areas in the third stage of transformation, a successful employment-oriented growth strategy in Africa will need to focus on increasing output of those specific items that can continue to bring income into specific rural areas: This means increasing output of those items that have a market outside the area. In the first instance, such a strategy will require investment to reduce the unit costs of production and distribution of tradable items. Once this is done, policy needs to focus on similar progress for nontradables. The instruments needed to implement such changes in commercializing agriculture are a spatially diffused rural infrastructure, functioning rural institutions, and a dynamic agriculture based on technological progress. Because the required interventions are often specific for a given commodity, location, or time, success will require that national and local decision makers have the will and the ability to assess the constraints and the potentials in production and marketing in each rural area individually. Both the political will and the capacity to make good decisions will be greater if decision makers have to answer to local constituencies.

Improving Local and National Institutions for Decision Making

When the former colonies of Africa gained their independence, one of the first actions of the military regimes that came to power in many of the new nations was to dismantle institutions of local self-government left over from colonial times and before.[37] These will have to be restored, for only participatory local institutions can mobilize the local knowledge and the immense resources that agricultural transformation requires. Both donors and national governments should be supportive of such institutions.

There is nevertheless considerable danger in having external actors too actively involved in what is fundamentally a political process. Although the imposition of political solutions from outside can bring short-term gains, in the long run it tends to crowd out the process of self-government that it is designed to foster. African rural nongovernmental organizations then start spending their time pursuing things that they can get external funds for, and central government interest quickly becomes cooptation. Ultimately, only African political processes can arrive at the right form of local government for a dynamic rural society. Donors can still prioritize their resource flows to those countries that have demonstrated real commitment to bringing farm people into the political class.

Another thing that donors and national governments can and must do is increase national capacities to contribute to the conceptualization of national problems. The degree of African intellectual input in constructing and analyzing the dominant paradigms of agricultural development since the 1960s, reviewed above, has been distressingly low, though it has grown rapidly. This fact alone distinguishes modern African experience from that of other parts of the developing world, and it accentuates the fact that the main challenge for African development strategy is to increase the capacity of African entities to analyze past experience and formulate new strategies for a better future.

A shortfall of input from Africans themselves also helps explain why the dominant paradigms for promoting agricultural transformation in Africa have shifted so much over such a short time. African societies are now addressing the issues of governance and political legitimacy. Donors can avoid hindering the efforts of African regimes to improve governance and achieve legitimacy in the eyes of their rural people, and they can do a great deal to increase human and institutional capacity for the formulation and maintenance of appropriate strategies for a major structural transformation in African agriculture. Like most African governments, what donors need is a vision of where the process should go and the political will to achieve it.

Notes

As this book went to press, a major new work on agricultural transformation has just been published. Between them, the authors of this report have 90 years of practical experience in the subject, and Dr. Delgado would like to acknowledge the intellectual debt of several generations of economists to them by citing their report here: Thomas P. Tomich, Peter Kilby, and Bruce F. Johnston, Transforming Agrarian Economies: Opportunities Seized, Opportunities Missed *(Ithaca, NY: Cornell University, 1995).*

[1] Steven Jaffee, "Enhancing Agricultural Growth Through Diversification in Sub-Saharan Africa," in *Trends in Agricultural Diversification: Regional Perspectives,* ed. Shawki Barghouti, Lisa Garbus, and Dina Umali, Technical Paper No. 180 (Washington, DC: World Bank, August 1992).

[2] See Christopher L. Delgado, "Agricultural Diversification and Export Promotion in Sub-Saharan Africa," *Food Policy,* Vol. 20, No.3 (June 1995), pp. 225-44. Better-off countries here refer to those countries the World Bank defines as "middle income," i.e., those countries whose 1993 GNP per capita was between $696 and $8,625, calculated using the *World Bank Atlas* (annual method). Lower income countries are defined as those whose 1993 GNP is $695 or less.

[3] Joachim von Braun, Raymond F. Hopkins, Detlev Puetz, and Rajul Pandya-Lorch, *Aid to Agriculture: Reversing the Decline,* Food Policy Report Series, (Washington, DC: International Food Policy Research Institute, 1993).

[4] Ibid.

[5] Philip Pardey, Johannes Roseboom, and Nienke Beintema, *Investments in African Agricultural Research,* Environment and Production Technology Division Discussion Paper No. 14 (Washington, DC: International Food Policy Research Institute, October 1995), p. 27.

[6] Per Pinstrup-Andersen, "Fertilizer Subsidies: Balancing Short-Term Responses with Long-Term Imperatives," in *Policy Options for Agricultural Development in Sub-Saharan Africa,* ed. Nathan C. Russell and Christopher R. Doswell (Geneva: Centre for Applied Studies in International Negotiations, 1993), pp. 99–106; Delgado, "Agricultural Diversification," op. cit.

[7] Peter C. Timmer, "The Agricultural Transformation," in *Handbook of Development Economics,* ed. Hollis Chenery and T. N. Srinivasan, Vol. 1 (Amsterdam: Elsevier Science Publishers, 1988), pp. 276–331.

[8] Derek Byerlee, "Technological Change, Productivity, and Sustainability in Irrigated Cropping Systems of South Asia: Emerging Issues in the Post-Green Revolution Era." *Journal of International Development,* Vol. 4, No. 5 (February 1992), pp. 477–96.

[9] Uma Lele and Steven W. Stone, "Population Pressure, the Environment and Agricultural Intensification: Variations of the Boserup Hypothesis," MADIA Discussion Paper No. 4 (Washington DC: World Bank, 1989).

[10] Timmer, op. cit.

[11] Steven A. Block, "A New View of Agricultural Productivity in Sub-Saharan Africa," *American Journal of Agricultural Economics,* Vol. 76 (August 1994), pp. 619–24.

[12] Christopher L. Delgado, John Mellor, and Malcolm J. Blackie, "Strategic Issues in Food Production in Sub-Saharan Africa," in *Accelerating Food Production in Sub-Saharan Africa,* ed. John Mellor, Christopher Delgado, and Malcolm Blackie (Baltimore, MD: Johns Hopkins University Press, 1987), pp. 3–22.

[13] "Close substitutes" is meant here in the economic sense, that a small rise in relative prices shifts consumption to alternative items and provokes resource inflow to the activity in question.

[14] Pinstrup-Andersen, "Fertilizer Subsidies," op. cit. A major reason why transport costs are so high is that bulky agricultural produce in much of Africa needs to be moved by truck, one of the most expensive forms of transport, over poor roads. Dunstan Spencer shows that in 18 countries in the humid and subhumid tropics of Africa, 388 kilometers of rural roads per thousand square kilometers of land area would be required to bring the rural road infrastructure up to the level of India in 1950, after adjusting for population density differences, whereas in fact in the early 1990s the African humid and subhumid tropics had only 63 kilometers of roads per thousand square kilometers. Dunstan Spencer, "Infrastructure and Technology Constraints to Agricultural Development in the Humid and Subhumid Tropics of Africa" Environment and Production Technology Division Discussion Paper No. 3 (Washington DC: International Food Policy Research Institute, 1994).

[15] Christopher L. Delgado, "Why Domestic Food Prices Matter to Growth Strategy in Semi-Open West African Agriculture," *Journal of African Economies,* Vol. 1, No. 3 (November 1992), pp. 446–71.

[16] Ibid.

[17] United Nations Development Programme, *Human Development Report 1993* (New York: Oxford University Press, 1993).

[18] World Bank, *World Development Report 1992* (New York: Oxford University Press, 1992).

[19] Per Pinstrup-Andersen, *World Food Trends and Future Food Security,* Food Policy Report (Washington, DC: International Food Policy Research Institute, 1994).

[20] World Bank, op. cit.

[21] J. Edward Taylor, "Undocumented Mexico-U.S. Migration and the Returns to Households in Rural Mexico," *American Journal of Agricultural Economics,* Vol. 69, No. 3, (1987),

pp. 626–38; Tom S. Walker and James G. Ryan, *Village and Household Economies in India's Semi Arid Tropics* (Baltimore, MD: Johns Hopkins University Press, 1990).

[22] Thomas A. Reardon, Christopher L. Delgado, and Peter Matlon, "Determinants and Effects of Income Diversification Amongst Farm Households in Burkina Faso," *The Journal of Development Studies,* Vol. 28, No. 2 (January 1992), pp. 264–96.

[23] Christina David and Keijiro Otsuka (eds.), *Modern Rice Technology and Income Distribution in Asia* (Boulder, CO: Lynne Reinner Publishers, 1994).

[24] See Christopher L. Delgado, "Africa's Changing Agricultural Development Strategies: Past and Present Paradigms as a Guide to the Future," Food, Agriculture and the Environment Discussion Paper No. 3 (Washington, DC: International Food Policy Research Institute, 1995).

[25] Ibid.

[26] Christopher L. Delgado and Chandra Ranade, "Technological Change and Agricultural Labor Use," in *Accelerating Food Production in Sub-Saharan Africa,* ed. John W. Mellor, Christopher L. Delgado, and Malcolm Blackie (Baltimore, MD: Johns Hopkins University Press, 1987).

[27] Christopher L. Delgado and John McIntire, "Constraints on Oxen Cultivation in the Sahel," *American Journal of Agricultural Economics,* Vol. 64, No. 2 (May 1982), pp.188–96.

[28] Thomas A. Reardon et al., "Agriculture-Led Income Diversification in the West African Semi-Arid Tropics: Nature, Distribution, and Importance of Production-Linkage Activities," in *African Economic Issues: What Have We Learned?* ed. Achi Atsain, Samuel Wangwe, and Anne Drabek (Nairobi: African Economic Research Consortium, 1994), pp. 207–30.

[29] Joachim von Braun, Tesfaye Teklu, and Patrick Webb, "Labor-Intensive Public Works for Food Security in Africa: Past Experience and Future Potential," *International Labour Review,* Vol. 131, No. 1 (1992), pp. 19–33.

[30] Uma Lele, *The Design of Rural Development: Lessons from Africa* (Baltimore, MD: Johns Hopkins University Press, 1975).

[31] John W. Mellor, *The New Economics of Growth: A Strategy for India and the Developing World* (Ithaca, NY: Cornell University Press, 1976); David and Otuska, op. cit.

[32] Clive Bell and Peter Hazell, "Measuring the Indirect Effects of an Agricultural Investment Project on Its Surrounding Region," *American Journal of Agricultural Economics,* Vol. 62, No. 1 (February 1980), pp. 75–86.

[33] Christopher Delgado, Peter Hazell, Jane Hopkins, and Valerie Kelly, "Promoting Intersectoral Growth Linkages in Rural Africa through Agricultural Technology and Policy Reform," *American Journal of Agricultural Economics,* Vol. 76, No. 5 (December 1994), pp. 1166–71.

[34] Raisuddin Ahmed and Cynthia Donovan, *Issues of Infrastructural Development: A Synthesis of the Literature,* Occasional Paper (Washington DC: International Food Policy Research Institute, November 1992).

[35] Steven Jaffee and John Morton (eds.), *Marketing Africa's High-Value Foods* (Dubuque, IA: Kendall-Hunt Publishing Co., 1995).

[36] Jaffee, op. cit.; Delgado, "Agricultural Diversity," op. cit.

[37] Ibid.

Chapter Five

Trade and Industrial Policy in Africa

Sanjaya Lall and Frances Stewart

INTRODUCTION

Industrialization is essential to long-run development. Every country that has achieved sustained growth has also seen a structural transformation of its economy away from primary production toward industry. Industrial expansion is necessary to raise incomes and employment, to diversify exports, to extend markets, and to avoid dependence on a few commodities. Industrial expansion is also needed so that countries can substitute domestic production for imports and enjoy the learning economies and the economies of specialization and of scale that are associated with industrialization. In nearly all economies, manufacturing has been the critical agent of the structural transformation from a primitive, low-productivity, low-income economy into one that is dynamic and diversified.

Against this background, it is disappointing that recent industrial performance in Africa has been extremely weak. Growth of manufacturing value added averaged only 3 percent per year in real terms from 1980 to 1993,[1] and its pace has slowed steadily over that period, from 3.7 percent per year in the first half of the 1980s to 2 percent in 1989–1993. Performance was worse still in the first part of the 1990s: Growth in manufacturing value added fell from 3.3 percent in 1989–1990 to 0.4 percent in 1991–92, with only a modest recovery to 1.5 percent in 1992–93. Moreover, these broad averages conceal continued stagnation or outright declines in manufacturing value added in a large number of individual countries. Over the past decade and a half many African countries have suffered a sustained "deindustrialization" in their manufacturing capacity—a loss matched by no other developing region in the world.

African economies, as a consequence, remain the least industrialized in the world: In 1990, industry accounted for about 30 percent of output in Africa, compared with 37 percent for all low- and middle-income countries worldwide. Manufacturing, the most dynamic element in industry, accounted for a particularly small share of total industrial output in Africa. This poor performance is especially marked in exports: Manufactured products accounted for only 8 percent of African exports in 1991, compared with 51 percent in the world's low- and middle-income countries as a group. This poor showing of manufactured exports, and the consequent continuing reliance on raw materials exports, is partly responsible for the worsening terms of trade that Africa has suffered over the past 20 years. It is also a reflection of the underdevelopment of African industry, as export performance is a powerful indicator of productivity and competitiveness.

This paper takes as its starting point that the objective of trade and industrial policies in Africa must be to build up an efficient industrial structure, and one that will, within a fairly short span of time, permit the expansion of manufacturing exports. Like most areas of policy in recent years, industrial policies in Africa have been dominated by the requirements of the stabilization and structural adjustment packages negotiated between the African countries and the International Monetary Fund (IMF) and the World Bank. In this policy area the World Bank has assumed the lead role. Its policies toward industry have shared the same philosophy as Bank policies in other areas: They have championed deregulation, a sharp curtailment of the role of the state as producer and regulator, devaluation of the exchange rate, and liberalization of import policies.

Not all countries, and indeed not all successful industrializing countries, have adopted the policy strategy advocated by the World Bank. In fact the Bank's policies have frequently stood in sharp contrast with the more interventionist policies practiced by some successful industrializers, such as Indonesia, Malaysia, the Republic of Korea, and Taiwan.[2] Their experience has given rise to a spirited debate between orthodox neoliberals at the Bank and elsewhere and so-called neostructuralists, who advance theoretical arguments for a more proindustry interventionist policy stance and for the need to be selective in creating the appropriate supply conditions.

In this paper we begin by considering the industrial strategy of the African countries in the years before reform and the inefficiencies in

African industry that apparently justified the reform package. Next we review some of the theoretical debate and consider the relevance of alternative approaches, based on the development of technological capabilities, to the African context. We then assess the performance of African industry during the 1980s, the period when the World Bank's structural adjustment packages were being put into effect. We also look at the record of industrial performance in one country, Ghana, considered by many to be one of Africa's model adjusting countries, having followed the World Bank's recommendations more closely and for a longer period than others.

INDUSTRIAL POLICY IN AFRICA IN THE 1960S AND 1970S

Industrial policy in much of Africa over the 1960s and 1970s was aimed at promoting investment both by the state and by local and foreign private enterprises. Heavy import protection, subsidized credit, and tax incentives encouraged private investment. For the most part (although this varied across countries), there was considerable state regulation: Large investors were required to obtain licenses to invest, import, remit foreign exchange, and so on. At first these policies achieved a respectable growth of industry. From 1970 to 1980 value added in industry grew by 5.3 percent per year, faster than the growth of GDP. But these gains were, as elsewhere in the developing world, associated with considerable inefficiencies, and the returns were not commensurate with the resources invested. The pattern of industrialization was, for the most part, inefficient by every measure: Industry was highly protected from foreign competition, and remained strongly dependent on imported inputs, had poor linkages with the rest of the economy, and exported little of its output.[3] Several African governments launched measures to increase local technological effort, but for reasons we explore below these remained a largely sterile exercise, with state-run research institutions doing poor-quality work largely irrelevant to and disconnected from industry.

The pervasiveness of public ownership in African industry (as well as in other sectors) was often blamed for much of the observed inefficiency (for example, by the World Bank's 1981 report entitled *Accelerated Development in Sub-Saharan Africa*).[4] A 1992 review by John Knight of Oxford University confirmed the large role of public enterprises in most African economies and provided evidence of their inefficiency.[5] African public enterprises have indeed produced very poor returns: In 1980, for example, the net losses of public enterprises in Niger and Mali amounted to 4 and 6 percent of those countries' respective GDPs; Kenya's large public investments produced a rate of return of only 0.2 percent per year. Other measures of efficiency also show weak performance; for example, in Tanzania public enterprises exhibited high capital intensity and low capacity utilization.[6]

Foreign direct investment (FDI) might have been an attractive alternative to public production, but the experience of foreign investment in Africa has been at best mixed.[7] The direct impact of FDI on countries' payments balances has frequently been negative, with outflows of dividends exceeding new inflows of capital. In Nigeria from 1977 to 1986 there was a cumulative outflow of $1.2 billion. In Kenya the net contribution was positive until the 1970s, but from 1979 to 1986 outflows of dividends and fee income greatly exceeded new inflows. This would not have mattered if inflows of FDI had been growing steadily and if its export-generating or import-substituting effects had been positive. However, neither seemed to be the case. From the mid-1970s on, the net stock of African FDI did not grow significantly; indeed, from 1976 to 1986 most countries experienced disinvestment for a variety of reasons—saturation of small local markets, political instability, inability to export, and deteriorating terms of trade, among others. Most FDI was concentrated in import-substituting industries; only in Malawi, Botswana, Senegal, and Zimbabwe was it associated with a significant increase in manufactured exports. Import substitution was, moreover, not very efficient, and there is abundant evidence that the technologies brought in by the new foreign investors were inappropriately capital-intensive and import-dependent.[8]

The low efficiency of FDI in Africa reflects the unfavorable situation that faced African industry in general: an unsupportive policy environment, enterprises lacking in capabilities, poor infrastructure, and a shortage of foreign exchange. More recent experience suggests that even with liberalization of trade and investment, it cannot be expected that FDI will provide an engine of growth for African industry or of manufactured exports. In the past decade or so, the flow of FDI has stagnated in Africa even as flows to other parts of the developing world have increased massively. Prospects for increasing FDI in the current environment remain gloomy, as international investors aim at richer markets with more advanced facilities, more abundant and sophisticated work force skills, and better infrastructure.

Joint ventures between foreign and domestic entrepreneurs are often suggested as a way of reaping the benefits of FDI while increasing the transfer of managerial and technical skills to local entrepreneurs. Joint ventures and other new forms of FDI have indeed been growing in importance in Africa.[9] In Nigeria, for example, income linked to such new forms of FDI accounted for 40 percent of total investment income paid overseas from 1976 to 1986.[10] But there is evidence that joint ventures have not fulfilled the hopes of the optimists. Almost none of the Kenyan joint ventures were viable in 1989. But if joint ventures clearly fall short of accomplishing "technology transfer without tears," there is some evidence that nominal domestic control (through ownership of capital) does slowly bring about indigenization of directorships and management, leading to much greater local control over decision making than occurs with undiluted FDI, without any obvious costs in terms of efficiency. There is no evidence that joint ventures perform any better than the wholly owned subsidiaries of multinational corporations in terms of technology choice or efficiency; but neither is there any evidence that they perform any worse.

Success in industrialization appears to vary with the size of the enterprise. Whereas there have been few examples of successful industrial development among large-scale enterprises in the formal sector, whether publicly or privately owned, the microenterprise sector appears to have been relatively successful.[11] According to a review of evidence presented by Carl Liedholm of the University of Michigan, small firms in Africa accounted for 60 percent or more of total industrial employment, and in Sierra Leone their share was 95 percent. The share of industrial value added of firms with fewer than 10 workers ranged from 26 to 64 percent across the countries of Africa. The vast majority of these firms are very small, employing five workers or fewer. All evaluations of their efficiency suggest that small enterprises in Africa exhibit social cost-benefit ratios that easily exceed unity and are invariably higher than those of formal-sector firms.[12] Unfortunately, much of their activity remains confined to local markets, operating at low levels of technology and with relatively little graduation to modern industrial methods or to export-oriented activity.

Despite some successes, therefore, the overall assessment of past industrialization in Africa must be negative. Why has Africa's record been so much poorer than that of other developing regions? The answers to this question are important, because the success of future remedies requires an accurate diagnosis of past deficiencies. In broad terms, four types of explanation have been advanced:

■ *Wrong incentives.* The inward-oriented, heavily protectionist trade policies, widespread state ownership, and interventionist industrial policies adopted by the African countries provide poor incentives for firms to become more efficient. As noted above, this is the dominant explanation in conventional economic analysis and informs much of the current policy reform effort, and in particular the World Bank's structural adjustment policies.

■ *External shocks.* Adverse external factors beyond the control of the African countries themselves, especially deteriorating terms of trade and a worsening debt situation, have caused an import "drought," which has starved industry of essential inputs and brought industrial development to a halt. This is the explanation favored by many African governments.

- *Structural deficiencies.* Weak industrial capabilities and deficient institutions frustrate the efforts of African enterprises to become efficient in modern industrial activity. This is the explanation advanced by "structuralist" economists and the one advanced here.
- *Bias against small enterprise.* Macro- and microeconomic policies are biased against the efficient indigenous small-scale sector, and this bias encompasses both incentives and institutions.[13] With appropriate policies, this sector could account for a much larger share of output and provide a breeding ground for efficient medium-sized firms, owned and controlled locally.

These explanations are not mutually exclusive, and indeed there is some truth to all four, but analysts differ as to which deserve the most emphasis. Under the currently dominant paradigm the first explanation—distorted incentives caused by government intervention in what ought to be free markets—is the most influential. Whether adopted willingly by governments or imposed on them, structural adjustment programs, as conceived and implemented by the World Bank, now constitute the dominant policy response to past failures of industrial performance, and economic performance more broadly, in Africa. In the next section we look at the assumptions of that strategy and its results.

THE RECORD OF STRUCTURAL ADJUSTMENT

Structural adjustment policies toward industry have their theoretical basis in the neoclassical competitive model and in Heckscher-Ohlin theories of trade. Countries, according to these models, should produce and export those goods and services in which they have comparative advantage; which goods and services those turn out to be depends on which factors of production a country has in abundance. The unregulated price mechanism is the best way of ensuring that this outcome prevails; world prices provide the competitive benchmark, and if agents within an economy are free to respond to world prices, taking into account the costs they face within the economy, then this optimum should be realized. Structural adjustment policies therefore recommend eliminating all distortions that prevent the realization of this competitive solution.

These distortions may emanate from trade or industrial policies or both. On the trade side, overvalued currencies, import quotas, and tariffs protect domestic industry from international competition; the lack of competition in turn leads to inefficiency. Resources are allocated to activities where they are not put to best use, and managers and workers lack the incentive to perform at peak capacity. Interventionist industrial policies—including price regulation, directed investment and credit programs, taxes, and subsidies—can have much the same effect. To achieve the competitive optimum envisioned by the model, therefore, both trade protection and domestic regulation of industry must be dismantled. In the words of a major World Bank study of Africa, it is a matter of "unleashing markets so that competition can help improve the allocation of resources . . . getting price signals right and creating a climate that allows businesses to respond to those signals in ways that increase the returns to investment."[14]

The structural adjustment model admits the possibility of market failure only in the provision of infrastructure and education, and indeed here the World Bank acknowledges the case for government intervention. In these areas, however, the Bank recommends functional or "market-friendly" interventions that do not discriminate between activities.[15] Interventions that favor some activities over others—for example, industry over agriculture, or the steel industry over textiles—are considered to distort efficient resource allocation. As a rule, no case is admitted for infant-industry protection or for other forms of selective intervention. And even in the few instances where it is agreed that failure in a particular market may call for selectivity in theory, it is argued that in practice governments cannot intervene efficiently—that the costs of government failure will exceed those of market failure.[16]

The "ideal" form of structural adjustment that will lead to healthy industrial growth follows from these assumptions. To simplify, this takes the form of three prescriptions:

■ Remove all forms of selective intervention and restore free-market-driven resource allocation (often referred to as "getting prices right"). In the trade arena, expose industrial activities to international competition, as a precondition for other adjustment measures. Allow free entry to foreign private investment, and exercise as little discretion as possible in international investment flows. In the domestic arena, promote unhindered market entry and exit, unrestricted ownership, and flexible labor markets; privatize public enterprises wherever possible, and restructure ("commercialize") them where not.

■ Carry out reforms quickly and across the board, since there is no economic justification for continuing to differentiate between activities. No "strategy" is needed to guide the restructuring or upgrading process at the level of the industry or the firm, since markets will give the correct signals on their own.

■ Implement measures to improve human capital and infrastructure, but do not link the pace of reform to this, since these will take much longer, and in any case factor markets will respond better if the overall price signals are correct.

All of these prescriptions rest on neoclassical (Heckscher-Ohlin) models, which in turn rest on a set of assumptions about the nature of the world economy and of national economies within it. The models assume perfect competition and the absence of significant economies of scale; instantaneous and costless access (including an absence of learning costs) to the same technology throughout the world; perfect information and no risk or uncertainty; "neutral" and exogenous changes in technology over time (that is, that technological progress does not favor one factor of production, like capital, over another, like labor, and its creation occurs outside the economic system); and identical preferences across countries. More recent trade theory has challenged these assumptions, which are clearly not an accurate representation of modern industry. Some of the models' assumptions are particularly inappropriate as a description of African economies.

A first problem with the Heckscher-Ohlin model is that modern industry is characterized by certain indivisibilities—large minimum investments necessary to get production up and running—which give rise to the very economies of scale that Heckscher-Ohlin assumes away. These indivisibilities are such that, in many industries, only a few (or one, or no) firms can produce efficiently in a market limited to a single small African economy. This observation has two consequences: First, it means that firms already established elsewhere in the world generally have a strong competitive advantage over African newcomers; and second, if an African firm succeeds nonetheless in establishing itself, the resulting market will not be a monopoly or an oligopoly.

Even more damaging to the theory's application to African reality are the assumptions of perfect information, instant, cost-free access to technology, and especially the absence of learning costs. The theory assumes that a technology will be equally productive wherever it is adopted; the only differences between locations involve the availability and cost of other factors. This is patently untrue. The capability to adopt and use a technology efficiently varies hugely, and a lack of such capability initially explains countries' inability to industrialize efficiently without protection—a point we will develop further below.

Finally, the assumptions of neutral technological change and identical preferences are also incorrect: Technological advances are largely dominated by the industrialized countries, and this fact conditions the direction of that change, which has tended to be toward ever more capital-intensive processes and ever more sophisticated products. Technologies suitable to small-scale producers, producing goods demanded by low-income consumers, are largely neglected.

In a widely quoted recent book, economist Adrian Wood has stressed the need to differentiate among labor force participants according to their levels of education and skills. In his view those without basic education (primary and secondary) will not be able to operate modern technology efficiently, so that the static comparative advantage of countries where the average educational attainment is relatively low may lie in raw material production rather than manufactures. This, broadly speaking, is the situation in Africa as compared with Asia and helps explain why free trade may lead to limited industrialization in Africa.[17]

More realistic assumptions about the nature of the economy, of technologies, and of learning have important implications for policy choices. First, it is essential to recognize the initial disadvantages of being a latecomer to industrialization. These disadvantages, which result from the presence of learning and scale economies, imply that some protection or subsidization of industry in its early phases may be essential. Where strong "learning" costs and scale economies exist, competitive solutions may simply prevent the activity from developing at all and might cause deindustrialization if protection were replaced by full, sudden exposure to global competition. Second, it is necessary to explore very carefully the policies needed to build up a competitive industrial sector, including complementary expenditures (that is, developing the supply side—skills, information, credit, infrastructure) and policies toward learning. These will be considered below. Third, the existence of economies of scale may handicap small economies and make import substitution a necessarily inefficient policy. Hence the need to combine policies of protection with policies that permit the exploitation of economies of scale and division of labor: This means either lowering barriers to trade among similar economies within a given region (while maintaining or perhaps raising them against richer, more industrialized competitors) or subsidizing exports in the early phase of industrial development. Fourth, there needs to be an active technology policy (e.g., technical extension, standards and metrology,[18] research and development, targeting foreign direct investment) aimed at helping develop and improve technologies that small-scale producers can put to use. This too could best be pursued on a regional basis.

Recent research on technological learning in developing countries suggests that industrialization is far more complex and varied than the neoclassical model assumes.[19] Becoming efficient in industry can be a slow, risky, costly, and prolonged process, beset by a range of market failures that call for interventions in both factor and product markets—for example, missing information markets, asymmetric information, externalities, technical linkages, unpredictable learning sequences, deficient capital markets, and absence of supporting institutions and skills. Often the learning process itself has to be learned: New firms in developing countries typically do not know what their deficiencies are, how to go about remedying them, or what the costs and duration of their efforts at self-improvement are likely to be. The process involves many externalities and generally calls for interactions with other firms and institutions. To create and reinforce these linkages, which are of multiple types, may require the intervention of government-supported institutions.

These insights lead to policies very different from those embodied in existing structural adjustment programs. They suggest that the rapid and sweeping liberalization recommended by the World Bank will not by itself "release the latent energies" of African economies and allow resources to move relatively costlessly from inefficient to efficient competitive activities. An effective supply response to rapid liberalization can only come from activities that already have established a competitive edge in world markets—either import-substituting activities in which firms have already mastered the requisite capabilities, or resource-based activities with a sufficient cost advantage that learning becomes of secondary importance. There exist a large number of other activities that are not now competitive but could become so given the time and resources to engage in further learning. These would simply be wiped out by rapid exposure to world competition, wasting the capabilities they have already built up and the physical investments they have already made. New ventures, involving more complex technologies, which could form the basis of industrial development and export diversification, might not be undertaken by a too-abrupt liberalization that makes no allowance for difficulties, costs, risks, and delays in the learning process.

However, protection by itself will not lead to efficiency if it leads to "infant" industries that never mature or if there are failures in factor markets. The adverse effects of protection on incentives for investing in learning have to be offset by other measures to stimulate competition, such as early entry into export markets. It is necessary to combine protection with policies to build up deficient factor markets and their associated institutions (this issue is considered further below). In particular, there needs to be an active technology policy to help develop and improve technologies suitable for small-scale producers producing appropriate technologies; these too could best be pursued on a regional basis.

ADJUSTMENT AND INDUSTRIAL PERFORMANCE IN AFRICA

It is not easy to identify the effects of adjustment on industrial performance. Structural adjustment programs differ greatly over time and between countries in their design, content, and implementation, depending on the bargaining power and conviction of the governments concerned and on exogenous events and political expediency.[20] Isolating the impact of adjustment from that of other factors affecting the economy at the same time raises numerous problems of method. One particularly vexing question is whether to include macroeconomic stabilization in one's definition of "adjustment." Although this may be appropriate for certain purposes, it does not reveal the specific impact of liberalization on industrial performance.[21]

These methodological problems have not prevented the World Bank from issuing a strong endorsement of its structural adjustment policies, the centerpiece of its policy reform. Its recent study, *Adjustment in Africa,* begins by asserting, "In the African countries that have undertaken and sustained major policy reform, adjustment is working," and goes on to note a particularly strong response to adjustment in the areas of industrial production and exports.[22] Since these conclusions are at variance with the aggregate figures cited earlier in this paper, and with many other assessments that find the responses of most African countries to structural adjustment programs to be weak and faltering,[23] particularly in manufacturing and export performance, it is worth examining the study's findings in greater depth.

Adjustment in Africa examines a sample of 29 countries in Sub-Saharan Africa that have undergone adjustment. At the time of the study many of these adjusting countries had not fully implemented the recommended reforms, so the study divides them into three groups: six with "large improvements" in macroeconomic policies, nine with "small improvements," and eleven that have experienced "deterioration" (the remaining three countries are unclassified). The impact of structural adjustment programs is assessed by comparing changes in growth performance in various sectors, with reference to these categories, between a pre- and a post-adjustment period (1981–86 and 1987–1991, respectively).

Measured in this way, the effect of structural adjustment policies on manufacturing emerges as positive: Countries with the greatest improvements in policies (that is, those that have undertaken the most adjustment) enjoyed the greatest median improvement in manufacturing performance, and those with the least, the least (Table 1). However,

TABLE 1. GROWTH IN MANUFACTURING VALUE ADDED AMONG AFRICAN COUNTRIES PURSUING DIFFERENT POLICIES, WORLD BANK FINDINGS FOR 1981–1991
(percent per year)

Country Group	Median Growth Rate 1981–1986	Median Growth Rate 1987–1991	Difference Between 1981–1986 and 1987–1991
Countries with Large Improvements in Policy	−0.3	4.4	5.8
Countries with Small Improvements in Policy	4.2	5.6	1.2
Countries with Deterioration of Policy	5.0	5.8	1.1
All Countries	3.0	5.5	1.9

Source: World Bank, *Adjustment in Africa: Reforms, Results, and the Road Ahead* (New York: Oxford University Press, 1994).

both the calculations and the conclusions drawn therefrom are subject to several criticisms:

- First, the groupings of countries according to improvement or deterioration in policy have little or nothing to do with structural adjustment. They are based entirely on changes in macroeconomic policy and not on adjustment in the sense of "getting prices right." The study provides no way of tracing the real effects of structural adjustment as distinguished from macroeconomic stabilization, since the groupings indicate nothing about which countries have implemented liberalization.
- Second, medians for groups have no statistical significance if individual variation within groups is greater than the variation between them. A statistical test on the data provided in the Bank study shows that *none* of the differences in growth rates between groups, or for the same group between the two periods, is significant. The one exception is the "deteriorating" group, which had a significantly higher average growth rate in the first than in the second period.

We recalculated various aspects of industrial performance in Africa using more recent data. The coverage was also extended to a total of 45 countries, including 16 that had not undergone adjustment (the full list of countries appears in the appendix to this paper). The grouping of adjusting countries according to improvement or deterioration of policies was, in the absence of other indicators of adjustment, based on the World Bank study. All the countries with "improved" policies were grouped together (and are referred to here as the "policy-improving countries"), since the differences between the Bank's subgroups registering large and small improvements were not found to be statistically meaningful. The periods used were also slightly different. We examined a longer overall period, 1980–1993, and we used 1990–93 as the later subperiod to capture the more recent effects of policy reforms. We report here the effects of adjustment on overall GDP growth, growth in manufacturing, and growth in exports.

The highest rate of GDP growth in both periods was achieved by the adjusting countries with improved macroeconomic policies. Over 1980–1993 and 1990–93, respectively, the policy-improving countries had weighted-average annual GDP growth rates of 2.7 and 3.4 percent, compared with 1.3 and 0.6 percent for the policy-deteriorating countries and 2.0 and 0.2 percent for the nonadjusting countries. The policy-deteriorating countries recorded the poorest GDP growth for the 1980–1993 period and the nonadjusting countries for the 1990–93 period. This provides *prima facie* evidence that macroeconomic policy improvement helped economic growth. However, there is no statistically significant difference between any of the group growth rates. Thus the differences in group performance are likely to have been caused by factors other than the macroeconomic policy differences that differentiate them.

Growth in manufacturing value added shows a slightly different trend, with the relative performance of the policy-improving countries showing a more marked improvement in the postadjustment period (Table 2). Both the nonimproving groups recorded more rapid growth in manufacturing value added over the period as a whole than in 1990–93, but the policy-deteriorating countries suffered an actual decline in manufacturing in the latter period while the nonadjusters maintained positive rates. In contrast, the policy-improving countries raised their manufacturing growth rates in the 1990s. A statistical significance test shows that this growth in the policy-improving countries was signifi-

TABLE 2. GROWTH IN MANUFACTURING VALUE ADDED AMONG AFRICAN COUNTRIES PURSUING DIFFERENT POLICIES, AUTHORS' UPDATES FOR 1980–1993
(percent per year)

Country Group	Average Growth Rate 1980–1993	Average Growth Rate 1990–1993
Policy-Improving Countries	2.70	4.41
Policy-Deteriorating Countries	1.64	−1.67
Nonadjusting Countries	2.12	0.05

Source: Authors' calculations.

cantly higher than in the policy-deteriorating countries in 1990–93. None of the other differences between groups are statistically significant.

There appears, therefore, to be a statistically sound reason to concur with the World Bank's finding that industry fared better in those countries that achieved policy improvements than in those where policy deteriorated. But again, this proves nothing about the impact of structural adjustment programs on industry, since the groupings reflect differences in macroeconomic management only. And, of course, the finding of statistical significance does not establish causation, since a number of other possibly important influences on manufacturing growth are not taken into consideration.

To examine more closely whether it is liberalization as such that is associated with good performance, it is useful to remove the veil of statistical aggregation and see precisely which of the main policy-improving countries actually experienced high rates of growth in manufacturing value added in 1990–93. Of the 15 countries in this group, only five—Burundi, Kenya, Mauritania, Nigeria, and Uganda—had annual increases in manufacturing value added of around 4 percent or more. Of these, Nigeria and Kenya dominate the group, accounting for 75 percent of the total manufacturing value added of all the policy-improving countries. Interestingly, neither of these countries is considered by the World Bank to have implemented import liberalization properly: Both reversed their trade reforms while their industrial sectors still enjoyed significant tariff protection. If they are excluded from the group total, the rate of growth in manufacturing value added for this group in 1990–93 falls to around 0.1 percent per year—in other words, virtual stagnation, and not significantly different from the performance of the nonadjusting countries. Thus, there are scant grounds for arguing that it was liberalization that led to improved manufacturing growth in this group of countries.

The value of manufactured exports of all the countries of Sub-Saharan Africa totaled to only $2.2 billion in 1992. The policy-improving countries accounted for $1.2 billion of this total, the policy-deteriorating countries for $1 billion, and the nonadjusters for only $46 million. The rates of growth for each group's exports for 1980–1992 and 1988–1992 are shown in Table 3; the period covered differs from that used in the previous calculations because of data availability.[24] The table shows that both the policy-improving and the policy-deteriorating groups improved their manufactured export performance in the later period. The best performers for the period as a whole, however, were the policy-deteriorating group, not the ones with better macromanagement, though the difference between them (10.03 and 9.35 percent, respectively) is quite small. The nonadjusting countries performed much worse than the others, and

TABLE 3. GROWTH IN MANUFACTURED EXPORTS AMONG AFRICAN COUNTRIES PURSUING DIFFERENT POLICIES, AUTHORS' UPDATES FOR 1980–1992
(percent per year)

	Median Growth Rate	
Country Group	1980–1992	1990–1992
Policy-Improving Countries	2.75	9.35
Policy-Deteriorating Countries	4.66	10.03
Nonadjusting Countries	−8.25	−15.77

Source: Authors' calculations.

their performance worsened over time. The only statistically significant group differences are those between the nonadjusting countries and the two groups of adjusting countries in the 1990s (but not for the period as a whole).

Can we infer that even mild forms of adjustment helped African exporters of manufactures (e.g., through devaluation and better access to imported inputs)? This is difficult to argue when the best performers are the countries that had worse macroeconomic policies than before. Since the policy-deteriorating countries maintained higher growth rates over the whole period, this seems to suggest that factors other than stabilization were at work in affecting export performance. The available data do not allow us to analyze what these were. More important for present purposes, the data do not allow us even to guess at the impact of import liberalization on growth of manufacture exports. What is evident, however, is that the manufactured exports of African countries remain very low. In 1992, the share of manufactures in total exports was 11 percent for the policy-improving countries, 16 percent for the policy-deteriorating countries, and only 2 percent for the nonadjusters. Although the growth rates for the adjusting countries appear healthy for 1988–1992, the base is very small, and it remains to be seen whether these rates will be sustained.

In sum, no general conclusions can yet be reached about the effects of adjustment on GDP or industrial growth, export performance, or competitiveness. Even the effect of stabilization on industrial performance is ambiguous: This is not to deny that good macroeconomic policies are desirable in Africa, but to suggest that causal inferences must be drawn with much more care. Clearly there are many missing factors at work, and it is not at all apparent what effect adjustment may have had on those.

THE RECORD OF ADJUSTMENT IN GHANA

A better way to analyze the impact of structural adjustment in Africa may be to look in detail at the experience of one African country that has undergone substantial reform of its trade and industrial regime. Ghana has the longest history of consistent adjustment in Sub-Saharan Africa (some other countries began adjustment programs earlier but did not fully implement them). In the World Bank's own assessment, Ghana is the African country that has advanced the furthest toward eliminating protection (and especially non-tariff-based protection) and moving toward free trade.[25]

The reforms undertaken by Ghana are impressive: A massive depreciation of the cedi from 2.75 to the dollar in 1982 to 920 to the dollar in early 1994; the removal of all quantitative restrictions on imports and the lowering of tariffs to a relatively uniform 10 to 25 percent range (and only luxury products are subject to tariffs at the high end); a reduction of corporate taxes (to 35 percent) and of the capital gains tax (to 5 percent); the removal of price controls and subsidies; the abolition of credit ceilings and guidelines; the privatization of state-owned enterprises; a revision of the foreign investment code; and the granting of incentives to exporters and to private investors in infrastructure.[26] By the start of the 1990s Ghana had a relatively stable, open, and liberal economy in place, and was often referred to as a "model adjuster" in Africa. It should therefore provide an ideal test case for assessing the impact of liberalization on industrial and export performance.

Ghana launched its policy reform with its 1983 Economic Recovery Program. In the initial stages, as far as manufacturing was concerned, this involved freeing up the allocation of foreign exchange for the acquisition of intermediate inputs and spare parts. Ghanaian industry faced no direct import competition at this stage. The first World Bank structural adjustment program started in 1986 and was followed by two others up to 1991. It was during this five-year period that the process of liberalization and market orientation was launched. There was a substantial increase in net inflows of capital from foreign sources (mostly in the form of aid), from $196 million in 1985 to an average of $878 million per year over 1989–1992.[27] This made it possible to finance imports and revive domestic demand.

What was the response of the industrial sector? Data from the Bank study seem to show the predicted positive response: Growth in manufacturing, which had been negative in the first half of the 1980s, rose to an average of 4.5 percent per year over 1987–1991. However, such averages are misleading. Manufacturing value added did rise rapidly after 1983, when imported inputs were made available to existing industries that were suffering substantial excess capacity: The rate of growth was 12.9 percent in 1984, 24.3 percent in 1985, 11.0 percent in 1986, and 10.0 percent in 1987. However, as liberalization spread to other imports and excess capacity was used up, exposure to world competition led to a steady deceleration of industrial growth. Growth in manufacturing value added fell to 5.1 percent in 1988, 5.6 percent in 1989, 1.1 percent in 1990, 2.6 percent in 1991, and 1.1 percent in 1992. Growth has thus followed an inverted U-shaped path, with a long taper in recent years—hardly a manufacturing sector in dynamic takeoff.

Employment in manufacturing fell from a peak of 78,700 in 1987 to 28,000 in 1993.[28] There was a rise in the number of small enterprises, but this was mainly in low-productivity activities aimed at local markets, sheltered from international competition. Foreign investment did not respond to the adjustment, and there was no increase in annual inflows after the structural adjustment programs ended. Moreover, the little investment that came concentrated on raw materials production rather than on manufacturing. Domestic private investment did not pick up sufficiently to lead to a surge of manufacturing growth.

At the same time, large swathes of the manufacturing sector were devastated by import competition. The long period of import-substituting industrialization in Ghana, led by state-owned enterprises, had left a legacy of inefficiency and technological backwardness. It also left some technological capabilities, but none that rapid liberalization could stimulate to reach world levels in a short period and with relatively low investment. The adverse impact of liberalization was strongest in the more modern, large-scale part of the industrial sector, which had the most complex technologies and so suffered most from the lack of technological capabilities. Industrial survivors and new entrants are for the most part in activities that have "natural" protection from imports: These are very small scale enterprises, making products for low-income consumers or for local markets, and larger enterprises protected by high transport costs or based on processing of local raw materials. Apart from aluminum processing—a well-established, foreign-owned enclave operation—and a few still-protected activities like government-owned petroleum refining, these include some food processing, furniture, cement, simple metal products, and production of uniforms for the army and schools.

As for manufactured exports, the expectation was that they would grow and diversify rapidly under the new incentive regime and absorb resources released from inefficient import-substituting activities. The data show that although manufactured exports have indeed grown since 1986, their value remains extremely small, totaling $14.7 million in 1991. There has been little sign of a broad-based response on the part of Ghanaian manufacturing enterprises, particularly in their main potential area of comparative advantage, cheap labor. Growth has come mainly from wood and aluminum products, both of which are long-established export sectors, and from firms already established in export markets, rather than from new products or producers.

Labor-intensive exports such as garments, footwear, toys, and other light consumer goods, which led the initial export thrust of the Asian newly industrializing economies, are conspicuous by their absence in Ghana. Such low-technology, "entry-level" activities, in which Ghana should be developing a competitive edge, have been unable to survive the import threat. The ability to compete internationally even in "simple" labor-intensive industries requires a level of productivity and of managerial and technical skill that is presently lacking in Ghana. The few relatively well-managed firms that exist are largely foreign owned; among local enterprises, the better ones are run by entrepreneurs that are well educated. The typical local firm, on the other hand, is managed by entrepreneurs with little education, has a poorly skilled work force, and lacks the means to raise their technological capabilities. Most lack the ability even to perceive and define their technological problems.[29]

The experience of Ghana illustrates clearly the more general dilemma of policy reform and industrial adjustment in Africa: An initially favorable response of manufacturing to adjustment may not lead to sustained growth and diversification if all structural adjustment programs do is "get prices right." Pervasive market failure raises the costs of adjustment to import competition and holds back the creation of new manufacturing activities and exports in response to the new incentives. The design of structural adjustment programs, by ignoring the enormous impediments to the development of new capabilities, places too much store by free markets that work rapidly and effectively.

Is Ghana an economically weak outlier whose experience has little relevance beyond its borders? It would appear not. Ghana is by African standards a fairly well-endowed and promising economy: It has a relatively good stock of human capital, and its favorable location, resource base, and infrastructure would place it in the top quarter of African economies. It has implemented a difficult program of stabilization and liberalization with admirable consistency, and over a longer period than any other African country. Its experience is likely to illustrate most clearly the response of the African industrial sector to adjustment.

POLICY IMPLICATIONS

What policy implications follow from this empirical and theoretical analysis of structural adjustment in Africa? Let us start with areas of agreement. Policy reform is necessary in Africa. Macroeconomic stabilization is a precondition for sustained development (the way in which it is achieved may be debatable, but this paper is not directly concerned with that issue). Old-fashioned import-substituting policies, which assigned a dominant role to an inefficient public sector, have proved inefficient not just in Africa but in the rest of the developing world, and they must be replaced by more outward-looking and competitive trade and industrial policies. At the same time, reform of the incentive regime must be integrated with interventions to improve factor markets.

Beyond these broad areas of agreement, however, controversy remains over the pace and content of the reform process. In particular, there is disagreement about the efficiency of factor and product markets and the role of public intervention in remedying market failures.

The satisfactory development of industry in Africa has two essential components. First, industrialization must be efficient, so that resources are not wasted and the sector eventually becomes a significant source of exports. Second, the capabilities of African firms and their work forces must be built up so that Africans rather than foreigners increasingly perform the major functions—managerial and technical. Foreign management and technical support should play a supporting but not a dominant role, not only for political reasons but for economic ones as well: Until indigenous African economic capabilities become strong, the choices of industry and in particular choices about technology and its adaptation suited to African conditions will not be made efficiently. Of course, building the skills that are the base of a country's industrial capabilities is a long and slow process. African countries have invested relatively large sums in education, but enrollments at all the higher levels of education remain well below levels reached in other developing regions. The quality and relevance of African education also generally lags other developing regions, and the ranks of technically qualified people who can undertake the efficient operation of industry remain thin.

It is difficult to devise policies that are likely to simultaneously increase efficiency and permit the buildup of African capabilities, because the means best suited to achieving these two objectives may be in conflict: Efficiency calls for strong external competitive pressures, whereas the nurturing of capabilities may require protection from those pressures, at least for a time. Protection of the enterprise provides a cushion for in-firm "learning" and skill acquisition. This has to be supported by factor market policies like education. But education and training cannot substitute for enterprise-specific investments in capability acquisition, thus the need for coordinated interventions in product and factor markets. The policies of the 1960s and 1970s emphasized protection of African industry but placed little emphasis on efficiency. The adjustment policies of the 1980s swung to the other extreme, focusing almost exclusively on efficiency and paying no attention to building capability, thus effectively killing the goose that could have laid the egg of efficient African industrialization.

For the future, then, it is necessary to chart a delicate course between these two extremes. There is no definitive guide on how to do so, although the experience of Taiwan, the Republic of Korea, and, in the African context, Mauritius provides some pointers. These countries first built up strong human capabilities through heavy investment in education; they protected import-substituting industrialization for a period (although not a prolonged one), and once industrial capability was established they changed the incentive system to favor manufacture of exports based on simple and labor-intensive technologies (mainly textiles and garments). They did not abandon protection of domestic industry, but instead provided incentives for efficiency through domestic competition and government pressure on firms, including, after a period of protection, pressure to enter export markets and thus face international competition. Efficiency was promoted through realistic exchange rates, fairly low levels of protection (except in some cases like automobiles), relatively low but steadily rising wage rates, and government supervision, while competitive pressures were exerted through domestic and international competition.[30]

The dual objectives of developing efficient industrialization and building up African capabilities suggest several policy conclusions, which are outlined below.

Ownership Patterns: Developing African Capacity

Policies toward ownership of African industry raise some difficult issues. On the one hand, the public sector, which has a dominant position in large-scale industry in a number of countries, has been a significant source of inefficiency, as already noted. But neither the local private sector nor FDI offers a simple, viable alternative to state ownership. The indigenous private sector for the most part lacks the resources and the skills to take over public industries (except in Nigeria, where there appears to be an impressive degree of local private entrepreneurship extending to medium-sized and large-scale enterprises).[31] In

Zimbabwe a large-enterprise sector exists but is dominated by whites, and in Côte d'Ivoire expatriate ownership and management is prevalent. The weakness of the medium- to large-scale indigenous private sector presents a major problem for privatization, both from a political and from an economic perspective.

This weakness might conceivably be overcome by foreign investment. FDI could become an important input in the upgrading of African industrial competitiveness, especially in export-oriented activities. Foreign investors are better able than local firms to overcome many of the market failures that now thwart industrial development, for the obvious reason that they have large internal markets within the firm for the capital, skills, information, and technologies needed. Yet Africa has so far remained marginal to the rapidly increasing flows of foreign investment to the developing world. Multinational companies are not prepared to invest in upgrading local industries when skills and capabilities are low, and the growth of globalization means that foreign investors are increasingly sensitive to differences in investment regimes, political climates, infrastructure, and taxes. It is evident that it is not just the "rules of the game" or the lack of fiscal incentives that are deterring foreign investors from Africa, but the general lack of competitive inputs and infrastructure in a liberalized climate where operations have to face severe import competition. In this setting, given that high and prolonged protection cannot and should not be used as a significant incentive for FDI, it is necessary to improve the "supply-side" factors if Africa is to benefit from the technological and other inputs that foreign investors can offer. Special incentives for FDI, such as tax relief, are justified only where FDI is likely to play a key role in promoting exports.

The minimal privatization achieved in Malawi and Zimbabwe suggests that there are severe political and economic obstacles to privatization, which will for the time being prevent it from being of more than minor significance.[32] Hence there is a need to focus on improving the efficiency of state enterprises, something that has tended to be neglected as policymakers concentrate on privatization. One possible approach is to promote joint ventures between the public sector and foreign (or local) private enterprises; such arrangements could help public enterprises become more efficient by bringing in foreign finance, technology, and management techniques. But they will succeed only if governments treat publicly owned firms (whether participating in joint ventures or not) in a much more arm's-length manner than has been the custom: Publicly owned firms should be expected to borrow on the same terms as other enterprises, should not get favorable tax or tariff treatment, should be subject to internal and external competition, and should be permitted to go bankrupt if they are no longer viable. Any subsidization should be explicit, limited, and clearly justified by reference to the public goods the enterprise provides. Given that building African capabilities is a primary objective, new forms of foreign investment such as joint ventures may offer a better vehicle for the transfer of technology and management skills than FDI.

Structured Markets

A wide range of policies typically discriminate heavily against the small business sector; this is invariably true of systems of administered credit and other controls, which favor larger enterprises.[33] However, the removal of administrative controls is not in itself sufficient to remove the bias against small business: Small enterprises remain at a disadvantage even after liberalization, because they lack the collateral to borrow from commercial banks and have inadequate resources to bid for foreign exchange. In Zambia, for example, a foreign exchange auction led to virtually all foreign exchange being allocated to large firms.[34]

Structured markets are needed: This means reserving a proportion of resources—credit, foreign exchange, and so on—for the small business sector, thus ensuring that a "market" solution generates adequate resources for the sector. For example, the Indian government was able to secure resources for the small business sector by requiring that the major banks allocate at least 1 percent of credit to small businesses. This led (among other things) to the establishment of the Self-Employed Women's Association. Similar provisions have recently been introduced in Indonesia. The other Asian newly industrializing economies have implemented measures to ensure that linkages to their small- and medium-sized enterprises were intensified, and that sufficient credit, technical assistance, and training were provided and access to international markets was made available.

In the past, efforts to support small enterprises in Africa have been largely confined to developing industrial estates and providing services and (subsidized) credit to a small number of such enterprises, leaving the vast majority to fend for themselves without any formal-sector credit, and with tariffs, markets, the pattern of infrastructure, and most government services biased against them. Much broader-based interventions are needed; this is partly a matter of systematically eliminating biases against the sector, and partly of promoting technology and credit institutions designed to serve small business. Imposing aggregate requirements for resource allocation to the small business sector facilitates the development of appropriate institutional structures without the need for detailed intervention, and without resort to subsidies, which are generally neither needed nor desirable and indeed have been rather ineffective. In the past, credit allocation by many African governments has not worked effectively, because it was used to generate and transfer rents rather than to create efficient enterprises. Any direction of resources therefore has to be accompanied by measures to increase competitive efficiency and to improve the supply of complementary factors such as skills, technology, marketing, and other assistance.

The success of some African governments—Kenya and Zimbabwe, for example—in reaching small-scale agricultural producers with technology, credit, and infrastructure indicates the potential for effective small enterprise policies. However, the technical extension services for small business that exist in much of Africa are largely ineffective, as are the available means to provide research support for industry. It is always difficult to remedy the information and technical market failures that affect small enterprises, but the experience of East Asia shows that strong efforts by the government can help with the most costly ones. The example of Taiwan, the newly industrializing Asian economy with the largest number of efficient and export-oriented small enterprises, is instructive here. Taiwan's industrial structure is dominated by small- and medium-sized firms, and government programs to promote subcontracting and technological development have been of special significance for industrial development.[35]

Incentive Reform

This paper's analysis of the development of industrial capability suggests that a gradual and controlled process of opening up, accompanied by a strategy of industrial restructuring and upgrading, is to be preferred to the rapid and sweeping exposure to market forces envisaged by the "ideal" structural adjustment program. The speed of liberalization should be based on a realistic assessment of which activities are viable in the medium term and geared to the learning and "relearning" needs of various activities. The strategy should be developed in collaboration with industry and should be preannounced so that enterprises have time to adjust.[36] Once announced, however, it is imperative to stick to the program so that there is no chance of backsliding and allowing inefficient performers to survive indefinitely. Kenya's preannounced liberalization was repeatedly diluted and negated, reducing the credibility of such gradual measures and removing the incentive for industrial enterprises to invest in the difficult and expensive process of capability development.

In implementing liberalization, the government should retain the power to guide resource allocation, but should do so in a clear and transparent manner and with strict requirements on industry to develop competitive capabilities. Unlike earlier strategies of import substitution, in which governments offered protection with little discrimination between activities, no time limit, and no requirement on firms to be efficient by international standards, this model of adjustment, based on strategies pursued in East Asia, places strong pressure on industries to invest in building new capabilities to face import and export competition, and to do so within a limited period. It is designed to overcome market failures, not to ignore them. It involves close monitoring of the progress of liberalization, and it requires that the government be able to address the supply-side needs of industries (see below) as it phases in liberalization.

It must be emphasized that to recommend a more gradual and nuanced strategy of liberalization is *not* to suggest that African countries simply reverse the adjustment process or postpone it indefinitely. What is needed is not to put off adjustment, but to prepare for it *actively* in the grace period provided by gradual rather than sudden liberalization. (Of course, whether external factors and aid donors allow such a grace period to the governments themselves is another matter—clearly some governments have more slack than others.) An important concern, however, is the strong risk of government failure. Many African governments are deficient in the capabilities needed to mount pervasive interventions in support of industrialization.

It is not recommended that African governments attempt the kind of detailed and pervasive interventions practiced in a country like Korea. Such a strategy imposes tremendous demands on the government and runs very high risks of hijacking and abuse. Fortunately, governments do not have to pick winners from among individual technologies, products, or firms: Taiwan has demonstrated that it is possible to intervene at a more general level. But whatever the level of the country's industrial development, there is a need for selectivity to reach the next level; simply "leaving it to the market" can achieve very little when there are pervasive market failures. It must be remembered that if the government is unable to provide any of the "supply-side" measures that industry needs to progress to the next level, the absence of interventions will not help development—weak governments may not do better by not intervening if they fail to provide the basic ingredients of industrialization.

It is evident that the launching pad for any reform must be improvements in governments' own capabilities. It goes beyond the scope of this paper to discuss this matter in detail, but evidence suggests that such capabilities can be improved by training, reorganization of the civil service, better performance incentives and monitoring, and greater insulation from the political process.[37] Unless these capabilities are developed, no strategy, including the "market-friendly" strategy that forms part of a structural adjustment program, has much chance of success. Until such capabilities are developed, governments should intervene with little selectivity. Our state of knowledge remains minimal about what level of capability on the part of a government permits what level of selectivity of intervention. This is a subject that deserves close study but is unfortunately ignored by donors who overlook the cost of market failure and insist that *all* selectivity is undesirable.

Regional Trade, Finance, and Infrastructure

Greater trade within the region would permit African countries to enjoy more specialization and economies of scale, and better access to technology and other modern infrastructure than is possible in these mostly small economies. Transregional infrastructure is notably deficient, and officially recorded intraregional trade accounted for only 6 percent of total African trade in the late 1980s. (The inclusion of unofficial border trade would, however, substantially increase this estimate.) African trade and financing restrictions have often hit intra-African trade harder than intercontinental trade, for which finance is easier to secure. Although it is common to pay lip service to the desirability of promoting regional trade arrangements, little has been achieved compared with other parts of the world. External finance could help in promoting these arrangements, financing regional infrastructure, and encouraging greater liberalization of restrictions on trade within the African continent. In practice, structural adjustment programs focus instead on across-the-board liberalization, to the complete neglect of regional provisions.

Supply-Side Measures

Important supply-side measures include skills development, technology support and extension services, provision of infrastructure, and financial support.

SKILLS DEVELOPMENT. The relationship between Africa's lagging industrial development and its weak base of human capital has been widely noted.[38] Africa has the smallest enrollments of all developing regions at practically all levels of schooling, including worker training and higher education.[39] It has a particularly small supply of trained engineers and technicians who are familiar with modern technologies and can restructure existing industry to cope with world competition. As already noted, the skill gap with the rest of the developing world has widened, and the evidence suggests that the quantity and quality of the training provided have fallen further and further behind. What is worse, education spending has been one of the main victims of the expenditure cuts entailed by stabilization programs. One of the main priorities of policy in the region must be to reverse this trend and to narrow the human capital gap with Asia and Latin America.

The provision of employee training by firms is a vital aspect of skill creation. Facilities for the continuing education of workers are weak or nonexistent in much of Africa, and enterprises themselves (apart from the major multinationals) invest little in training their employees in modern technologies. Even the multinationals operating in Africa train only to the level needed to achieve basic operational efficiency. An apprenticeship system exists, especially among small enterprises, but is largely geared to the transmission of traditional skills at fairly low levels of technological sophistication.[40] The level of skills will need to be raised at all levels if African industry is to compete at home or overseas in the emerging liberalized environment. This requires the improvement or the establishment of specialized worker and other training institutes geared to evolving industrial needs, and the provision of greater incentives for in-firm training. The case of Singapore suggests, for instance, that strong efforts to provide tax incentives and subsidies for training in the specific technologies needed by industry, combined with the import of high-level foreign teachers, can be extremely effective in improving the base of industrial skills.[41]

TECHNOLOGY SUPPORT AND EXTENSION. The development of technological infrastructure and the provision of technical extension services to industry, especially to small- and medium-sized enterprises, is another crucial part of supply-side support for industrial upgrading during adjustment. Technological infrastructure includes such basic services as quality assurance and metrology, research support, information about sources of technology, and assistance in the purchase of foreign technology. International trade in manufactured products increasingly requires stringent quality management. An important development is the International Standards Organization's ISO 9000 quality management standards, which are mandatory for health-related industrial products exported to the European Union and are fast becoming an important competitive asset for *all* exporters. The promotion of ISO quality standards is now a major objective of many developing countries, especially in East Asia. Yet in 1993, the whole of Africa (excluding South Africa) had fewer than ten ISO 9000 certificates, whereas Singapore alone had over 600.

Liberalization by itself cannot lead firms to the level of quality they need to survive in world markets. Government and industry must make a concerted effort to strengthen standards and metrology institutions, to provide consultation to firms seeking certification, and to persuade firms to invest in this process. None of this is happening in most of Africa, and certainly the structural adjustment programs make no provision for it.

Large firms in Africa conduct practically no in-house research and development. Nor is there much interaction between the industrial sector and the infrastructure that does exist in many countries to provide research and development and technical support to enterprises. Many existing research institutes are poorly funded and as a result have inadequate equipment and unmotivated staff. They do not go out of their way to search for and offer solutions to the technical problems of industry, preferring a more isolated, "ivory tower" existence. Much the same is true of technology information services designed to help local firms, especially small- and medium-sized firms, locate and purchase foreign technologies.

A strong and proactive technology infrastructure is invaluable for upgrading the competitive capabilities of industry. All the governments of East Asia invested a great deal in providing a range of technological and information services to their enterprises; many of these services were subsidized because of their public-good nature or because of the inability of the targeted firms themselves to pay the full cost. If adjustment is to be successful in Africa, such services need to be established and strengthened. The main thrusts here should be to select industry "clusters" that are of greatest importance to each country and to concentrate infrastructure resources on identifying and meeting their most pressing technological needs.

INFRASTRUCTURE. The need for better infrastructure in Africa is widely accepted. Although recent adjustment efforts have stressed this need, in practice the constraints imposed by stabilization have deprived governments of the necessary resources. One possibility is for governments to experiment with ventures with private investors in large infrastructure projects under a variety of contractual forms (such as build-operate-transfer and build-own-operate arrangements). Other countries have been able to attract substantial amounts of investment through such vehicles and so relieve their own financial and manpower constraints while ensuring more efficient management.

FINANCING AND OTHER SUPPORT. The need to provide adequate financial support for industrial restructuring and upgrading is obvious. Unfortunately, adjustment in Africa takes place mostly under conditions of extreme financial stringency, which compounds the adverse effects of rapid liberalization. Information services for potential exporters are also generally weak.

Many of these needs are fully admitted by institutions such as the World Bank. However, the problem in the context of structural adjustment programs is that measures to meet these needs are not integrated with reforms to the incentive system, and indeed the stabilization measures frequently lead to cuts in important components. This must be because the proponents of rapid liberalization believe either that the benefits of exposure to market forces accrue regardless of whether or not the supply response is boosted, or that supply-side improvements should only be undertaken after the market is giving the "right" signals. However, this paper has argued that this approach is costly and inefficient, and based on faulty reasoning about the nature of the market failures that today confront industrial enterprises trying to become competitive.

CONCLUSION

There is no longer any controversy about the need for reform and stabilization in Africa. The debate is instead over just how efficient markets are and what role governments should play in improving them. The argument advanced here is that market failures are rife and that structural adjustment must be pursued more gradually, with greater control, strategy, and involvement on the part of the government. Stabilization efforts can undermine adjustment and long-term development where they involve cuts in expenditure on education and infrastructure. This argues for more generous financial support for the programs, which should be designed with an emphasis on raising revenue and redirecting expenditure, so that investments in infrastructure and human capital, which are essential for industrial development, can be promoted.

Although African governments are at present limited in their capacity to carry out interventionist industrial policies effectively, the sort of government interventions recommended here are broad-brush in nature, involving identification of and support for sectors where industrial comparative advantage is likely to emerge, not detailed interventions in particular industries. A first priority in adjustment programs should be to improve African governments' intervention capacities, as well as to provide external support for the development of appropriate industrial strategies. Without such action, liberalization policies are likely to lead only to continued industrial stagnation in Africa.

APPENDIX. POLICY-IMPROVING, POLICY-DETERIORATING, AND NONADJUSTING COUNTRIES IN THE AUTHORS' SAMPLE		
Policy-Improving Countries	Policy-Deteriorating Countries	Nonadjusting Countries
Burkina Faso	Benin	Angola
Burundi	Cameroon	Botswana
The Gambia	Central African Republic	Cape Verde
Ghana	Chad	Comoros
Kenya	Congo	Djibouti
Madagascar	Côte d'Ivoire	Equatorial Guinea
Malawi	Gabon	Ethiopia
Mali	Guinea	Lesotho
Mauritania	Guinea-Bissau	Liberia
Niger	Mozambique	Namibia
Nigeria	Rwanda	São Tomé and Principe
Senegal	Sierra Leone	Seychelles
Tanzania	Togo	Somalia
Uganda	Zambia	Sudan
Zimbabwe		Swaziland
		Zaire

Notes

The authors are grateful to Benno Ndulu and Nicolas van de Walle for comments on an earlier draft, and to Sunil Mani for help in collecting and analyzing data.

[1] The data in this paragraph are from African Development Bank, *African Development Report* 1994 (Abidjan: African Development Bank, 1994).

[2] See S. Lall, "Industrial Policy: The Role of Government in Promoting Industrial and Technological Development," *UNCTAD Review* (1992), pp. 65–89; A. Amsden, *Asia's Next Giant: South Korea and Late Industrialization* (New York: Oxford University Press, 1989); R. Wade, *Governing the Market* (Princeton, NJ: Princeton University Press, 1990); and H. Pack and L. E. Westphal, "Industrial Strategy and Technological Change: Theory Versus Reality," Journal of Development Economics, Vol. 22, No. 1 (1986), pp. 87–128.

[3] S. Lall, "Structural Problems of African Industry," in *Alternative Development Strategies in Sub-Saharan Africa,* ed. F. Stewart, S. Lall, and S. Wangwe (London: Macmillan, 1992), pp. 103–44.

[4] World Bank , *Accelerated Development in Sub-Saharan Africa* (Berg Report) (Washington, DC: World Bank, 1981).

[5] J. Knight, "Public Enterprises and Industrialisation in Africa," in Stewart, Lall, and Wangwe, op. cit.

[6] J. James, "Bureaucratic, Engineering, and Economic Man: Decision Making for Technology in Tanzania's State-Owned Enterprises," in *Theory and Reality in Development,* ed. S. Lall and F. Stewart (London: Macmillan, 1986), pp. 217–39; and S. Wangwe and M. Bagachwa, "Impact of Economic Policies on Technological Choice in Tanzanian Industry," in *The Other Policy,* ed. F. Stewart, H. Thomas, and T. de Wilde (London: Intermediate Technology Publications, 1990).

[7] See evidence of L. Mytelka, "Ivorian Industry at the Cross-Roads," L. Cockcraft, "The Past Record and Future Potential of Foreign Investment," and J. Ohiorhenuan and

I. Paloamina, "Building Indigenous Technological Capacity in African Industry: The Nigerian Case," in Stewart, Lall, and Wangwe, op. cit.

[8] Mytelka, op. cit.; Ohiorhenuan and Paloamina, op. cit.

[9] Cockcroft, op. cit.

[10] Ibid.

[11] See C. Liedholm, "Small-Scale Industries in Africa: Dynamic Issues and the Role of Policy," and M. D. Bagachwa and F. Stewart, "Rural Industries and Rural Linkages in Sub-Saharan Africa: A Survey," in Stewart, Lall, and Wangwe, op. cit.

[12] Bagachwa and Stewart, op. cit.

[13] "Incentives" refer to the competitive environment, and "institutions" to the "rules of the game" and the institutions set up to support firms.

[14] World Bank, *Adjustment in Africa: Reforms, Results, and the Road Ahead* (New York: Oxford University Press, 1994), p.61. For a discussion of what structural adjustment policies involve and how they differ from stabilization programs, see the article by the main author of the World Bank's Africa study: I. Husain, "Structural Adjustment and the Long-Term Development of Sub-Saharan Africa," in *Structural Adjustment and Beyond in Sub-Saharan Africa,* ed. R. van der Hoeven and F. van der Kraaij (London: Curry, 1994), pp. 150–71.

[15] See, for instance, World Bank, *World Development Report 1991* (New York: Oxford University Press, 1991); and World Bank, *The East Asian Miracle: Economic Growth and Public Policy* (New York: Oxford University Press, 1993).

[16] For instance, World Bank, *The East Asian Miracle,* op. cit. For reviews of the study, see *World Development,* (April 1994); and Nguyuru H. I. Lipumba, *Africa Beyond Adjustment,* Policy Essay No. 15 (Washington, DC: Overseas Development Council, 1994).

[17] Wood follows the Heckscher-Ohlin model but believes that the relevant factors explaining a country's comparative advantage are land and educated labor—not capital, because capital is internationally mobile. See Adrian Wood, "Skill, Land, and Trade: A Simple Analytic Framework," IDS Working Paper No. 1 (Sussex: Institute for Development Studies, 1994).

[18] "Metrology" is the science of measurement: It provides the precise weights, lengths, pressures, temperatures, volumes, and so forth, needed for industrial and commercial operation. Metrology institutions are separate bodies in advanced countries and newly industrializing economies with international recognition so that products are accepted as meeting standards. Without metrology, there would be no conformity of measures and it would be impossible to make high precision products.

[19] Lall, "Industrial Policy," op. cit.; and Lall, "Structural Problems of African Industry," op. cit.

[20] See P. Mosley, J. Harrigan, and J. Toye, *Aid and Power: The World Bank and Policy-Based Lending* (London: Routledge, 1991).

[21] The discussion here therefore focuses on longer-term adjustment measures that are meant to increase the role of market forces in the economy rather than simply achieve internal and external (macroeconomic) balance.

[22] World Bank, *Adjustment in Africa,* op. cit.

[23] For a flavor of the recent debates on structural adjustment in Africa, see I. A. Elbadawi, "Have World Bank-Supported Adjustment Programs Improved Economic Performance in Sub-Saharan Africa?" Working Papers Series No. 1001 (Washington, DC: World Bank, 1992); I. A. Elbadawi, D. Ghura, and G. Uwujaren, "Why Structural Adjustment Has Not Succeeded in Sub-Saharan Africa," Working Papers Series No. 1000 (Washington, DC: World Bank, 1992; G. K. Helleiner, "The IMF, the World Bank, and Africa's Adjustment and External Debt Problems: An Unofficial View," *World Development,* Vol. 20, No. 6 (1992), pp. 779–92; G. K. Helleiner, "From Adjustment to Development in Sub-Saharan Africa," *UNCTAD Review* (1992), pp. 143–54; T. Killick, *The Adaptive Economy: Adjustment Policies in Small, Low-Income Countries,* EDI Development Series (Washington, DC: World Bank, 1993); Mosley, Harrigan, and Toye, op. cit.; P. Mosley and J. Weeks, "Has Recovery Begun? 'Africa's Adjustment in the 1980s' Revisited" *World Development,* Vol. 21, No. 10 (1993), pp. 1583–1606; H. Stein, "The World Bank and the Application of Asian Industrial Policy to Africa: Theoretical Considerations," *Journal of International Development,* Vol. 5, No. 1 (1994); pp. 1–19;

H. Stein, "Decentralization, Adjustment, the World Bank, and the IMF in Africa," *World Development,* Vol. 20, No. 1 (1992), pp. 83–95. For a perceptive and critical review of the recent World Bank study, see P. Mosley and J. Weeks, "Adjustment in Africa," *Development Policy Review,* Vol. 12, No. 3 (1994), pp. 319–27.

[24] Data for manufactured exports are taken from the World Bank, *World Development Report 1994* (New York: Oxford University Press, 1994). Figures for exports are missing for some countries, especially in the nonadjusting group.

[25] World Bank, *Adjustment in Africa,* op. cit., p. 67; and C. Leechor, "Ghana: Forerunner in Adjustment," in *Adjustment in Africa: Lessons from the Country Studies* ed. I. Husain and R. Faruqee (Washington, DC: World Bank, 1994).

[26] African Development Bank, op. cit., pp. 57–62.

[27] Ibid., Table 27.

[28] Ibid., p. 61.

[29] S. Lall, G. B. Navaretti, S. Teitel, and G. Wignaraja, *Technology and Enterprise Development: Ghana Under Structural Adjustment* (London: Macmillan, 1994).

[30] See Amsden, op. cit.; Wade, op. cit.

[31] T. Forrest, *The Advance of African Capital: The Growth of Nigerian Private Enterprise* (Edinburgh: Edinburgh University Press, 1994).

[32] C. Adam, W. Cavendish, and P. Mistry, *Adjusting Privatisation: Case Studies for Developing Countries* (London: Curry, 1992).

[33] Wangwe and Bagachwa, op. cit.; D.B. Ndlela, "Macro-policies for Appropriate Technology in Zimbabwean Industry," in Stewart, Thomas, and de Wilde, op. cit.

[34] P. Ncube, M. Sakala, and R. Ndulo, "The International Fund and the Zambian Economy," in *The IMF, the World Bank, and Africa,* ed. J. Havenik (Uppsala, Sweden: Scandinavian Institute for African Studies.

[35] There are some 700,000 small- and medium-sized enterprises in Taiwan, accounting for 70 percent of employment, 55 percent of GNP, and 62 percent of total manufactured exports. In 1981 the government set up the Medium and Small Business Administration to coordinate the efforts of several support agencies that provide financial, management, accounting, technological, and marketing assistance to these firms. The government pays 50 to 7.0 percent of the fees for management and technical consultancy services provided to small businesses. The China Productivity Center (CPC) sends out teams of engineers to visit plants throughout the country, where they demonstrate advanced automation techniques and solve relevant technical problems. Over a two-year period, the CPC visited over 1,000 plants and made over 4,000 suggestions for improvement.

[36] See S. Lall, "Trade Policies for Development: A Policy Prescription for Africa," *Development Policy Review,* Vol. 11, No. 1 (1993), pp. 47–65.

[37] The World Bank's *East Asian Miracle* study, op. cit., provides many useful insights into how Asian governments improved their intervention capabilities.

[38] See, among others, S. Lall, "Structural Problems of African Industry," op. cit.; and World Bank, *Sub-Saharan Africa: From Crisis to Sustainable Growth* (Washington, DC: World Bank, 1989).

[39] For instance, Korea alone had 411,000 enrollees in technical subjects at the tertiary level in 1990, compared with 111,000 for the whole of Africa.

[40] Lall, Navaretti, Teitel, and Wignaraja, op. cit.

[41] Singapore is a regional leader in employee training programs outside the firm. The Vocational and Industrial Training Board established an integrated infrastructure that has trained and certified over 112,000 individuals—about 9 percent of the work force—since its inception in 1979. To provide state-of-the-art training in special technologies and equipment, Singapore has also set up a number of training centers in advanced manufacturing skills, subsidized by the government in collaboration with multinational companies such as the Dutch firm Philips NV and the Indian firm Tata. More recently the government-financed Skills Development Fund has focused on the training needs of smaller firms.

Chapter Six

The Politics of Economic Renewal in Africa

E. Gyimah-Boadi and Nicolas van de Walle

This chapter contends that the major obstacles to Africa's economic renewal are institutional. In particular, pro-growth economic policies will not emerge there without the development of more effective political institutions. Our objective is to analyze the circumstances under which such institutions are likely to emerge in Africa.

During the past 10 years, a considerable degree of consensus has been reached among professional economists regarding the broad contours of the appropriate package of economic policies for Africa. The sharp disagreements of the past over the proper economic role of the state or over the nature and implications of some of the behavioral parameters of African economies (for instance, various elasticities of supply and demand) have been greatly narrowed. The consensus is far from perfect, of course, but widespread agreement exists that African governments need to achieve macroeconomic stability through smaller budget deficits and realistic exchange rate policies, that they should devote more resources to infrastructure and the social sectors, and that they need to promote agricultural productivity and export growth, especially in manufacturing. In sum, there is as close to a consensus as there has ever been regarding the desirable end state of the current economic policy reforms in Africa.

Yet progress toward that end state has been slow and uneven across Africa, as documented by a growing literature.[1] On the policy reform front, significant progress has been achieved on the liberalization of prices and the setting of realistic exchange rates, somewhat less progress on fiscal adjustment, and very little on public enterprise reform or other institutional issues. African economies have continued to find the renewal of economic growth elusive, and the record in the 1990s is turning out to be disappointing, if not as disastrous as that of the 1980s, justifiably dubbed "the lost decade." The current reform experiments, it is now allowed, need more time to bear fruit, and many economists stress the need for patience and perseverance. Nonetheless, confidence in ongoing economic reform programs has waned in recent years, particularly within Africa itself. A perusal of the increasingly lively African press confirms, for instance, a growing impatience with the slow progress of economic reform and the sense, in the words of the Senegalese daily, *Le Soleil,* that "structural adjustment has so far not produced any results."[2] Somewhat ironically, then, the growing professional consensus among donors and a small number of African technocrats about needed economic policies has been paralleled by a progressive loss of confidence among the African public in the current reform programs.

The other chapters in this book reflect the new consensus; each advances arguments regarding the kinds of macroeconomic and sectoral policies that are appropriate to pull the African continent out of its current stagnation. The objective of this study, in contrast, is to assess—in the context of this loss of confidence in adjustment—the continuing institutional obstacles to the emergence of what we call "developmental states" capable of sustaining growth-inducing policies. Throughout, we seek to distinguish structural constraints that are difficult, if not impossible, to change in the short run from factors in which human agency plays a more important role and that policymakers can thus affect more easily. Putting African states on the path to becoming developmental states essentially entails making progress on the latter in order to loosen the constraints imposed by the former.

The next section expands on the themes of this introduction and defines what is meant by developmental states. We then provide a diagnostic of the current impasse in Africa by discussing the major political and institutional obstacles to economic reform. This is followed by a section in which we discuss the necessary prerequisites for the emergence of political institutions capable of promoting economic reform. We conclude by outlining some implications for the design of economic reform programs, before summarizing the main points of the discussion.

A DEVELOPMENTAL STATE IN AFRICA

The importance of effective states for the development process in Africa is widely accepted again, after being eclipsed during the 1980s.

Political scientists have long argued that the weakness of state institutions hinders economic development in Africa.[3] Nonetheless, the first generation of adjustment programs largely ignored institutional issues; donors focused on price liberalization and deregulation, which was probably inevitable, given the depth of the fiscal crisis facing most African states at that time and the evident deficiencies of the essentially statist development strategies pursued after independence. Two factors have swung the pendulum slowly back.[4] First, development practitioners have begun to assimilate the lessons of the *orthodox paradox* first postulated in academic circles a decade ago: Successful economic liberalization requires a relatively efficient, capable, and willing state.[5] In fact, in the absence of such a state, institutional deficiencies and political factors have constituted the Achilles' heel of African adjustment programs. The most effective political opposition to economic reform has typically come from within the state apparatus, while institutional reforms such as privatization or civil service reform have proven to be the most difficult to implement.[6] By the end of the 1980s, donors such as the World Bank realized that "underlying the litany of Africa's development problems is a crisis of governance" and that these problems will not be overcome without fundamental improvements in the effectiveness of states.[7]

Second, an influential literature has emerged regarding the economic success of East Asia, arguing that, far from being paragons of laissez-faire economic policies, the governments of economies like Korea, Singapore, or Taiwan have systematically intervened in markets to steer the behavior of economic agents toward desirable ends.[8] A debate has ensued about the implications of these success stories for Africa.[9] Indeed, what is striking about a comparison between these economies and those of Sub-Saharan Africa are not the differences in economic policies pursued during the 1960s and 1970s, although these were not trivial, but rather the much lower levels of internal discipline and capacity that African governments brought to the implementation of policy. The same policies (for example, widespread public ownership or strategic trade policies) that were highly successful in East Asia achieved little in Africa other than encouraging rent seeking and engendering large fiscal deficits. Thus, if one lesson from the comparison of Africa and East Asia is that Africa's economic salvation will not necessarily be found in laissez-faire liberalism alone, another equally important lesson is that East Asian-type interventionist policies are not likely to succeed in Africa without dramatic improvements in state performance. In sum, Africa's development has been in part frustrated by an ineffectual state apparatus that has proven unable or unwilling to create and sustain a policy climate that promotes productive investment, exports, growth, and human welfare.

States that are able to do these things have been called developmental states and are characterized by three key features in particular.[10] First, the developmental state is endowed with a professional, disciplined, and skilled central administration. Typically relatively few in number and highly cohesive, its members are selected through a rigorous recruitment process and engage in relatively little corruption and rent seeking. Such a bureaucracy provides the state its capacity, which is the ability to implement the government's economic policies with a minimum of slippage, a prerequisite of sustained development.

Nonetheless, a capable civil service is not the sole characteristic of developmental states, because such states could conceivably employ their capacities for despotic purposes, rather than for promoting economic growth and the general welfare. In addition, a second characteristic of developmental states is that the central state does not rule through coercion alone but is blessed with a broad degree of popular legitimacy throughout the national territory. Regardless of the nature of the regime, there should be a broad degree of support for the government and its policies. This legitimacy is typically ensured by extensive contacts and networks that link the state with various civic and societal groups; as a result, the state's considerable effectiveness is used to respond to various collective needs. For instance, a pro-growth policy environment may be explained by the numerous personal links that create a climate of trust and cooperation among civil servants, politicians, and businesspersons. The civil service may be a stepping stone to a career in politics or business, and extensive networks maintain the relations among these three groups.[11]

This does not mean that developmental regimes are more likely to emerge in one type of political regime than another. Although it is generally recognized that authoritarianism and the repression of labor were integral aspects of the East Asian regimes, empirical research has never established a clear link between growth and type of regime, and there is thus no reason to think that authoritarianism is a necessary or sufficient condition for long-term economic development in Africa.[12] We return to this issue below.

Finally, and a corollary to these first two features, developmental states are characterized by a deep political commitment to economic growth. As Ziya Onis of Boğaziçi University in Instanbul has remarked, it "constitutes the foremost and single-minded priority of state action."[13] There is widespread support, both in the population at large and within political, business, and military elites, for systematically favoring investment over consumption in order to promote growth and competitiveness. The commitment to growth distinguishes developmental states from the mature industrial states of the Organisation for Economic Co-operation and Development (OECD), where dominant political interests favor consumption. The reasons for this commitment may vary, but it typically results from structural and historical factors. For example, many observers have pointed to the external threat posed by hostile communist neighbors to explain the commitment to economic growth in economies like Korea and Taiwan.[14]

We believe that a range of different economic policies are compatible with the developmental state. Certainly, the newly industrializing economies of East Asia did not base their economic performances on a single set of policies, favoring instead distinct economic strategies that were based on perceptions of long-term comparative advantage and their own distinctive histories.[15] What they did share, however, was a commitment to small fiscal deficits and to deferring consumption to promote savings and investment. Thus, the emergence of developmental polities in Africa will necessarily entail the realization of at least some of the objectives of current stabilization and adjustment programs.[16] For example, it is clear that current attempts to reorient public spending away from recurrent consumption and toward long-term investments in physical and human capital are critically important.

These three characteristics of the developmental state are missing today from most African polities south of the Sahara. To be sure, the quality of the civil service, the social legitimacy of the central state, and the commitment to economic growth vary greatly across Africa. In fact, cross-national differences in the quality of governance have probably increased over the past 10 years. Some polities are closer than others to meeting the criteria of developmental states. Nonetheless, with the possible exception of a small number of states, such as Botswana, no state in Africa qualifies as developmental.[17]

A wide-ranging literature has sought to explain the underlying causes of Africa's current economic impasse, focusing on the historical impact of colonialism, for example, or on the precapitalist ethos that pervades African societies.[18] Our concern here is more practical: How can African polities be made more developmental? What obstacles and constraints embedded in their societies must be overcome? Under what circumstances and how quickly will more effective states committed to long-term economic growth emerge? And what plausible strategies can be adopted to help governments to become more effective?

OBSTACLES AND CONSTRAINTS

There is one key long-standing obstacle to the emergence of developmental states in Africa and one newly emerging one. The first is the weakness of the state itself; the second is the legacy of failed reforms.

State Weakness

First, African reformers are constrained by the weak capacity of the contemporary state. This is, of course, a variant of the orthodox paradox: Who will implement the measures needed to bring about more effective states? Given all of its deficiencies, where will the state find either the capabilities or the commitment needed for reform to succeed? Deborah Brautigam's chapter in this book provides an exhaustive look at state capacity issues; we limit our comments to a brief assessment of the implications of a weak state.

Most governments in the region are severely limited in their capacity to formulate and implement policies. The states that emerged at independence were weakly institutionalized, undercapitalized, and lacking in trained personnel. The quality of the civil services that emerged after independence varied appreciably across African states, of course. Some states were able to establish reasonably effective central administrative structures.[19] Nonetheless, in most states, institutional effectiveness was limited. Moreover, the tremendous erosion of real wages in the civil service during the 1970s and 1980s, as well as a wide variety of managerial deficiencies and the impact of macroeconomic disequilibria, undermined the effectiveness of African civil services. As the breakdown of efforts to implement economic reforms in many countries suggests, capabilities for gathering, processing, and communicating information, for collecting revenues, or for planning and controlling expenditures are typically in short supply. Moreover, as emphasized by political scientist Joel Migdal, political elites in these countries have only rarely been committed to strengthening the bureaucracy; the preferred instruments of political control, clientelism, patronage, and prebendalism reproduced state weakness over time, even as they helped individual leaders to weather economic recession and remain in power.[20]

State weakness in Africa is a structural phenomenon. In other words, it results from deep-seated and long-standing factors and is unlikely to be significantly improved in the short run. To be sure, increasing state capacity has long been an objective of donor assistance and, as Deborah Brautigam makes clear in her chapter, the donors are today supporting a number of ambitious reform efforts. In general, however, most observers agree that foreign aid has not increased state capacity appreciably.[21] It is even argued that aid has often had a negative impact, notably by undermining the cohesion of the public service, lessening the state's accountability, and slowing down the learning process.[22] A recent World Bank study admitted that even in the most successful operations, there was little evidence that the civil service became significantly more effective.[23] The case of Ghana, which has received generous donor support and is rightly considered as a front-runner in adjustment, is instructive in this matter. Under the Ghanaian adjustment program, the public sector was downsized, including reductions of about 60,000 staff between 1987 and 1992 and divestiture of 22 percent of state-owned enterprises by mid-1994. To improve analytical, implementation, monitoring, and administrative capacities, a special compensation package, with donor support, was instituted to attract high-caliber Ghanaian professionals to take up positions in the public service at differential salaries. Decompression of public service salaries has moved the differential between the top and bottom grade from about 2.5 to 1 in 1984 to about 10 to 1 by 1991. In addition, government departments now have computers and office equipment. In spite of these measures, a 1994 World Bank report concluded that Ghana's public service remains "one of the largest in Sub-Saharan Africa and lacks the necessary incentive framework and supervision to ensure satisfactory performance."[24]

Reforms to increase state effectiveness have been complicated by several factors. First, reforms are costly. A reform program in Tanzania, for instance, estimated that public sector salaries would have to increase fivefold to reach the level of remuneration of the early 1970s. Yet, persistent and large budget deficits constrain the choices available to most African states. In the not atypical case of Tanzania, a budget-neutral program would have necessitated a 30 percent retrenchment of existing staff to increase salaries for remaining staff just 168 percent. Governments have balked at the perceived political cost of such large layoffs. Yet, in the absence of retrenchment, the wage bill would have to increase an estimated 5 percent a year for 35 years to return average wages to early 1970s levels.[25]

To finance such expensive reforms, governments will have to change current spending patterns, increase revenues, or seek external (public or private) finance. Seeking external finance is the least realistic option, because additional external finance is not likely to be available in the medium term, at least in all but a handful of countries.[26] Cutting spending and increasing state revenues are politically difficult, because they imply taking on entrenched interests. Although, as the chapter by Ibrahim Elbadawi in this volume makes clear, many countries in the region have the potential to increase state revenues, the state's capacity to extract finances has actually declined in most countries in the past two decades.

Thus, in all likelihood, building more effective state administrations will require time and sacrifice in most countries in the region. Again, we must ask, from where will the necessary discipline come to free up the necessary resources? Such a question points to the second major obstacle to state reform: the sociological nature of African politics, in particular its roots in neopatrimonialism.[27] Even if ideological factors have also played a key role, policies of state intervention in the economy have typically served to expand patronage, rent seeking, and corruption, which have been critical to securing political order, at least in the short run.[28] Current patterns of spending and revenue may well suit state elites, who often lack the incentives to promote more developmental states. Moreover, a negative synergy probably exists between weak capacity and neopatrimonial politics. Administrative rationality is systematically undermined by rent seeking and corruption, with which it cannot easily coexist. The incompatibility between neopatrimonial practices and the state's capacity to enforce laws and contracts, or to perform basic administrative and accounting functions, provides perverse incentives to the beneficiaries of these practices.

Some observers have argued that a response to these socio-political realities is to implement what Paul Collier of Oxford University has labeled "agencies of restraint," defined as "institutions which protect public assets from depletion, prevent inflationary money printing, prevent corruption, protect socially productive groups from exploitation, and enforce contracts."[29] Properly constituted, these serve as autonomous centers of power and countervail the tendency on the part of political regimes to make economically ruinous decisions and allocations. The classic agency of restraint is the independent central bank, which can resist politically motivated calls for unsustainable monetary expansion. As an example of such an agency at work in Africa, Collier mentions the relative fiscal discipline displayed by governments in francophone Africa, which, as members of the monetary zone of central francophone Africa, have limited autonomy over domestic fiscal matters. Similarly, the constitutional restrictions imposed on the new Zimbabwean government by the Lancaster House at independence effectively forbade the confiscation of landed assets of settler farmers for the next 10 years; it thus protected the property and productivity of the white settler farmers by providing government with a plausible defense against strong domestic pressure from key constituencies to expropriate settler property.

Unfortunately, few African rulers appear willing to accept restraints on their own power in the interest of the public good. Notwithstanding the potential long-run benefits that may accrue to their economies from such institutions, African rulers have usually preferred to maintain maximum discretion over economic decisions. For instance, although a completely independent central bank could well help them to resist populist pressures to undertake unsustainable spending or inflationary monetary policies, most African governments have been unwilling to cede the necessary autonomy to their national banks; some have indeed established special and off-budget foreign accounts to circumvent their own financial requirements. In general, many governments have regarded constitutional restrictions on official power, independent judiciaries, and public accounting bodies as impediments to the exercise of effective power and not as guarantors of predictability and stability.

Rulers rarely limit their own power willingly, and strong agencies of restraint will not emerge in Africa until nongovernmental domestic actors can impose them on recalcitrant rulers. So far, such restraints have been maintained largely thanks to outside donor efforts and have been resented and sometimes even undermined by top officials, in part because the measures did not enjoy broad local legitimacy. This has in fact been the case for the Franc Zone; long subsidized by the French treasury, its undeniable success at keeping inflation low in its member countries was undermined in the early 1980s, because governments systematically circumvented the zone's rules to address short-term budgetary disequilibria.[30]

Reform Fatigue

The resource scarcities and sociopolitical factors just described have constituted long-standing obstacles to economic and institutional reform. They are structural in the sense that there is no reason to believe that their importance will diminish quickly or easily. Instead, the building of more effective institutions will be a long and arduous process. Today, in addition, the legacy of failed reforms is emerging as a second obstacle in certain countries. It is important to realize the impact of the failures of economic reform during the past two decades. In this respect, there are admittedly large differences among the countries in the region, but where governments have been engaging in economic reform for a considerable time, and have slowed down or reversed the implementation of reform measures more than once, their commitment to reform is no longer fully credible. Economic agents are skeptical that new reform measures will be sustained and shape their behavior accordingly. For example, the disappointing response of economic agents to reform measures is in part related to their belief that progress is reversible and will not be sustained. Various interest groups have learned that mobilizing against reform measures can lead the government to reverse course or provide some kind of compensation; similarly, government threats against these groups become less credible over time. To counter this loss of credibility, governments must find a way to signal their newfound resolve, or else reform will be costlier, longer, and more difficult, because both economic and political expectations take long to change.

In nearly all instances, the reforms achieved have generated considerable political controversy and induced reform fatigue. Many of the reforms embodied in the developmental state are unpopular today, linked as they are in the public mind with the economic crisis itself. Economic stabilization and adjustment policies were bound to be unpopular, given their impact on the purchasing power of large segments of the population. In many respects, a decade is too short a time period in which to judge a reform effort, particularly in low-income economies. Nonetheless, the "partial reform" syndrome present in many countries has compounded the political difficulties of reform; one of the ironic consequences of stretching out structural adjustment programs over time is that many Africans do not distinguish ongoing reform programs from the economic crisis they are supposed to overcome. The counterfactual has been buried under the inflated and contradictory claims of donors and governments that have oversold the achievements of adjustment to the public for more than a decade. Today, reform is blamed for a country's ills, even when it has never been implemented. This also makes reform harder today than it was two decades ago.

The willingness of donors to allow the reform process in some countries to proceed without much apparent government ownership contributes further to this paradoxical situation. Governments make little or no commitment to reform, which they publicly blame on donor conditionality. Over time, they can shift the blame for the economic crisis to the reform program, whether or not it has been implemented. The longer the reform process stagnates, the more extensive and intrusive donor involvement becomes, as donors come to believe that to implement reform better, they must micromanage the process.[31] This feeds the fears, especially among the local intelligentsia and policy elites, about the ideological and nationalistic implications of reforms. The suspicion persists that reforms are exposing African economies unduly to an international economic system that is inherently punitive to African interests and threatens to recolonize the continent.[32] Whatever the merits of such a view, it is reinforced by the absence of clearly successful reforms in Africa to date, notwithstanding several heralded cases.[33] In sum, the longer African countries are officially "adjusting" without producing clear success stories, the more the economic and political credibility of the reform effort will be undermined.

PREREQUISITES OF THE DEVELOPMENTAL STATE

Are African countries incapable of the kind of fundamental reform that would lead to developmental polities? Are they completely hemmed in by the logic of the orthodox paradox, to adopt the pessimistic terminology of one recent collection of essays on the continent?[34] In this section, we discuss domestic factors that have been offered as necessary prerequisites for the emergence of developmental states in Africa. In each case, we assess their ability to help overcome Africa's structural constraints.

Democratic Pluralism

In recent years, democratization and the empowerment of civil society have been advocated as prerequisites of African economic development.[35] There are reasons to believe that greater political pluralism could improve economic management in the long term and provide an impetus for reforms in the short term. First, the record of economic management in Africa's relatively established democracies, Botswana and Mauritius, has been better than the record of authoritarian regimes in the rest of the continent. In fact, in a number of African countries, the desire for improved economic management was a key factor motivating both domestic and external advocates of democratization.[36] Most significantly, the governments of the new democracies strengthened or at least maintained their commitment to the economic reforms supported by international financial institutions (IFIs), often despite their considerable unpopularity.

Second, there are grounds to believe that democratic pluralism can increase governmental accountability. An independent judiciary and empowered legislature as well as an active political opposition, a free press, and independent civic organizations such as student associations, trade unions, and professional groups all monitor government performance and increase the sanctions on state corruption and incompetence. Moreover, greater participation by nongovernmental agents enriches the policy process and increases the national sense of ownership over policy outcomes, lending greater legitimacy to government decisions.[37] Thus, although democratic pluralism was not a feature of the East Asian developmental states, it may help to correct the tendency of governance in Africa to degenerate into counterproductive neopatrimonialism and predatory rule. Certainly, Patrick Molutsi of the University of Botswana and John Holm of Cleveland State University argue that government officials in democratic Botswana have come to believe that broad consultation and participation improve their own decision-making processes.[38]

However, the escalation of popular protest against economic austerity in some of the new democracies of Africa seems to confirm earlier claims that democratic pluralism does not facilitate the sound management of African economies. The emergence of civil society has often been felt in the negative sense of mobilizing constituencies in defense of status quo policies that undermine long-term productive investment. Thus, in nearly all cases where the forces of civil society (trade unions, student organizations, traders associations, professional bodies, and so forth) are mobilized in Africa, they are articulating opposition to adjustment reforms, sometimes quite effectively. In Ghana, in response to union and student unrest, the Rawlings government broke its otherwise impressive record of fiscal prudence in the run up to the 1992 elections, when it triggered a fiscal shock and undermined macroeconomic stability by making across-the-board wage increases of between 70 and 100 percent and annulling the planned increase in petroleum taxes. It later suspended planned public sector job retrenchments and increased student allowances in direct response to popular pressures. In 1995, the government withdrew the value added tax it had introduced in the annual budget, as a concession to paralyzing labor strikes and violent demonstrations against the measure.[39] Similarly, in Mali, President Konaré's attempts to reform education sparked public protests by well-organized and now legalized student groups, while in Benin the National Assembly and President Soglo have engaged in a protracted feud over the annual budget and the ratification of reforms negotiated with IFIs.[40]

It is true that the ability of popular groups and other societal interests to pressure governments and the state for or against reforms is limited, given their own organizational weaknesses.[41] But it is also true that elected governments cannot easily resort to the strong-arm tactics that their authoritarian predecessors used to overcome opposition and must devote greater resources to dialogue and persuasion. Thus, on balance, the recent wave of democratization probably will not appreciably change the dynamics of economic decision making in Africa.

Despite its achievements, democratization across the region has not fundamentally altered the structural dynamics of African political systems. First, whether incumbent autocrats managed to retain power after multiparty elections, as in Ghana, Kenya, and Togo, or whether opposition parties emerged victorious as in Malawi or Zambia, neopatrimonial patterns of rule are likely to persist in the near future, manifesting themselves as high-level corruption, excessive patronage, and expensive perks for the political class. Several new democracies have retained governments of more than 80 ministers and deputy ministers, for instance, or have maintained the bloated presidential establishments of their authoritarian predecessors, despite the negative fiscal implications of such practices.

Second, many of the key institutions of democratic politics remain weak. The powers of the judiciary, the legislature, the press, and civil society have been entrenched in the new liberal constitutions, and donors have begun channeling direct assistance to state institutions, the press, and a host of civic associations—all in the justified belief that they can temper executive power.[42] Again, it is true that African associational life has surged in the last decade, with the ranks of civic associations swelling into myriad groups dedicated to political participation and the promotion of democracy. Indeed, many played a prominent role in the rebirth of political freedom on the continent.[43]

Unfortunately, civil society, legislatures, and legal systems will take time to shake off long-standing traditions of subservience to the executive. A combination of organizational, financial, and legal handicaps will limit their effectiveness in the immediate future and hamper their ability to provide a counterweight to presidential power or to promote the accountability and transparency of governmental operations in the new democracies. Although more and more donors have come to regard civil society as a legitimate area of external intervention, they are not always able to bypass the state to give direct support to local nongovernmental organizations (NGOs). Indeed, there is little evidence that the neopatrimonial states in the region are content to eschew their hegemonic tendencies and allow NGOs to prosper at their own expense. Most independent associations have to gird themselves against governmental efforts to cripple, control, or co-opt them. Given these political dynamics, as well as long-standing weaknesses in the private sector and traditions of state intervention in the economy, many civic associations have little real autonomy from the state.[44] Until they become considerably stronger, they are poorly placed to enforce standards of public accountability and transparency among politicians and state officials.

Civic groups themselves are often fractured along ethnoregional or religious lines and exhibit clientelist and personalistic characteristics in their own internal management.[45] Such groups may fail to foster a sense of trust and reciprocity between citizens and the state; moreover, in some ethnically divided countries, the emerging issue is how to reconcile the empowerment of civil societies with the need to contain vicious and atavistic tendencies.

In sum, we should not overestimate the changes brought about by democratization. With the political status quo remaining largely unchanged and the prospects for democratic consolidation uncertain, the net development benefits derived from democratization may well be positive, but they are not likely to be significant, at least in the short run. The prospects for democracy and its benefits are probably best in countries that have had semi-competitive traditions in the past, and where the judiciary, the legislature, and civic organizations are strong enough to begin to counterbalance the power of the executive. In the long run, as the democratic order institutionalizes itself in these states, it will promote developmental state institutions that can promote economic prosperity. In countries where institutional actors have emerged from authoritarianism too weak to contest the hegemony of the executive, democratization is unlikely to improve the quality of economic governance much in the near term. In these states, the task of building democratic institutions has just begun.

A Social Coalition for Growth

A change in the social coalitions that dominate African politics has often been identified as a necessary condition for the adoption and, especially, the long-term implementation of pro-growth and market-based economic development strategies in Africa. This essentially entails replacing the dominant social coalition of the first 25 years of independence that supports the current policy mix with a new pro-reform coalition incorporating groups with a stake in more growth-oriented policies—business groups, exporters, and commercial agriculture, for example. In the absence of such an alternative coalition, it is argued, leaders find it impossible to sustain reform.[46]

What are the prospects for the emergence of such a pro-reform coalition? The hold of the old anti-developmental coalition on political power and policies has been undermined by the economic stagnation of the past two decades, as well as by its own organizational and financial handicaps and, to a degree, by the economic reforms of the past 10 years. The relative ease with which several African governments were able to carry out macroeconomic stabilization during the 1980s (and in the case of francophone Africa, the 50 percent devaluation of currency in January 1994) may be a measure of the weakened ability of African trade unions, urban elites, and other societal groups to mount an effective opposition against reforms.[47]

Nonetheless, the anti-reform coalition remains politically strong enough in some countries and on some issues (such as cuts in military spending and public sector job retrenchment) for governments and donors to consider it prudent to make strategic side payments and other concessions to key elements within these groups. For example, to keep unions quiescent, retrenched public sector employees have been promised generous compensations or severance wages and encouraged to buy shares in privatized state companies. Such compensatory concessions have been substantial enough in some cases to have either blocked implementation of the reforms or substantially reduced their fiscal and efficiency gains.[48]

A new pro-growth, pro-market coalition is emerging in some countries out of the ranks of persons who are dissatisfied with the anti-developmental economic policies of the past. Some observers have identified such a potential coalition in Ghana, which would include senior public servants, cash crop farmers, exporters, and businessmen.[49] However, this coalition is nascent at best, and its consolidation largely dependent on three factors. First, the economic and political reforms need to be credible to economic agents, and be sustained long enough to provide tangible benefits to large segments of the population, for interests to organize in their defense. In the absence of such benefits, the disparate members of a potential pro-growth coalition will not unite.

Second, these coalitions need to be organized and led. On the whole, African economic reformers have proven to be poor coalition builders. Many have military backgrounds or were nurtured in authoritarian political systems; steeped in the political culture of personal rule, they have demonstrated little talent for building effective political coalitions to back their economic reforms. After eleven years of sustained economic reform in Ghana, analysts are unable to assert positively that a pro-reform coalition has emerged to support the Rawlings-era changes in policy.[50] The existence of a base of rural support is sometimes inferred but is hard to verify in the absence of accurate polling. Indeed, to win its first real test at the polls in 1992, the Rawlings regime resorted to methods that undermined its economic reform program: It promulgated public sector salary increases and announced a number of high-profile and expensive development projects in rural areas.

A third obstacle to the emergence of a pro-growth coalition may be found in the uneasy relations between rulers and the business elite in many African countries. On one level, certainly, many businessmen cultivate close contacts with the state to exploit the rents created by government economic policies. Because the state is a vector of accumulation, the members of political business elites overlap considerably in most countries of the region, sometimes within the same families.[51] Nonetheless, most governments have entertained contentious relations with the business community as a whole. Rulers, often with intellectual roots in nationalism and Fabian socialism, view business as suspect, foreign, and thus threatening and seek to control it. Large portions of the business community resent the government's constant interference, the anti-business slant of much public rhetoric, and their own lack of influence. In many countries, moreover, indigenous business elites tend to come from ethnic or regional outgroups or are associated with the political opposition. The incentive for rulers to handicap or at least to deny rewards to business elites and other real or imagined political opponents in the private sector may override any desire to create a pro-growth coalition. Moreover, important segments of the business community are from the nonindigenous Indian, Lebanese, or Pakistani communities; they are often intimidated by nationalist rhetoric and must maintain an extremely low political profile.

The political transition of the early 1990s has created somewhat new dynamics for state-business relations. The business community played an important role within the pro-democracy coalition in some countries. Business influence has increased, notably through its financing of political parties and of newspapers that have taken advantage of the new freedom of the press. Countries like Zambia are trying to forge a sense of partnership between government and business, through a regular process of consultation and dialogue. But building trust and overturning the legacies of the past relationship will take time and are difficult tasks in the uncertain context of economic recession and policy change.

Policy Learning

Another prerequisite for the emergence of developmental states in Africa is the emergence of a broader and more sophisticated debate among African elites about economic policy dilemmas. To this day, because of the absence of such debate, little consensus has emerged over the fundamental issues at stake in the economic reform process or on the general direction the economy should take. It is true that the past two decades have seen the emergence of a small cadre of technocrats with a sophisticated understanding of the broad parameters of African economies, the impact of policies, or the nature of tradeoffs they face. Many heads of states and their top advisers share in this understanding. Nonetheless, in all but a handful of countries, almost 20 years of economic crisis and attempts at reform have produced remarkably little understanding of economic policy among the population at large.

The reasons for this state of affairs are fairly clear. Authoritarian political leaders in Africa have rarely found it in their interest to encourage policy debates other than in a blatantly self-serving manner; instead, they have circumscribed participation in policy discussions to a small number of technocrats and political cronies. In Cameroon, for instance, virtually all important decisions have been made by the presidency. Cabinet meetings are purely ceremonial, and senior civil servants have on occasion first heard of sectoral policy changes on the radio.[52] The nongovernmental actors with a direct interest in promoting debate on economic matters, notably professional associations, unions, or business associations, have been muzzled if not eliminated in many countries.

Restricting debate helps to limit accountability, by allowing the government to avoid clearly expressing its policy preferences. The donors have accepted and sometimes even encouraged the insulation of decision making, which suited their own technocratic managerial cultures and which could be justified as necessary, given the unpopular nature of many of the policies they felt should be implemented. In fact, the IFI-sponsored adjustment programs and their policy conditionality further limited debates by shifting much decision making to Paris or Washington.

For the short-term stabilization reforms that dominated the first phase of adjustment, the insulation of decision makers could be justified, because doing so facilitated decision making, and implementation of those decisions rarely benefited from broad participation. But, this bias has also prevented a national debate about economic issues and the progressive education of the population on policy matters. The media has rarely examined economic issues in a serious manner, while single-party parliaments typically have not scrutinized government fiscal or monetary decisions in more than a perfunctory manner. Before the current wave of democratization, few government parties provided a forum for policy debate; change has come slowly with the arrival of multiparty politics, because most new parties are characterized by low levels of institutional development and ideological coherence, and few elections have addressed policy issues.

As a result, Africans are generally poorly informed about the economic crisis and the dilemmas their leaders face. A broad-based public discourse about economic policy is a necessary, if not a sufficient, condition for sustainable policy reform. In most African countries today, a process of policy learning is required before pro-growth policies are likely to be implemented and sustained. Considerably more investment in broad-based education on economic policy is appropriate, notably in the civil service, the parliament, the media, and the schools and universities. Governments should undertake direct dialogue with unions, professional associations, and other NGOs about policy. Only through public discourse can nations engage in broad-based policy learning, the process by which publics and elites change their perceptions about available options and the economic implications of those options for the nation. Open debate is important in determining how policymakers and the intelligentsia understand the issues and subsequently help to shape public opinion.

Such a process is not sufficient, however, and can backfire, at least in the short run, as it did in Nigeria in 1986, when the regime of Ibrahim Babangida conducted a national debate on adjustment only to witness a clear popular rejection of the reform program backed by the International Monetary Fund (IMF) in favor of the unsustainable status quo policies.[53] Other factors were at work in Nigeria; participatory decision making cannot be turned on and off like a faucet by an authoritarian regime that otherwise is intolerant of pluralism. Nonetheless, the Nigerian example does suggest that it is important not to exaggerate the importance of ideas in policy debates. People's understanding of what are fairly complex economic issues is highly imperfect and needs to be improved, but opposition to changing the current policies in Africa is often motivated less by ignorance than by keen appreciation of the benefits of the status quo and the costs of change. Nonetheless, greater public participation in economic policy debates and decision making is probably necessary if Africans are to accept the sacrifices that will be necessary to put their economies on a path of rapid growth.

The recent democratization achieved in many countries should thus facilitate policy learning in the medium term. It is true that the transition processes themselves did not articulate a vision of economic renewal or alternative economic programs. Although economic mismanagement, specific austerity measures, and accompanying hardships were key factors in the popular mobilization to oppose dictatorial rule in Africa, the discussion of possible alternatives to the current policy regime has been strikingly absent from transition discourse. Typically, the economic crisis was blamed on the corruption and mismanagement of incumbent autocratic regimes, and it was implied that a change in stewardship would bring relief and make adjustment unnecessary. Ironically, leaders like President Alpha Konaré in Mali or President Albert Zafy in Madagascar campaigned against reform programs, but once in office, they have sought to come to agreement with the IFIs. Nonetheless, democratic governments have to rely on persuasion to be effective and thus have a much greater incentive than authoritarian ones to support institutional arrangements that promote dialogue and trust.

Effective Leadership

The structural constraints discussed in the previous section as well as the institutional factors discussed in this section all point to the importance of effective political leadership. Needless to say, we offer no recipe for its emergence, but we do posit that political leadership is probably a necessary condition for the emergence of effective state structures and a pro-growth policy environment. Finding ways to overcome the orthodox paradox will include the right kind of leadership.

All of the factors identified as key to the success of economic reform in the recent literature are, in fact, dependent on effective political leadership. These include the government's level of understanding of economic issues, its commitment to reform, the insulation of key technocrats, and its ability to build coalitions on behalf of reform.[54] For instance, technocratic change teams have been viewed as key to the implementation of economic reform programs. Where they have been led by outstanding individuals with a sophisticated understanding of economic issues or close relationships with the IFIs, such men as Prime Minister Alassane Ouattara in Côte d'Ivoire, President Nicéphore Soglo in Benin, Finance Minister Kwesi Botchwey in Ghana, Finance Minister Bernard Chidzero in Zimbabwe, and Minister of Finance and Economy Mamoudou Touré in Senegal may have been effective implementers of reforms, but their power was delegated principally from the political leadership (of Houphouët Boigny, the interim government, Jerry Rawlings, Robert Mugabe, and Abdou Diouf, respectively). Typically without a significant political base of their own, they were dependent on the head of state; when they lost his support, the reform program typically lost momentum. Invariably, such technocrats were more single-mindedly committed to the reform process than their patrons.

The question is how new political and economic values can be engendered among African leaders, whose understanding of economic issues is often weak and who view policy reform as inimical to their own interests. There is no clear answer to this question, since idiosyncratic national factors necessarily play a large role in the career of any political leader. It has been argued that a complete economic breakdown, or what Callaghy has called the trough factor, is needed to induce a greater willingness to undertake fundamental reforms insofar as only then do the costs of doing nothing come to be perceived as larger than the dangers of doing something.[55] In countries like Uganda or Ghana, it was the depth of the crisis that convinced President Lt. General Yoweri Museveni and President Jerry Rawlings of the need for fundamental policy change and made their tough reform programs politically viable.

It is striking how few African leaders seem to have developed a positive political strategy to sustain fundamental reforms. In some cases, the only apparent strategy has been to blame the IFIs or neocolonialism for unpopular measures. Such strategies are useful at first, because they allow governments to shift part of the responsibility for people's hardships to the donors. Over time, however, they have the negative effect of forcing the government to appear essentially passive vis-à-vis the reform process and to reject any ownership of the measures taken. In so doing, an opportunity is lost both to engage in a popular debate about the crisis and to legitimate the reform process.

Yet, for leaders who are committed to economic restructuring, a host of rhetorical strategies are available to lessen resistance to painful economic reforms and to restore credibility to the process. For instance, leaders who are able to explain the need to forgo current consumption to their citizens in a coherent manner may induce a greater propensity to save among the citizenry; they may invoke the "metaphor of the household" to stress the importance of the nation living within its means in a way that ordinary citizens can appreciate; other appeals to the patriotism and good sense of citizens can be useful to sustain unpopular programs ahead. Thus, leaders have sold economic reforms to their citizens by employing versions of the metaphor of the household, especially ones that present structural adjustment reform as the only realistic and pragmatic option available. Faced with a resounding rejection of his plans to introduce a structural adjustment program supported by the IMF and the World Bank in Nigeria, President Babangida resorted to arguments about the imperatives of good housekeeping and the need to preserve the dignity of the nation as the main justification for the introduction of an ostensibly home-grown version of economic reform in 1986.

Similarly, leaders who can convey the impression that the burdens of adjustment and belt-tightening are being shared equitably among citizens may be better able to weaken the resistance to reforms. For example, Rawlings's shrewd use of the argument that his austerity measures hurt the rich more than the poor, and the urban elites more than rural people, are cited among the key factors in the relative success of reforms in Ghana.[56] In this regard, budgetary cuts in nonessential items may be symbolically important for boosting the popularity of the reform effort. For instance, given the absence of any real external threats to national security, the excessive secrecy that surrounds military allocations and procurement practices, and the considerable resentment aroused among civilian populations, cuts in military expenditures are both justified and likely to be popular. The case for reducing diplomatic services and presidential budgets and staffs can be made on the same grounds and will be less dangerous to political stability. In Zambia, for example, the diplomatic corps still receives a larger share of the budget than does public education, once teacher salaries are excluded.[57]

The credibility of reform can similarly be increased if leaders are perceived to be doing all they can to eliminate waste and fraud in public spending. Indeed, the reputation of personal integrity on the part of Rawlings and Museveni has been mentioned as an important factor in the relatively successful implementation of economic reforms in Ghana and Uganda.[58] Similarly, the perception of corruption within the regime of Frederick Chiluba undermined the reform process in Zambia after 1993.[59]

The limits of leadership as a factor should be made clear. Exhortation and charisma matter much more when reform does not mobilize significant new organizational or financial resources. Leaders can exhort the population to make sacrifices for the sake of short-term stabilization, they can push through unpopular stroke-of-the-pen reforms such as devaluation, but they cannot conjure up more effective agricultural extension systems or judiciary institutions. There, the effect of leadership is at best more subtle and can be felt only after a period of years.

Nor is leadership likely to make much of a difference if it is not backed up by organization and mobilizational capacity. That is the purpose of political parties, which can communicate the message of the government from the presidential palace to the village as well as inform the leadership of public opinion. When effective, political parties mobilize popular support on behalf of governmental policies. They serve as a useful intermediary between elites and the masses, helping the government to modulate its discourse and anticipate problem areas. Party rank and file can represent a useful sounding board for policy proposals and debates, helping to legitimate new and controversial policies. Particularly in periods of rapid policy change, an effective party structure clearly provides an extremely useful and perhaps necessary resource for governments.

Dominant parties clearly played such a role in economies as varied as Korea, Mexico, and Taiwan. Unfortunately, years of no-party or single-party rule have left African political parties organizationally and ideologically weak. New parties have sprung up in the past five years all over the continent, but many of them are little more than pressure groups put together to challenge autocratic rulers or to counteract opposition challenges. ADEMA in Mali or Forces Vives in Madagascar won impressive electoral victories in the founding elections of democracies but were never more than loose electoral alliances and have splintered badly since then.[60] Both the new parties, like Ghana's New Patriotic Party or Kenya's Ford-Kenya and Ford-Asili, as well as older single parties like Kenya's KANU and Zambia's UNIP, are organized around individual personalities or ethnoregional groups. They typically lack a coherent ideology or economic program and do not provide an institutional framework for making and implementing policy.[61]

IMPLICATIONS OF THE ARGUMENT

The previous two sections have concluded that there are significant obstacles to the emergence of developmental states in Africa and that the failure of repeated attempts at reform over the past two decades further complicates matters. We have also identified a number of prerequisites for the creation of developmental states, such as effective leadership or the appearance of a pro-growth social coalition, but we are forced to admit in each case that the emergence of these prerequisites is far from certain in the near future. In each case, resource scarcities are problematic, or the political incentives to supply the prerequisite are largely absent.

The stock we have placed on leadership in the last section is perhaps a measure of the current uncertainty. Perhaps creating and mobilizing individual leaders of the kind that social science cannot predict will be necessary to put Africa on the path of rapid growth. In the face of the powerful structural constraints posed by state weakness and various resource scarcities, it is clear that the burden of change must fall on the shoulders of individual men and women. The prerequisites we identified in the last section will require effective leadership to overcome the problems noted. Leaders are needed to articulate the interests around which social coalitions will form; they play a critical role in the promotion of policy dialogue that can legitimate politically difficult reform; and the quality of governance in the new democracies depends in no small measure on what political leaders choose to make of the fledgling institutions at their disposal. In sum, progress on each of the factors identified is possible but is inextricably tied to effective leadership.

We thus do not view African states as completely hemmed in. With patience and creative leadership, the bases of rapid economic growth can be put into place in the coming years. The recent wave of political reform has spawned the emergence of a generation of new leaders, many of whom appear significantly more committed to change than their political elders. Nonetheless, the major implication of this paper is that we should not expect more than slow progress toward the developmental state in the near future. In a number of countries, state collapse appears to have been averted, the economy has stabilized, and the process of building the developmental state can commence. Even with effective leadership, it will be a long and arduous process, and our analysis suggests that a positive outcome is far from assured. In these countries, the population is already exhausted from years of austerity, and the extent to which the progress made can be sustained remains an open question. The international resources to facilitate reform are not likely to increase, limiting the ability of states to undertake many of the reforms outlined in other chapters of this book, however desirable we believe they are, unless governments expand their extractive capacity significantly. Finally, the logic of neopatrimonial politics will limit the domestic resources available and more generally continue to conspire against the emergence of the developmental state.

Several other implications emerge from the analysis. First, macroeconomic stability should be an urgent priority for all African states. Disequilibrium, with its runaway inflation and huge fiscal deficits, fuels a climate of uncertainty that has a negative impact on low-income economies like those in Africa. Our analysis suggests that it is also having a devastating impact on state capacity and effectiveness that African states can ill afford. Stabilizing public finances in particular should be an urgent priority: Not only does the specter of state collapse lurk in virtually every nation in the region, but the longer the current economic crisis lasts, the more depreciated will the already limited existing state capacities become.

Second, governments and donors should not defer institutional reform to a second phase of the reform process. The enhancement of state capacity through, for example, civil service reform should come early in the reform process and should take precedence over measures of economic liberalization (for example, trade reform), particularly when the latter are likely to have negative fiscal consequences. We repeat that we do not believe that most of the current state structures in Africa are capable of sustaining all but the simplest economic reforms. Strengthening them should therefore be a top priority. Donor initiatives to promote state capacity, such as the Africa Capacity Building Foundation, are steps in the right direction, but the capacity-building imperative should be integrated into all aid activities, rather than be separated into a stand-alone sector. It remains striking the extent to which standard donor practices, such as the reliance on long-term resident experts, undermine capacity building.

Third and related to this, efforts should also focus on instruments to improve state performance from the outside or demand side. Thus, in addition to programs like civil service reform or support of the judiciary, governments and donors should enhance current efforts to strengthen the local organizations and social forces that are likely to benefit from better state performance. Donors need to sustain their recent discovery of civil society with the long-term objective of creating a network of organizations in each country that can impose accountability and transparency on the state. In the same spirit, we subscribe to the call for supporting various national and regional agencies of restraint, from independent central banks to regional economic integration schemes, because they will also serve to temper neopatrimonial impulses and restrain the state. Donor support for these agencies is important, notably by providing the financial support without which many will not be politically viable. Nonetheless, successful agencies of restraint require broad domestic legitimacy and thus need to be negotiated and sustained by African political elites among themselves. Enlightened leaders need to foster the nonpartisan dialogue, either in the legislature or in other national fora, that will result in national agreement for the creation of such agencies. They also need to demonstrate that they will respect the autonomy of such agencies, even at the expense of their own short-term political interests, to set the precedents that begin the process of their institutionalization. Pressure from an empowered civil society can help to convince leaders, but ultimately only their own altruistic resolve will pave the way for the emergence of the needed agencies of restraint.

Fourth, an equally obvious implication of our argument is that the state apparatus in most African countries will need to devote its limited resources and capacities to a circumscribed set of essential functions for the foreseeable future. For example, we do not believe that most states in Africa have the capacity to undertake the kind of highly interventionist trade and industrial policies practiced by states in East Asia. Our view is purely pragmatic: We accept the argument that such interventionism may be necessary to sustain rapid economic growth but do not think that states that have not demonstrated the capacity to perform basic functions such as collecting adequate revenues, ensuring law and order, and providing basic physical infrastructure will be able to implement interventionist sectoral policies. Primary attention must be devoted to these essential functions. In the meantime, government can, however, endeavor to enhance its capacities to engage in rational budgeting and planning in the core economic ministries, so that it can generate a national development strategy based on a pragmatic appraisal of its own capabilities.

Finally, the past pattern of donor-government relations, characterized by a combination of ineffectual conditionality and micromanagement of the reform process, not only is counterproductive in the short run but also hampers the long-term prospects for policy change by obscuring the real choices facing African societies. The way out of this conundrum is for donors both to limit their adjustment lending to a more selective set of governments that have demonstrated their commitment to adjustment and, at the same time, to allow these governments greater room to experiment with policy and gain policy learning. This admittedly tricky combination constitutes a challenge for the donors, but it will lead to much healthier relations with African governments and citizens.

Building the developmental state in Africa will take much more time than has typically been allowed for in public policy debates about economic reform in Africa. Creating capable institutions both in and out of the state will require years of effort. In the meantime, rapid growth of the kind witnessed in East Asia is not likely to be attainable by most countries in the region. With effective leadership, however, sustainable macroeconomic stability and slow but steady growth are possible.

Notes

The authors wish to thank Dan Green, John Heilbrunn, Peter Lewis, and Benno Ndulu for their useful comments but absolve them of any responsibility for the views expressed here.

[1] Recent assessments include World Bank, *Adjustment in Africa: Reforms, Results, and the Road Ahead* (NewYork: Oxford University Press, 1994); Nguyuru Lipumba, *Africa Beyond Adjustment,* Policy Essay No. 15 (Washington, DC: Overseas Development Council, 1994); G. K. Helleiner, "The IMF, the World Bank, and Africa's Adjustment and External Debt Problems: An Unofficial View," *World Development,* Vol. 20, No. 6 (1992), pp. 779–92; Giovanni Andrea Cornia, Rolph van der Hoeven, and Thandika Mkandawire, eds., *Africa's Recovery in the 1990s: From Stagnation and Adjustment to Human Development* (New York: St. Martin's Press, 1993); and Nicolas van de Walle, "Adjustment Alternatives and Alternatives to Adjustment," *African Studies Review,* Vol. 37, No. 3 (December 1994), pp. 103–16.

[2] See "Nouvelles Promesses," *Le Soleil* (21 June 1995).

[3] For example, see Goran Hyden, *No Shortcuts to Progress: African Development Management in Perspective* (Berkeley, CA: University of California Press, 1983); and Thomas M. Callaghy, "The State and the Development of Capitalism in Africa: Theoretical, Historical, and Comparative Reflections," in *The Precarious Balance: State and Society in Africa,* ed. Donald Rothchild and Naomi Chazan (Boulder, CO: Westview Press, 1988), pp. 67–99.

[4] Readers interested in a more complete history of this intellectual cycle should consult Tony Killick, *A Reaction Too Far* (Boulder, CO: Westview Press, 1990); and Christopher Colclough and James Manor, *States or Markets? Neoliberalism and the Development Policy Debate* (New York: Oxford University Press, 1991).

[5] The term orthodox paradox was coined by Miles Kahler; see Miles Kahler, "Orthodoxy and Its Alternatives: Explaining Approaches to Stabilization and Adjustment," in *Economic Crisis and Policy Choice: The Politics of Economic Adjustment in the Third World,* ed. Joan M. Nelson (Princeton, NJ: Princeton University Press, 1990), pp. 33–61; variants on the same argument are made by Jeffrey Herbst, "The Structural Adjustment of Politics in Africa," *World Development,* Vol. 18, No. 7 (1990), pp. 949–58; and Thomas M. Callaghy, "Lost Between State and Market: The Politics of Economic Adjustment in Ghana, Zambia, and Nigeria," in Nelson, op. cit.

[6] For example, Henry Bienen has argued that the opposition to trade reform has originated primarily within African governments themselves. See Henry Bienen, "The Politics of Trade Liberalization in Africa," *Economic Development and Cultural Change,* Vol. 38, No. 4 (July 1990), pp. 713–32. An interesting case study along these lines is presented in Tor Skalnes, "The State, Interest Groups, and Structural Adjustment in Zimbabwe," *Journal of Development Studies,* Vol. 29, No. 3 (April 1993), pp. 401–28.

[7] See World Bank, *Sub-Saharan Africa: From Crisis to Sustainable Growth* (Washington, DC: World Bank, 1989).

[8] See Robert Wade, *Governing the Market: Economic Theory and the Role of Government in East Asian Industrialization* (Princeton, NJ: Princeton University Press, 1991); Alice Amsden, *Asia's Next Giant: South Korea and Late Industrialization* (New York: Oxford University Press, 1989); Frederic C. Deyo, ed., *The Political Economy of the New Asian Industrialism* (Ithaca, NY: Cornell University Press, 1987); and Albert Fishlow et al., *Miracle or Design? Lessons from the East Asian Experience,* Policy Essay No. 11 (Washington, DC: Overseas Development Council, 1994).

[9] See, for example, Howard Stein, ed., *Asian Industrialization: Lessons for Africa* (London: Macmillan, 1993); and David Lindauer and Michael Roemer, eds., *Asia and Africa: Legacies and Opportunities in Development* (San Francisco: Institute for Contemporary Studies, 1994).

[10] The term development states is usually attributed to Chalmers Johnson, about postwar Japan. See his *MITI and the Japanese Miracle* (Stanford, CA: Stanford University

Press, 1982). See also Gordon White and Robert Wade, eds., *Developmental States in East Asia* (London: Macmillan, 1988).

[11] Such state-society relations have been called "embeddedness." See, for example, Peter Evans, "The State as Problem and Solution: Predation, Embedded Autonomy, and Structural Change," in *The Politics of Economic Reform,* ed. Stephan Haggard and Robert Kaufman (Princeton, NJ: Princeton University Press, 1992), pp. 139–81.

[12] See Wade, *Governing the Market,* op. cit., pp. 228–55. Insightful recent reviews of the literature on this issue can be found in Alberto Alesina and Roberto Perotti, "The Political Economy of Growth: A Critical Survey of the Recent Literature," *World Bank Economic Review,* Vol. 8, No. 3 (September 1994), pp. 351–71; Larry Sirowy and Alex Inkeles, "The Effects of Democracy on Economic Growth and Inequality: A Review," *Studies in Comparative International Development,* Vol. 25, No. 1 (Spring 1990), pp. 126–57; and Adam Przeworski and Fernando Limongi, "Political Regimes and Economic Growth," *Journal of Economic Perspectives,* Vol. 7, No. 3 (Summer 1993), pp. 51–69; in addition, an investigation of these issues in the African context is provided by John Healey and Mark Robinson, *Democracy, Governance, and Economic Policy: Sub-Saharan Africa in Comparative Perspective* (London: Overseas Development Institute, 1992).

[13] Ziya Onis, "The Logic of the Developmental State," *Comparative Politics,* Vol. 24, No. 1 (October 1991), p. 111.

[14] An excellent analysis is provided in Bruce Cumings, "The Origins and Development of the North East Asian Political Economy," *International Organization,* Vol. 38 (Winter 1984), pp. 1–40. See also Stephan Haggard, *Pathways from the Periphery: The Politics of Growth in the Newly Industrializing Countries* (Princeton, NJ: Princeton University Press, 1990).

[15] In addition to the works already cited, see Robert Wade, "East Asia's Economic Success: Conflicting Perspectives, Partial Insights, Shaky Evidence," *World Politics,* Vol. 44, No. 2 (January 1992), pp. 270–320.

[16] See the chapter by Ibrahim Elbadawi in this volume. See also Janine Aron, "Africa in the 1990s: The Institutional Foundations of Growth," in *Africa Now: People, Policies, and Institutions,* ed. Stephen Ellis (London: James Currey, 1996).

[17] See Charles Harvey and Stephen Lewis, *Policy Choice and Development Performance in Botswana* (New York: St. Martin's Press, 1990); and Louis Picard, *The Politics of Development in Botswana: A Model for Success?* (Boulder, CO: Lynne Rienner, 1987).

[18] See Crawford Young, "Africa's Colonial Legacy," in *Strategies for African Development,* ed. Robert J. Berg and Jennifer Seymour Whitaker (Berkeley, CA: University of California Press, 1986), pp. 25–51; and Hyden, *No Shortcuts to Progress,* op. cit.

[19] This is argued notably for Kenya and Côte d'Ivoire; see David Leonard, *African Successes: Four Public Managers of Kenyan Rural Development* (Berkeley, CA: University of California Press, 1991); and Richard Crook, "Patrimonialism, Administrative Effectiveness, and Economic Development in Côte d'Ivoire," *African Affairs,* Vol. 88, No. 351 (April 1989), pp. 205–28.

[20] Joel S. Migdal, *Strong Societies and Weak States* (Princeton, NJ: Princeton University Press, 1988).

[21] The record of donor efforts to enhance state capacity is assessed in Elliott Berg, *Rethinking Technical Cooperation: Reforms for Capacity Building in Africa* (New York: United Nations Development Programme, 1993); and Uma Lele, ed., *Aid to African Agriculture: Lessons from Two Decades of Donors' Experience* (Baltimore, MD: Johns Hopkins University Press, 1990). Among an earlier literature, see David Leonard, "The Political Realities of African Management," *World Development,* Vol. 15, No. 7 (1987), pp. 899–910; and Elliott Morss, "Institutional Destruction Resulting from Donor and Project Proliferation in Sub-Saharan African Countries," *World Development,* Vol. 12, No. 4 (1984), pp. 465–70.

[22] For a discussion of this point, see Nicolas van de Walle, "The Politics of Aid Effectiveness," in Ellis, op. cit.

[23] David L. Lindauer and Barbara Nunberg, eds., *Rehabilitating Government: Pay and Employment Reform in Africa* (Washington, DC: World Bank, 1994).

[24] See World Bank, *Ghana: Country Brief* (Washington, DC: World Bank, June 1994). Similarly unremarkable results are reported of Uganda's equally comprehensive donor-

supported public service reform and capacity-building effort. See Robert Sharer, Hema De Zoysa, and Calvin McDonald, *Uganda: Adjustment with Growth, 1987–94,* Occasional Paper No. 121 (Washington, DC: International Monetary Fund, March 1995), chap. 5.

[25] See Mike Stevens, "Public Expenditures and Civil Service Reform in Tanzania," in Lindauer and Nunberg, op. cit., pp. 74–7.

[26] Public finance from the Western donors seems to be on a long-term downward trend. For overall levels of aid flow and an assessment of their evolution, see the Organisation for Economic Co-operation and Development, *Development Cooperation: Efforts and Policies of the Members of the Development Assistance Committee* [the DAC report] (Paris: OECD, annual). Moreover, little of the dramatic increase in private capital flows has yet been directed toward Africa, despite signs of interest by investors (see, for instance, "Global Fund Managers Make Tracks for Africa," *Financial Times* (1 February 1996). In any event, private capital is unlikely to be available to finance the various public goods that most experts agree are underprovided today. Some observers have been more sanguine about the ability of southern Africa to attract capital. See "Investing in Africa: A New Scramble," *The Economist* (21 August 1995), pp. 17–9.

[27] Among a huge literature, see the following key works: Jean François Bayart, *L'etat en Afrique* (Paris: Faired, 1989); Richard Joseph, *Democracy and Prebendal Politics in Nigeria: The Rise and Fall of the Second Republic* (Cambridge, UK: Cambridge University Press, 1987): Crawford Young and Thomas Turner, *The Rise and Decline of the Zairian State* (Madison, WI: University of Wisconsin Press, 1985); Christopher Clapham, ed., *Private Patronage and Public Power* (London: Frances Pinter, 1982); and Rothchild and Chazan, eds., *The Precarious Balance,* op. cit.

[28] See Richard Sandbrook, *The Politics of Africa's Economic Stagnation* (Cambridge, UK: Cambridge University Press, 1985); and Aristide Zolberg, "The Structure of Political Conflict in the New States of Tropical Africa," *American Political Science Review,* Vol. 62, No. 2 (1968), pp. 70–87.

[29] See Paul Collier, "Africa's External Economic Relations, 1960–90," in *Africa: 30 Years On,* ed. Douglas Rimmer (London: Heinemann, 1991), pp. 155–68.

[30] See Nicolas van de Walle, "The Decline of the Franc Zone: Monetary Politics in Francophone Africa," *African Affairs,* Vol. 90 (July 1991), pp. 383–405; a good study of the zone's procedures and their impact before the crisis is provided by Patrick Guillaumont and Sylviane Guillaumont, eds., *Stratégies de développement comparées: Zone franc et hors zone franc* (Paris: Economica, 1988).

[31] A similar argument is advanced in David Gordon, "Debt, Conditionality, and Reform: The International Relations of Economic Policy Restructuring in Sub-Saharan Africa," in *Hemmed in: Responses to Africa's Economic Decline,* ed. Thomas Callaghy and John Ravenhill (New York: Columbia University Press, 1993), pp. 90–129.

[32] The views of the Economic Commission for Africa, and especially that of its long-serving executive secretary (until recently), Adebayo Adedeji on IFI support of structural adjustment programs are fairly representative of the anti-SAP views held by African intellectuals and policy elites. For a recent statement of those views, see Adebayo Adedeji, "An Alternative for Africa," *Journal of Democracy,* Vol. 5, No. 4 (October 1994), pp. 119–32; also see Giovanni Cornia, Rolph van der Hoeven, and Thandika Mkandawire, "Overview of an Alternative Long-Term Development Strategy," in Cornia, van der Hoeven, and Mkandawire, op. cit., pp. 159–90.

[33] The list of successful cases of structural adjustment is usually quite short and hedged with various qualifications, and even then it is the subject of some controversy. See, for example, World Bank, *Adjustment in Africa,* op. cit. and Lipumba, op. cit.

[34] Callaghy and Ravenhill, op. cit.

[35] See Richard L. Sklar, "Democracy in Africa," *African Studies Review*, Vol. 26 (1983), pp. 11–24.

[36] For discussions of this issue from different vantage points, see Peter Gibbon, Yusuf Bangura, and Arve Ofstad, eds., *Authoritarianism and Democracy and Adjustment* (Uddevalla, Sweden: Nordiska Afrikainstitutet, 1992); and Adrian Leftwich, "Governance, Democracy, and Development," *Third World Quarterly,* Vol. 14, No. 3 (1993), pp. 605–24; see also

Ernest Harsch, "Structural Adjustment and Africa's Democracy Movements," *Africa Today,* Vol. 40, No. 4 (1993), pp. 7–29.

[37] A good review of these issues is provided by Derick W. Brinkerhoff, "Perspectives on Participation in Economic Policy Reform in Africa," *Studies in Comparative International Development* (forthcoming 1996).

[38] See Patrick Molutsi and John Holm, "Developing Democracy when Civil Society Is Weak," *African Affairs,* Vol. 89 (1990), pp. 323–40.

[39] A recent analysis of the relationship between democratization and economic reform in Ghana is provided by Todd J. Moss and David G. Williams, "Can Ghana's Economic Reform Survive the 1996 Elections?" *CSIS Africa Notes,* Vol. 175 (August 1995).

[40] These events in Mali are described in "Difficile apprentissage de la liberté," *Jeune Afrique,* Vol. 1735 (7 April 1994). On Benin, see the interesting assessment by Curt Grimm, "Increasing Participation in the Context of African Political Liberalization: The Benin Budget Crisis of 1994 and Its Implications for Donors," paper presented at the annual meetings of the African Studies Association, Toronto, Canada, November 1994.

[41] See Nicolas van de Walle, "Political Liberalization and Economic Reform in Africa," *World Development,* Vol. 22, No. 4 (April 1994), pp. 483–500.

[42] Pierre Landell-Mills, "Governance, Cultural Change, and Empowerment," *Journal of Modern African Studies,* Vol. 30, No. 4 (1992), pp. 543–67.

[43] See especially, Rothchild and Chazan, op. cit.; Michael Bratton, "Beyond the State: Civil Society and Associational Life in Africa," *World Politics,* Vol. 41, No. 3 (1989), pp. 407–30; John Harbeson, Donald Rothchild, and Naomi Chazan, eds., *Civil Society and the State in Africa* (Boulder, CO: Lynne Rienner, 1994); Michael Bratton and Nicolas van de Walle, "Popular Protest and Political Transition in Africa," *Comparative Politics,* Vol. 24, No. 4 (1992), pp. 419–42.

[44] For such an argument about African civil society, see Peter Lewis, "Political Transition and the Dilemma of Civil Society in Africa," Vol. 27 (Summer 1992), pp. 31–54; and René Lemarchand, "Uncivil States and Civil Societies: How Illusion Became Reality," *Journal of Modern African Studies,* Vol. 30, No. 2 (1992), pp. 177–91; see also E. Gyimah-Boadi, "Civil Society and Democratic Consolidation in Africa," *Journal of Democracy* (forthcoming April 1996)

[45] For such an argument about farm associations in Zimbabwe, see Michael Bratton, "Micro-Democracy? The Merger of Farmer Unions in Zimbabwe," *African Studies Review,* Vol. 37, No. 1 (April 1994), pp. 9–38; for a useful general discussion of the nonliberal and antidemocratic tendencies inherent in key elements of African civil societies, see Ken Post, "State, Civil Society, and Democracy in Africa: Some Theoretical Issues," in *Democracy and Socialism in Africa,* ed. Robin Cohen and Harry Goldbourne (Boulder, CO: Westview, 1991), pp. 34–52; see Celestin Monga, "Civil Society and Democratisation in Francophone Africa," *Journal of Modern African Studies,* Vol. 33, No. 3 (1995).

[46] Robert Bates has long argued that the prevailing pre-reform economic policies reflect the interests of the dominant social coalition. See Robert Bates, *Markets and States in Tropical Africa: The Political Bases of Agricultural Policies* (Berkeley, CA: University of California Press, 1981); Robert Bates, "Pressure Groups, Public Policy, and Agricultural Development: A Study in Divergent Outcomes," in *Agricultural Development in Africa: Issues of Public Policy,* ed. Robert Bates and Michael Lofchie (New York: Praeger, 1980). See, for instance, Callaghy, "Lost Between State and Market," op. cit.

[47] For example, see Jeffrey Herbst, *The Politics of Economic Reform in Ghana, 1982–1991* (Berkeley, CA: University of California Press, 1993), chap. 4.

[48] M. Dia, *A Governance Approach to Civil Service Reform in Africa,* Technical Paper No. 225 (Washington, DC: World Bank, 1993), p. 10.

[49] See J. Clark Leith and Michael Lofchie, "The Political Economy of Structural Adjustment in Ghana," in *Political and Economic Interactions in Economic Policy Reform* (Oxford: Basil Blackwell, 1993), pp. 225–386; also E. Gyimah-Boadi, "Economic Recovery and Politics in the PNDC's Ghana," *Journal of Commonwealth and Comparative Politics,* Vol. 27, No. 3 (1990), pp. 228–43.

[50] See Herbst, *Politics of Economic Reform,* op. cit., pp. 76–94; and Leith and Lofchie, "Political Economy of Structural Adjustment in Ghana," op. cit.

[51] Richard Sklar, "The Nature of Class Domination in Africa," *Journal of Modern African Studies,* Vol. 17, No. 4 (1979), pp. 531–52.

[52] Personal communication to Nicolas van de Walle during an interview in Yaoundé in May 1993.

[53] See Jeffrey Herbst and Adebayo Olukoshi, "Nigeria: Economic and Political Reforms at Cross Purposes," in *Voting for Reform: Democracy, Political Liberalization, and Economic Adjustment,* ed. Stephan Haggard and Steven Webb (New York: Oxford University Press, 1994), pp. 472–77.

[54] See, for instance, Joan Nelson, "The Political Economy of Stabilization: Commitment, Capacity, and Public Response," *World Development,* Vol. 12, No. 10 (1984), pp. 983–1006.

[55] See Callaghy, "Lost Between State and Market," op. cit. A similar argument is made in Merillee S. Grindle and John W. Thomas, *Public Choices and Policy Change: The Political Economy of Reform in Developing Countries* (Baltimore, MD: Johns Hopkins University Press, 1991).

[56] See Richard Jeffries, "Leadership Commitment and Political Opposition to Structural Adjustment in Ghana," in *Ghana: The Political Economy of Recovery,* ed. Donald Rothchild (Boulder, CO: Lynne Rienner, 1991), pp. 157–72; and Richard Jeffries, "Ghana: The Political Economy of Personal Rule," in Donal Cruise O'Brien et al., eds., *Contemporary West African States* (Cambridge, UK: Cambridge University Press, 1989), pp. 75–98; also Kevin Shillington, *Ghana and the Rawlings Factor* (London: Macmillan, 1992), pp. 129–44.

[57] See World Bank, *Public Expenditure Review of Zambia,* Report 11420-ZA (Washington, DC: World Bank, 1992).

[58] For a skeptical view of such claims, see Mike Oquaye, "The Ghanaian Elections—A Dissenting View," *African Affairs,* Vol. 94, pp. 259–75; also E. Gyimah-Boadi, "Explaining the Economic and Political Successes of Rawlings: The Strengths and Limitations of Public Choice Theories," in *The New Institutional Economics and Third World Development,* ed. Colin Lewis, John Harriss, and Janet Hunter (London: Routledge, 1995).

[59] See "Disaffected in Zambia," *The Washington Post* (12 September 1995); and Julius O. Ihonvbere, "From Movement to Government: The Movement for Multi-party Democracy and the Crisis of Democratic Consolidation in Zambia," *Canadian Journal of African Studies,* Vol. 29, No. 1 (1995), pp. 1–25.

[60] See Nicolas van de Walle, "Economic Reform and the Consolidation of Democratic Rule in Africa: Three African Case Studies," paper delivered at the annual meetings of the International Political Science Association, Berlin, August 21–25, 1994.

[61] See Robert Buijtenhuijs, "Les partis politiques africains ont-ils des projets de société? L'exemple du Tchad," *Politique Africaine,* Vol. 56 (December 1995), pp. 119–36.

About the ODC

ODC is an international policy research institute based in Washington, D.C. that seeks to inform and improve the multilateral approaches and institutions—both global and regional—that play increasingly important roles in the promotion of development and the management of related global problems.

ODC's program of multilateral analysis and dialogue is designed to explore ideas and approaches for enhancing global cooperation, to build networks of new leadership among public and private actors around the world, and to inform decision making on selected development topics of broad international concern.

ODC is a private, nonprofit organization funded by foundations, corporations, governments, and private individuals.

Stephen J. Friedman is the Chairman of the Overseas Development Council, and the Council's President is John W. Sewell.

Board of Directors

About the Authors

Project Directors

BENNO NDULU is the Executive Director of the African Economic Research Consortium in Nairobi, Kenya, on leave from the University of Dar es Salaam, Tanzania, where he was Professor of Economics and chaired the department. He is widely published in international journals and books, focusing on macroeconomic policy adjustment and growth; trade, agricultural, and industrial policy; governance and economic management; and macroeconomic modeling. He serves on several editorial boards including those of *World Development* and the *Journal of African Economies*. He has been consultant and adviser to a wide range of countries and international organizations on matters related to economic policy and development. He is currently a director on the board of Tanzania's Central Bank and Chairman of the Tanzania Revenue Authority.

NICOLAS VAN DE WALLE is an Associate Professor of Political Science at Michigan State University and the Davidson Sommers Fellow at the Overseas Development Council, where he is directing a project on aid effectiveness in Africa. In recent years he has conducted field research in Botswana, Cameroon, Senegal, and Zambia. He has served as consultant to UNDP, UNIDO, USAID, the Global Coalition for Africa, and the World Bank. He has published widely on democratization issues as well as on the politics of economic reform in Africa. His publications include: *Democratic Experiments in Africa: Regime Transitions in Comparative Perspective* (Cambridge University Press, forthcoming 1996, with Michael Bratton); *Improving Aid: The Challenge to Donors and African Governments* (ODC, forthcoming 1996); *Of Time and Power: Leadership Duration in the Modern World* (Stanford University Press, 1990, with Henry Bienen); "Crisis and Opportunity in Africa: Economic Reform and Democracy," (*Journal of Democracy*, April 1994); and "Political Liberalization and Economic Reform in Africa" (*World Development*, April 1994).

Contributing Authors

SIMON APPLETON is Microeconomic Coordinator at the Centre for the Study of African Economies at the University of Oxford and Lecturer in economics at Pembroke College, Oxford. He spent a year at

Kenyatta University, Nairobi, as a World Bank McNamara Fellow, researching gender differences in primary school examination performance. His research interests include gender, poverty and human resources, and applied microeconomics.

DEBORAH BRAUTIGAM has been an Associate Professor at American University's School of International Service in Washington, DC, since 1994. She has also taught a Silpakorn University in Thailand and Columbia University. She was a Council on International Affairs Fellow at the World Bank in 1991, where she contributed to the Bank's work on governance and development. Her articles have appeared in the *Journal of Comparative and Commonwealth Politics, World Development, Studies in Comparative International Development, Journal of Developing Areas, and Journal of Modern African Studies*, as well as a number of edited collections. Her current research, a study of the institutions of democracy and distribution in Taiwan and Mauritius, continues her long-term interest in the comparative political economy of Asia and Africa.

CHRISTOPHER L. DELGADO is Research Fellow in the Markets and Structural Studies Division of the International Food Policy Research Institute (IFPRI), Washington, DC. He has worked on African agricultural and economic policy issues since joining the Institute in 1979. Author or editor of three books and 80 professional papers on economics and agricultural economics, he is currently leader of IFPRI's Multi-Country Project on Agricultural Diversification and Export Promotion. He has conducted long-term research and taught at the Center for Development Studies and Education in N'Djamena, Chad, the University of Ouagadougou, Burkina Faso, the Center for Research on Economic Development at the University of Michigan, and The Johns Hopkins University Nitze School of Advanced International Studies (SAIS). He is currently Book Review Editor of *Agricultural Economics: Journal of the International Association of Agricultural Economists* and Associate Editor of Oxford University Press's *Journal of African Economies*.

IBRAHIM ELBADAWI, a Sudanese national, is the Research Coordinator of the African Economic Research Consortium in Nairobi, currently on leave from the World Bank where he worked in the Macroeconomic and Growth Division. Before joining the World Bank in 1989, Dr. Elbadawi taught economics at Northwestern University, the University of Gezira in Sudan, and Yale University. His research focuses on the issues of exchange rate economics, structural adjustment, macroeconomic policy and agriculture, international migration and remittances, and economic growth in Sub-Saharan Africa and to a lesser extent in the oil-surplus economies of the Arabian Gulf. His publications include several articles in international journals.

E. GYIMAH-BOADI is a Ghanaian political scientist currently teaching at the School of International Service at the American University in Washington, DC. In 1994–95, he was a Guest Scholar at the Woodrow Wilson International Center for Scholars. His publications include: "Civil Society and Democratic Consolidation in Africa" (*Journal of Democracy*, April 1996); "Explaining the Economic and Political Successes of Rawlings: The Strength and Limitations of Public Choice Theories," in Barbara Harris, Janet Hunter, and Colin Lewis (eds.), *The New Institutional Economics and Third World Development* (Routledge, 1995); "Ghana's Economic Decline and Development Strategies" (with Donald Rothchild) in John Ravenhill, *Africa in Economic Crisis* (Macmillan Press, 1986); and an edited volume, *Ghana Under PNDC Rule* (Codesria Books, Dakar, 1993).

SANJAYA LALL is University Lecturer in development economics and a Fellow of Green College at the University of Oxford. He has published widely on international investment, industrial and technological development, and trade policy in developing countries. He has been as staff member of the World Bank and has consulted for many international organizations. His current research focuses on technology policies and the role of the government in industrialization, with particular reference to Southeast Asia and Sub-Saharan Africa.

JOHN MACKINNON is a Research Officer at the Centre for the Study of African Economies at the University of Oxford. He has taught economics at the Universities of Oxford, Warwick, East Anglia, Makerere, and Addis Ababa. Previously he worked for two years in Vanuatu. He served as an advisor to UNCTAD on health issues and a consultant to the World Bank in Uganda on poverty alleviation and social sectors. He carried out research on health in Uganda and Ethiopia, including a study of the determinants of child mortality and malnutrition using household survey data in Uganda. His other research interests include the characteristics of poverty in African economies, the theory of land markets, and the macroeconomic effects of climatic shocks in agricultural economies.

FRANCES STEWART is Director of the International Development Centre, Queen Elizabeth House, and Fellow of Somerville College at the

Unversity of Oxford. She was President of the United Kingdom and Irish Development Studies Association form 1990–92 and is currently British Council Member of the United Nations University. Her many publications include: *Technology and Underdevelopment* (Macmillan, 1977); *Planning to Meet Basic Needs* (Macmillan, 1985); co-author with G. A. Cornia and R. Jolly, *Adjustment with a Human Face*, (Oxford University Press, 1987)); and *Adjustment and Poverty: Options and Choices* (Routledge, 1995). In addition, she has served as consultant to UNICEF and UNDP (on *Human Development Report*), among others.